IT IS SO ORDERED

IT IS SO ORDERED

A CONSTITUTION UNFOLDS

....

WARREN E. BURGER

Chief Justice of the United States
1969–1986

Chairman of the Commission
on the Bicentennial of the Constitution
1985–1992

WILLIAM MORROW AND COMPANY, INC.
New York

Library of Congress Cataloging-in-Publication Data

Burger, Warren E., 1907–
    It is so ordered : a constitution unfolds / Warren E. Burger.
      p.   cm.
    Includes bibliographical references and index.
    ISBN 0-688-09595-X
    1. United States—Constitutional history.   2. United States—Constitu-
      tional law—Cases.   I. Title.
  KF4541.B85   1995
  342.73 ' 029—dc20
  [347.30229]   94-36252
                                                CIP

Printed in the United States of America

First Edition

1 2 3 4 5 6 7 8 9 10

BOOK DESIGN BY MICHAEL MENDELSOHN / MM DESIGN 2000, INC.

For Elvera

FOREWORD

THIS BOOK IS IN NO SENSE intended as a serious, scholarly, or comprehensive study of constitutional law, but rather as a story for nonlawyers about some of the great cases and controversies that have shaped America's judicial, political, and economic history. The great American author Barbara Tuchman wrote: "I did not write to instruct but to tell a story." It has been said that history, like beauty, often lies in the eye of the beholder.

Every lawyer and law student knows the cases reviewed in this book, nearly all of them decided by the Supreme Court of the United States, but there are many otherwise well-educated people who are only vaguely aware of them. And few are conscious of the setting in which these issues arose or the interrelationship of these cases and how they affected our system of ordered liberty—or of the personalities involved. Yet the fundamental role that the Constitution plays in each of our lives today, whether we are aware of it or not, is a direct result of the meaning these cases gave to that glorious charter. Through these and other significant cases, the Supreme Court has given life to the Constitution. Thus I have titled this book *It Is So Ordered*, the phrase that concludes many of the Supreme Court's opinions.

Taken together, these great cases have served as the key building blocks that have allowed our country to grow from a wilderness society of three and a half million people along the Atlantic seaboard in 1787 to a world power, spanning an entire continent, of over a hundred million people by World War I and more than two hundred and fifty million today. Among other things, these tales may serve to remind us that democracy, with its often untidy, inconvenient "checks and balances," is not always neat and orderly; sometimes critics say there is too much "check" and not enough "balance." Democracy is people—men and women with all their virtues and flaws—trying to work together to produce ordered liberty.

Some of these cases resulted from clashes between the three

branches of the federal government, while others arose from conflicts between federal and state governments. These controversies generated enormous political and economic reform with lasting consequences. And the Supreme Court, being composed of mortals, makes mistakes at times. These cases reveal the Court at both its best and its worst. Under Chief Justice John Marshall, for example, the Court asserted its independence and judgment against the political pressures of the day. The opinion of John Marshall for a unanimous Court in 1803 in *Marbury* v. *Madison* infuriated President Thomas Jefferson. It focused Jefferson's latent hostility toward Marshall and toward the independence of the judiciary, which led in time to what has been called the most massive political assault on the Supreme Court in history, alongside of which President Franklin D. Roosevelt's court-packing campaign looks pale in comparison. Fortunately, both attacks failed. In 1816 *M'Culloch* v. *Maryland* sustained Congress' power to create a national banking system and made clear that no state had the power to tax federal entities. That decision was vigorously opposed by Thomas Jefferson, Andrew Jackson, and even James Madison. In 1824 *Gibbons* v. *Ogden* confirmed that the Commerce Clause of the Constitution established the "common market" for America contemplated by Alexander Hamilton but vigorously opposed at that point by most of the states.

In 1807 John Marshall, our fourth Chief Justice, presiding as a federal trial judge in Richmond, Virginia, over the trial of Aaron Burr, applied Lord Edward Coke's doctrine that even a king is not above the law. This doctrine ensured that governmental power could not be used against political adversaries as English kings had used their authority to send "uncooperative" politicians to the Tower of London. Marshall's conduct in the trial of *United States* v. *Aaron Burr* enraged Jefferson even more than the *Marbury* decision. Jefferson's admirers prefer to overlook these episodes in the life of that great man; but great men are not perfect, and the Chief Justice, sitting as a trial judge, made clear that presidents, Jefferson not excepted, could be required to give evidence needed by the courts in the administration of justice, whether they liked the idea or not.

The reader will find that in discussing these cases I have commented not only on such historic figures as Jefferson, Marshall, and

Burr but also on many other Founding Fathers. In fiction and history these men are portrayed as heroes—and heroes they surely were. Never in all the past—to borrow from Henry Steele Commager—was there such a galaxy of leaders as those who met in 1787 in Philadelphia. Unlike some of history's revolutionaries, our Founding Fathers were people of intellectual substance who possessed the combined genius and political experience necessary to create an enduring system of government. Some were rich, and all were successful, but they had been willing to risk all of that, as well as the gallows and firing squad, as revolutionaries.

Sometimes it is said that philosophers and scholars do not make revolutions. But history, especially the history of America from the years 1774 through 1781, does not support that proposition. Many of our Founding Fathers—Benjamin Franklin, for example—were philosophers, scholars, and practical politicians, and most of them were also soldiers. This company included men deeply read in philosophy and history, who understood the great thinkers of the past, not only those of the eighteenth century in France, England, and the Scottish Enlightenment, but also those of ancient Greece and Rome. Thirty-three of the fifty-five who labored in drafting our Constitution were lawyers. The American Revolutionaries were passionate men, and they put their fortunes, their lives, and their futures at risk. Some of them, George Washington included, hoped at the outset to work out an accommodation or new working relationship with the mother country. But others, like Tom Paine and John Adams' cousin Sam Adams, were propagandizers or "provocateurs of revolution" who planned events like the Boston Tea Party and the Liberty Tree. They organized the Sons of Liberty and the "Boston mob" that led to the so-called Boston Massacre, in order to arouse the people and bring them into the frame of mind that would support a revolution against their king. Eleven years before the Declaration of Independence, the Stamp Act had provoked colonial opposition, and promoters of revolution like Sam Adams exploited those events. Calmer heads had hoped that the problems could be worked out and that King George's men in London could be made to listen to the reasoning of Edmund Burke, who was arguing the cause of the colonists in the House of Commons.

In the end, however, it is our Constitution and the important cases that shaped its legal image over the years that are at the core of this book—from *Ware* v. *Hylton* in 1796 to the Supreme Court's landmark decisions under the Great Chief Justice, John Marshall; from the Court's failures in *Dred Scott* and *Plessy* v. *Ferguson* under Marshall's successors to the Court's refusal in the *Steel Seizure Case* to sanction President Harry Truman's efforts to quash the steel strike of 1952. Since this is a story and not a formal history, there is but a single footnote. I reached back in memory for many of these stories. Now, with syntax repaired, and with a few quotations from the pens of these great figures, it still remains a story. I hope it will help the reader remember those who designed and built our democracy, which has become an ensign of freedom throughout the world. But most of all, I hope this book inspires the reader to further examine what has been written about these men and these events—and especially about John Marshall, the Great Chief Justice who ranks with the top dozen of the Founding Fathers but has not always been seen as such.

CONTENTS

Nothing in all history . . . ever succeeded like America . . . .
—HENRY STEELE COMMAGER

IT IS SO
ORDERED

CHAPTER ONE

IN THE BEGINNING

....

New Jersey is our country!
—New Jersey volunteers,
reporting to General George
Washington at Valley Forge

FOR MORE THAN TWO CENTURIES Americans have taken for
granted the Constitution and the unique system of government
it created, treating it as we treat good health and good weather,
whose sources are thought irrelevant while they are being enjoyed—if
they are given any thought at all. The success Henry Steele Commager
spoke of came from the document described by William Gladstone,
prime minister of England, as the "most remarkable [document] to
have been produced by the human intellect, at a single stroke."

Called a "miracle" at the time, that characterization has been repeated for more than two hundred years, and one of the great books on
the Constitution, written by Catherine Drinker Bowen, used as its title *Miracle at Philadelphia*. Political leaders, philosophers, and historians
from other countries have seen our experience more clearly than many
American observers. Perhaps this came about because, as Commager
implied, people in no other country ever achieved so much so swiftly
in terms of freedom, material rewards, and peaceful development—the
Civil War excepted. This was the case from the earliest years when
many of the immigrants from countless countries—including deported
convicts—made a good life here and moved, as some did, from having

3

nothing to enjoying positions of wealth or political power. That African Americans in particular did not share wealth or power on an equal basis is one of the sad chapters in our extraordinary story. We must never forget that the mass of immigrants from Africa, ancestors to more than thirty million of today's Americans, did not come to our shores by their own choice, as did the early Caucasian arrivals and the later-arriving Asians and Hispanics. The immigrants from Africa were brought here in chains; the scar inflicted by those chains is something we have yet to deal with fully.

When Benjamin Franklin and George Washington were young, in the mid-eighteenth century, American colonists were doing quite well as British subjects—better than most of those who stayed behind in the "old country." A few chafed over relatively small things. The hated stamp tax was not really that great a burden. London had been sending troops at great expense for a long time to defend the colonists from the French and to check the Native Americans who, understandably, considered this to be their land and resented the intruders. But having tasted more freedom than almost any people who had ever lived on this planet before them, the hardy Americans wanted more. More land, more freedom, more of the good things. Freedom generates appetites for more and more freedom. People take great risks to get and keep it.

Some colonists joined in the protests against England simply to secure their full rights as Englishmen. A clumsy government in London under a monarch and a parliament that lacked a true understanding of the situation in America gave men such as Tom Paine and Sam Adams what they needed to stir masses of people to rebellion. Modern promoters and "spin doctors" are amateurs compared with Paine, Adams, and Thomas Jefferson.

Once hostilities began in earnest, the Articles of Confederation of 1778 sought to establish a "national government" of sorts, yet the Articles hardly created a true nation. They were barely more than a multilateral treaty between thirteen independent, sovereign states. By the very terms of that document each state reserved its sovereign and independent status. The Articles did not become binding until all thirteen "sovereigns" ratified them, which was not done until 1781, the year of Lord Cornwallis' surrender to General Washington at Yorktown. But during the Revolutionary War the thirteen sovereigns undertook to

operate more or less under the terms of the Articles. It was the loose-
ness of this system that led General George Washington and Colonel
Alexander Hamilton, who had to deal with wartime conditions in the
field, and James Madison, even without that wartime experience, to
conclude that drastic changes must be made.

The Articles of Confederation described the Union as the "United
States," but that Union could not levy taxes or raise armies except by
voluntary action. The result was that Washington had seen his comrades die of malnutrition and cold at Valley Forge, Pennsylvania. It
was at Valley Forge that volunteers from New Jersey resisted taking an
oath to the "United States," saying, "New Jersey is our country!" The
troops suffered and were deprived of necessities because the Confederation Congress could not compel the thirteen sovereign states to support the military forces and carry on the war. One must go to Valley
Forge and see the huts and hovels, in each of which up to a dozen soldiers were quartered, to grasp the hardships of that war. Washington
and the other leaders knew that a strong central government was imperative for survival. If the thirteen states had continued in this independent and sovereign status after 1781, with or without the Articles of
Confederation, they would have been natural prey for the great powers of the world—including France, our wartime ally. Each of the great
powers would be reaching for pieces of this great continent, which was
largely unknown and the natural resources of which were not fully
appreciated.

Having borne the heavy load of command without adequate support, George Washington understood the situation better than most.
He despaired as he watched some of the states, after the British surrendered at Yorktown, follow the historic pattern of victorious allies
falling out under postwar conditions. Boundary and commercial disputes had states on the verge of calling out troops against one another.
Virginia and Maryland were arguing seriously over boundary lines,
control of the Chesapeake Bay, and fishing rights on the Potomac
River. George Washington's intervention—calling Virginia and
Maryland delegates to an informal "peace conference" at Mount Ver-
non in 1785—resolved those issues. But such disputes, along with
Shays' Rebellion in Massachusetts a year later, confirmed Washington's, Hamilton's, and Madison's fears for the future under the Articles

of Confederation. Jefferson, of course, did not participate at that stage, for he was in Paris as our envoy to France.

Alexander Hamilton's concern for open commerce and trade among the thirteen independent, sovereign states, as well as their foreign trade, was shared by Washington and Madison. With the prompting of these men, a conference among the states was scheduled for September 1786 in Annapolis, Maryland, to discuss trade issues. Delegates from only five states participated. Those of some states simply did not show up, but four states affirmatively refused to send delegates, thinking the convention a dangerous business. The best the conference in Annapolis could do was to adopt a "report" directed to the Confederation Congress and the governors of the states, urging that a convention of representatives from all of the states meet in Philadelphia in May 1787. The focus at this point was still on issues of trade and commerce among the states, but Washington, Hamilton, and Madison knew that commercial and political problems had to be resolved together. To these men, politics and commerce were Siamese twins, not to be separated. Some historians label the meeting in Annapolis "the most successful failure in American history" because it led to the later convention in Philadelphia that drafted our Constitution.

The Articles of Confederation of 1778 had created a Congress that was a semi-executive, semi-legislative body in which each state had an equal vote and each had a veto power over the actions of that body. George Washington called it "little more than a shadow without the substance" of a national government—hardly enough to call the Union a Nation. The thirteen "United States" under the Confederation had less real power than today's European Union with its common market. For such an alliance to win a rebellion against the world's greatest power was itself a miracle, one that might not have happened had George III not been forced to "keep his powder dry" with an eye on France and Spain. And it might not have happened if France had not joined us toward the end of the war.

But once victory was won, new problems loomed. It is difficult in our time to grasp the fear the American people held of a strong national government and a standing army. In their experience, standing armies had always been the tools of oppression, responsible to none but the monarch. That fear of central government had been one of the con-

cerns of the Annapolis conference. Thus, when the Confederation
Congress responded to the conference's call for the states to send delegates to Philadelphia in May 1787, its resolution spoke of making "al-
terations and provisions" in the *existing* constitution, that is, the Articles
of Confederation. According to the resolution, the "sole and express
purpose" of the Philadelphia meeting was to "revis[e] the Articles
of Confederation." We know the Philadelphia Convention as the
"Constitutional" Convention only by virtue of what it produced
on September 17, 1787. When that "product" was sent back to the
Congress to begin the ratification process, there were protests in the
Congress that the delegates to Philadelphia should be censured for exceeding their "mandate"—censured for writing a new constitution!

The process of drafting and ratifying the Constitution shows that
our nation, as a true nation, got off to a slow start—and almost didn't
get started at all. Not all of the thirteen states even responded and sent
delegates to Philadelphia: Rhode Island was thinking of "going it
alone." And without the united support of Massachusetts, Virginia, and
New York, given their size, population, economic status, and key sea-
ports, there could be no real future for a Union of the one-time
colonies of George III. Yet, as described below, these and other states
only narrowly ratified the new charter. There were some hopeful signs,
however. George Washington, a symbol of national unity, was chosen
unanimously to be chairman, or president, of the meeting.

The modern media would have revolted over one of the first actions of the meeting, which was to close the sessions in what is now
known as Independence Hall in Philadelphia to all "outsiders," including representatives of the press. In that hot summer of 1787 all precau-
tions for secrecy were taken: even the windows of the building were
boarded up. The delegates concluded that secret discussions were imperative to foster deliberation and compromise. A delegate who spoke
positively to a point on Monday would find it easier to modify his position on Friday if his arguments had not in the meantime been published in the press and bandied about in the taverns of Philadelphia.
The importance that delegates attached to this aspect of the Convention is illustrated by the fact that James Madison, often called the "architect" of the Constitution, did not allow his copious notes of the
debates to be made public until long after his death. The belief that se-

crecy of debate was required was illustrated, moreover, by one of the
few statements made by George Washington during the course of
the Convention. One delegate carelessly left in the hall some notes
about the meeting. They were found and turned over to George
Washington. The next day Washington scolded the unnamed delegate
for his carelessness.

If there was to be any chance of reconciling the major differences
among the delegates, compromise was essential. Small states were wary
of large states. The interests of the delegates representing the plantation
states of the South and the mercantile-agricultural states of the North
had to be reconciled in some way. Some of their differences seemed ir-
reconcilable, slavery being the major one. The northern states were
largely antislavery while the plantation states were in favor of slavery
because their economies were dependent on it, or so they thought.

As the Convention began, everyone knew that the states, suspicious of central power, were reluctant to give up any part of their sovereignty. Yet the wisest leaders among them knew that a strong
national government was imperative for the new Union. They knew
that if some of the powers of the states were not "surrendered" and delegated to the new national government, there could be no effective
Union—no true nation. They knew that the lack of national authority
had almost led to defeat in the Revolutionary War. They knew that
just the year before, Shays' Rebellion in Massachusetts had threatened
governmental operations in that state. Colonel Daniel Shays, one of
George Washington's soldiers, gathered a mob of farmers and others
who could not pay their debts. So acute was their pain, so strong their
passion that the mob formed into a small army. They closed some of
the Massachusetts courts by force, thereby temporarily halting foreclosures and imprisonment for debt. Only when the "rebels" tried to seize
a military arsenal were they defeated by superior military forces. That
event underscored the need for a true national union, as well as the
connection between political and commercial problems.

One of the most difficult questions to be resolved by the delegates
was the representation of states in the new national legislature. The
small states understandably demanded equal representation, as they had
been given under the Articles of Confederation. The large states, of
course, insisted that representation be on the basis of population. The

final result was a bicameral legislature—with a Senate having equal representation for each state and a House of Representatives in which representation was based on population. That solution seems so logical that it is difficult to realize how sensitive the issue was at the time. The solution became known as "The Great Compromise."

There was constant pressure from George Mason and John Randolph of Virginia, and others, for a Bill of Rights in the Constitution itself. There was no real objection to the substance of the concept, but most of the states at that time already had their own bills of rights and the potential for a conflict between national and state definitions of rights, among other things, was disturbing to some. Another concern was the risk that if they undertook to declare and define some rights, the omission of others might undermine the stated objectives. But it is fair to say that at the close of the Convention there was something like a "gentleman's agreement" that a national Bill of Rights would be promulgated as soon as possible. This promise was to become a significant factor in the ratification process. Although he opposed a Bill of Rights at Philadelphia, James Madison, as a newly elected representative from Virginia, introduced the Bill of Rights in the first Congress in 1789, and ten of the twelve proposed amendments based on Madison's proposals were finally ratified in 1791. One of the twelve, concerning changes in congressional pay, was not ratified at the time but finally became part of the Constitution by the assent of the necessary three fourths of the states in 1992, thus becoming the Twenty-Seventh Amendment. Even today there is debate over whether some of the amendments were needed. Some described these amendments as merely "hortatory," but they still reflected the state of mind of the draftsmen. Let there be no doubt that this is a Constitution that will protect individual rights, said one proponent.

It is not surprising that in subsequent years there were to be bitter political controversies and great cases arising out of the Constitution. The Constitution itself was the subject of profound debate at Philadelphia and in the state ratification conventions that followed. The fear of creating a "monster" national government was a constant specter at Philadelphia. At one point a delegate said in despair that "[i]f no state will part with any of its sovereignty, it is in vain to talk of a national government." In the state conventions during the ratification process and on countless occasions since then, the debate has continued as to whether the Constitution was "correctly" written. Sometimes the criticism is addressed to the Constitution's basic structure. Some critics would have preferred to have a parliamentary system rather than three separate, co-equal branches of government—co-equal, that is, in constitutional theory. Having three independent branches of government was bound to invite controversy, it was argued. This critique is correct to a point. Perhaps a fair response to the critics, however, is that the whole idea of our system of government is to invite debate, after which the people through their representatives can decide upon a tolerable result. As one delegate wrote after Philadelphia, the Constitution was the result of "bargain and Compromise." Admittedly, the success of our system calls for informed and concerned voters, but when the voters take their job seriously, the system works—even if it is not tidy— and freedom is preserved. Although Winston Churchill had not yet said it, it was clear from the beginning of America that "democracy is the worst form of Government except all those other forms that have been tried from time to time."

When the Convention adjourned, the delegates soon discovered that the creation of the Constitution was, to put it mildly, no overwhelmingly popular act. It was almost three months after the Miracle at Philadelphia, on December 7, 1787, when Delaware became the first state to ratify the proposed Constitution. Although all thirty delegates to Delaware's ratification convention approved the new charter, such sentiment in favor of the Constitution was by no means unanimous in the other states. Massachusetts, the sixth state to ratify, did so on February 6, 1788, by the slight margin of 187 votes to 168 votes. Article VII of the proposed Constitution provided that the new national government would be established when nine of the thirteen states ratified it. On June 21, 1788, New Hampshire had the historic honor of becoming the ninth state to do so, by a vote of 57 to 47. Even after New Hampshire adopted the Constitution, the status of the Union remained in doubt because the powerful states of Virginia and New York, not to mention North Carolina and Rhode Island, still had not voted to join. But on June 25, 1788, only four days after New Hampshire's vote, Virginia—by far the most populous state at the time—became the tenth state to adopt the Constitution, voting 89 to

79 in favor of ratification. Following Virginia's heated ratification debate, New York narrowly adopted the new charter on July 26, 1788, by a vote of 30 to 27. North Carolina and Rhode Island had options to join the Union or to remain as they were: "independent" and "sovereign." It was not until November 1789 that North Carolina ratified the Constitution; Rhode Island followed in 1790.

Even before North Carolina and Rhode Island had joined the Union, the first Congress of the eleven states was called and was scheduled to meet at Federal Hall in New York on March 4, 1789. However, there were not enough members to form a quorum in either the House or the Senate, and as a result the Senate was prevented from conducting any business until April. That delayed the receipt of the vote of the Electoral College. The Senate finally counted the votes on April 6, 1789, thus confirming that George Washington had been unanimously elected the first president of the United States pursuant to Article II of the Constitution. Because of the delay, the presidential inaugural date set by the Confederation Congress for March 4 was deferred until April 30, 1789. Without a president to appoint members of the judicial branch established by Article III, there were no federal judges or Supreme Court justices at the beginning of the new nation.

The judicial branch was minuscule in the small governmental structure. The Constitution established a Supreme Court but did not specify its composition, and it left the creation of "inferior," or lower, courts to the discretion of Congress. Thus, neither the first justices nor other judges could be appointed until the Congress met to decide how many justices, trial courts, and appellate courts were needed. On September 24, the Judiciary Act of 1789, largely drafted by Senator Oliver Ellsworth, who would later become the third Chief Justice, created the federal judicial branch. The Act provided that "the supreme court of the United States shall consist of a chief justice and five associate justices." The Act also created thirteen district court judgeships, assigning one trial judge each to nine of the eleven states that had so far ratified the Constitution and two judges each to Virginia and Massachusetts, in anticipation that the new states of Kentucky and Maine would later be formed out of their territory.

February 2, 1790, is a very important date in our history, a date even the judiciary had not acknowledged until recently, when we looked back at our beginnings. On that date the Supreme Court of the United States first met. When Washington was finally chosen as president and a quorum of the Congress was obtained, he nominated John Jay of New York to be the first Chief Justice of the United States, with John Rutledge, James Wilson, William Cushing, John Blair, Jr., and Robert Harrison (who declined to serve on account of poor health) as associate justices. They were promptly confirmed and a date was fixed for the first session: February 1, 1790. But because of the extremely difficult travel conditions of that day, only three justices—Chief Justice John Jay and Associate Justices James Wilson and William Cushing—showed up on the first day of February. They met in New York City, then the capital of the new nation, in a small room on the second floor of a nondescript commercial building with a fancy name—the Royal Exchange—across the street from the Fulton Fish Market. Because three justices were one less than required for a quorum, the Court adjourned to February 2, when Justice John Blair arrived. On that day, the Court officially opened its first session. No cases were yet scheduled on the docket, of course, so the justices attended to administrative matters, such as appointing the Court's clerk and adopting the Court's rules.

The Court in those early years met in humble surroundings, and in the minds of many in that day the Court would not occupy a very important position in the government of the nation. During the debate over the Constitution, Alexander Hamilton alluded in *The Federalist Papers* to the judiciary's inherent weakness, having "no influence over either the sword or the purse." John Jay would resign from the Court to become governor of New York because, according to him, the tribunal would never amount to much, a view he reiterated to President Adams when Jay was asked to return as Chief Justice in 1800. States were still considered in many respects to be sovereign nations, and being governor was thought of as being in essence the president of a state. For example, Ben Franklin had been called "President," not "Governor," of Pennsylvania. John Rutledge, one of the original associate justices, resigned to become chief justice of the Court of Common Pleas in his native South Carolina. But although Jay, Hamilton, and Rutledge were key Founding Fathers, history has proven them, and especially Jay, to be poor prophets in regard to the future of the Supreme Court. They did not anticipate John Marshall, the Great Chief Justice. They lacked Marshall's vision of what the Court could become and, perhaps, of the Court's key role in making the American experiment work.

CHAPTER TWO

MR. MARSHALL GOES
TO COURT

....

Bracken v. Visitors of William & Mary College, 1790

To all to whom these Our present Letters shall come, greeting: Foras-
much as our well-beloved and trusty Subjects, constituting the General As-
sembly of our Colony of Virginia, have had it in their Minds, and have
proposed to themselves . . . to make, found, and establish a certain Place of
universal Study, or perpetual College of Divinity, Philosophy, Languages,
and other good Arts and Sciences, consisting of one President, six Masters or
Professors, and an hundred Scholars, more or less, according to the Ability of
the said College. . . . And . . . it shall be called and denominated for ever,
The College of William and Mary in Virginia . . . .

—King William III and Queen
Mary II, February 8, 1693,
making the Bishop of London
the first chancellor of the
College of William and Mary

U P TO THE TIME when Thomas Jefferson and his committee
drafted the Declaration of Independence and the war between
the thirteen new states and the mother country began, the
original charter of the College of William and Mary, granted by King
William and his queen, was honored. The college is located at Wil-

14

liamsburg—at that time the capital of Virginia—and substantial financial support came from the Parliament in London. But with the royal source of income cut off by the war, the college undertook some necessary reorganization, and George Washington became its first American chancellor.

The college taught the "Lattin," Greek, and Hebrew tongues together with divinity, philosophy, and mathematics. It also conducted a grammar school. The Board of Visitors, the governing body of the college, decided to abandon that school. John Bracken, the grammar school's master, or professor, objected. He insisted that the action could not be taken without the approval of the Virginia legislature because the changes in the status of the school from the original royal charter had placed the college under legislative mandate. The Board of Visitors was unpersuaded. The college had already dropped its divinity school, with its focus on the Church of England, even though the school of divinity was specifically mentioned in the charter. To preserve the grammar school and, of course, his position, Bracken engaged one of the distinguished lawyers in Virginia, John Taylor, to plead his case. The college engaged a young Williamsburg lawyer, John Marshall, who had studied briefly on its campus under George Wythe. Marshall was a college dropout, but a very successful practitioner.

When the case came before Virginia's highest court in 1790, Taylor argued that the powers vested in the Board of Visitors came from the original royal charter of 1693; in Taylor's view the Board could not abandon the grammar school "without the approval of the [state] legislature" because, by virtue of the financial support granted from the state after royal support ceased, the college had become an arm of the state. In other words, the legislature of Virginia had stepped into the royal shoes and therefore the state had to be consulted.

Taylor's argument derived from the charter of the College of William and Mary, which he described as a "magnet, from whence every part of th[e] business [of the college] must take its direction." He contended that the charter was the "constitution of the College," and as with all constitutions, it "ought to be preserved inviolate." It was clear, Taylor said, that the people of a nation can change their constitution and adopt another, but a subordinate body politic within that nation can do no such thing. In Taylor's view the Board of Visitors was just such a body and its actions were "defined and limited by, and subordinate to, the charter." He said that this must be so if there was to be anything fundamental and permanent about the structure of the college. Little did Taylor know that by turning the argument about the grammar school at the College of William and Mary into a constitutional debate, he was presenting the young and talented John Marshall with one of his first opportunities to articulate the rules of constitutional interpretation that he would later use to mold the constitutional law of the United States.

Marshall responded to Taylor's argument by saying that the College of William and Mary was a private entity whose internal affairs were not subject to control by the state of Virginia even though the college received some of its support from the state. After 1776, relations between the college and the Crown were at an end; the Bishop of London had been removed as chancellor and George Washington became the first American chancellor. Since it was no longer a Crown college, no Bishops of London or Archbishops of Canterbury would ever again hold the office of chancellor. The college was plainly a charitable institution under its 1693 charter, Marshall argued, supported in part by the Crown. Now, he said, it is the same body—with support in part from the legislature of Virginia—with its charter unchanged.

Marshall contended that these changes, along with the needs of the college, supported the action of the Board of Visitors in abandoning one of its schools. He also rejected the notion that the Board of Visitors' act of abolishing the master's position violated the college charter. In Marshall's view, the Board's legislative powers "extended to the modification of the schools, in any manner they should deem proper, provided they did not depart from the great outlines marked [for the college] in the charter." Marshall said that such discretion must be given to the Visitors because the knowledge of a particular branch of science, which at one time might be deemed all important, might at another time be thought of as not worth acquiring. He argued that "only great leading and general principles, ought to be immutable" when interpreting the charters of durable institutions such as the College of William and Mary.

Marshall accepted Taylor's suggestion that the Visitors were bound by the charter, but his interpretation of that charter was different from

Taylor's. Marshall identified certain principles in the document that Taylor did not. Rather than focus on those provisions that apparently limited the Visitors' powers, Marshall emphasized those sections of the charter from which the power to abolish the master's position could be derived. He began with the appointment clause, which gave the Visitors the

> power to make such rules, laws, statutes, orders and injunctions, for the good and wholesome government of the College, as to them and their successors shall, from time to time, according to their various occasions and circumstances, seem most fit and expedient.

Because the charter accorded the Visitors "the power of making . . . laws for the government of the College," Marshall argued that the Visitors also had, with respect to the masters, "the power of appointment and the power of deprivation."

In response to Taylor's argument that the Board of Visitors' act of abolishing the position of master of the grammar school was beyond the Board's powers, Marshall said simply that the grammar school itself was not established by the charter. Rather, the charter gave the trustees the power

> to erect, found and establish a certain place of universal study, or perpetual college for divinity, philosophy, languages and other good arts and sciences, consisting of one president [and] six masters or professors.

The charter required, therefore, only that there should be "a president and six professors[;] and, perhaps, that divinity, philosophy and the languages should be taught in the College." The requirement that languages should be taught in the college was satisfied, said Marshall, if either "the modern [or] the ancient languages" were taught, but there was no express requirement in the charter for a grammar school.

In sum, Marshall told the court that the Board's act abolishing the grammar school was a perfectly legitimate exercise of legislative power, because the Board had "power to make such laws for the government of the College, from time to time" so long as those laws were in "no way contrary" to the charter. This reasoning foreshadowed the analysis that Marshall as Chief Justice would later apply to the power of Congress under the United States Constitution.

In essence, Marshall's argument was that the royal charter of 1693 was an organic document—a charter or a constitution creating a form of government—and that it authorized, but did not command, the college to have a grammar school. It followed that the legislative arm of the college could make changes to meet changed conditions and that the action of its governing body in abandoning the grammar school in 1779 was within its authority under the charter. Marshall concluded that it was not for judges to worry whether the Board of Visitors—the legislative body of the college—had made a wise and sound decision, but only whether it had acted "within the great outlines" of the charter. The future Chief Justice was not simply arguing a case; he was articulating a view of separation of powers and judicial restraint in reviewing legislative action that was to become the hallmark of one great line of interpretation by the Supreme Court. Courts do not evaluate the wisdom of an act of Congress, any more than, in John Marshall's view, they should have reviewed the wisdom of the decision of William and Mary College's Board of Visitors. Rather, the courts are to determine whether the legislature's action is authorized by the organic document, be it the charter of a college or—as Marshall would apply the principle years later—the Constitution of the United States.

The highest court of Virginia agreed with John Marshall. It issued a one-sentence holding:

> Let it be certified that, *on the merits of the case,* the General Court ought not to award a writ of mandamus to restore the plaintiff to the office of grammar master and professor of humanity in the said College.

Thus Mr. Bracken lost his job as master of the grammar school, but there were no hard feelings about it. The esteem in which he was held was shown years later when he was made president of the college.

The case of Mr. Bracken was of greater significance than most historians realize because it foreshadowed the greatness of Chief Justice

John Marshall as a jurist. It revealed Marshall's view that an organic law is to be applied by an institution's governing body with a mind to the objectives of the law's creation, confined only by the explicit limitations within that law. The Court could just as easily have expressed its holding in the terms Marshall would use years later as Chief Justice: if the "end" of the Visitors' actions (eliminating the grammar school) was a "legitimate" exercise of their discretionary legislative power, then the "means" by which they accomplished that end (abolishing the position of master of the grammar school) were valid inasmuch as they were plainly "adapted" to accomplish the end and were not contrary to any express provision in the charter. Under Marshall's expansive interpretation of the charter, the power of the governing body—the legislature of the college—included the power to say when and how the college was to be run. His approach to these fundamental questions as well as his concept of organic law emerged in this relatively unimportant case about the job of a master of a small grammar school. Interpreting the charter in terms of "great outlines" and "general principles," Marshall was laying the foundation for his method of interpreting the United States Constitution in such historic cases as *Marbury* v. *Madison, M'Culloch* v. *Maryland,* and *Gibbons* v. *Ogden,* all of which are discussed in later chapters. As we shall see, in such cases and applying those principles, Marshall gave meaning—too broad a meaning, some of his critics contended—to many of the Constitution's more generally worded provisions.

CHAPTER THREE

TREATIES SHALL BE THE SUPREME LAW OF THE LAND

....

Ware v. Hylton, 1796

*[A]ll Treaties made, or which shall be made, under the Authority of the
United States, shall be the supreme Law of the Land; and the Judges in every
State shall be bound thereby, any Thing in the Constitution or Laws of any
State to the Contrary notwithstanding.*
  —Article VI, U.S. Constitution

*Our Federal Constitution establishes the power of a treaty over the constitu-
tion and laws of any of the States; and I have shewn that the words of the 4th
article [of the Treaty of Paris] were intended, and are sufficient to nullify the
law of Virginia . . . .*
  —Justice Samuel Chase,
  in *Ware* v. *Hylton,* 1796

FROM THE EARLIEST DAYS of the colonies, Americans borrowed
money from sources in England, sometimes to expand a plantation, sometimes to build a house, sometimes to build a ship. The
powers in control who influenced economic policy in England had
never let the colonists become economically independent, but were
willing to finance certain limited businesses. The per capita debt in the
thirteen colonies owed to lenders in England was very high at the time

20

of the Declaration of Independence. During the revolutionary period this problem went unresolved. The British were not lending to revolutionaries, nor were the Americans sending money to pay off their debts to British creditors. Americans who sided with England, the Tories, often left the country and had their property confiscated. While the war lasted, the rights of debtors and creditors were laid aside. In 1777, while Thomas Jefferson was governor of Virginia, the Virginia legislature enacted a law that permitted American borrowers to satisfy their debts to creditors in England by making payments into a trust fund that would be later used to repay the British creditors. These payments were, of course, in American currency.

But at the war's end, one of the obstacles to a peace treaty between the United States and England was the settlement of the economic relationships that had been ignored during hostilities. The British insisted that any treaty provide that all money owed by Americans to British creditors be paid in sterling. The British drove a hard bargain, for the Americans, though victorious in the war, faced a serious threat from British troops poised on Canada—not all that far from Boston. Those troops would not be removed unless the debt problem was resolved. So the Americans agreed to the British terms in the Treaty of Paris, concluded in 1783.

American creditors were highly critical of the treaty and its costly concession to the British. The Constitution had placed treaty obligations on essentially the same level as its other provisions limiting state power and hence superior to state legislative acts. The Virginians who owed money to British creditors were naturally unsympathetic to the notion that they had to give those creditors a higher standing than they would give to their fellow Americans from whom they had borrowed money. Nevertheless, British creditors were coming after the millions of pounds of sterling they had lent to the former colonists.

The first Supreme Court case to construe the Treaty Clause was initially tried in the federal circuit court in Virginia. It was heard by two Supreme Court justices and the district judge assigned to the state and federal district of Virginia. In that court John Marshall and his colleagues who represented the Virginia debtors argued that the Treaty Clause did not apply to debts created before the adoption of the Constitution. They won. An appeal was taken by the British creditors to the United States Supreme Court, which was sitting in Philadelphia, the seat of the government at that time. Before his arguments in this case, Marshall had established a solid reputation in the Virginia bar, but this would be the first and only time that Marshall would argue before the Court over which he later presided.

Marshall spent many weeks in Philadelphia to prepare for a Supreme Court that, in 1796, had been hearing cases for only a few years. During those weeks he met many of the leaders of the Federalist party whom he had known only by reputation. In that day it was common, as it is to this day in England, for lawyers and judges to share social engagements even while litigating. During the time the Virginia debtors' case was pending before the Supreme Court in Philadelphia, the members of the Philadelphia bar and the judges were frequently living and dining at the same boardinghouses and taverns. Some had heard of Marshall's strong advocacy of the Constitution in the Virginia ratification convention in opposition to Patrick Henry, George Mason, and others. All of these men, who were waiting for their cases to be called by the Court, were leading members of the bar and active in public affairs. But it was characteristic of Marshall that he did not let his political and legislative conflicts interfere with personal relationships.

In 1796 lawyers did not file written briefs on appeal, as they do today, but rather argued the case without time limit. An argument in the Supreme Court in 1796 was more like a debate before a congressional committee than the half-hour argument permitted in today's Supreme Court. With its light docket in the eighteenth and nineteenth centuries, the Court let the lawyers take their time. It took a total of six days, with interruptions and recesses, for counsel to argue the case of *Ware* v. *Hylton*. Superb lawyer that he was, Marshall must have known that, given the Treaty Clause, he had a very difficult case. The very Constitution he had helped to ratify had an explicit provision that on its face contradicted his position. Virginia's law had to comply with the Treaty Clause in Article VI of the Constitution, which provides that

> all Treaties made, or which shall be made, under the Authority of the United States, *shall be the supreme Law of the Land;* and the Judges in every State shall be bound thereby, any Thing in the

Constitution or Laws of any State to the Contrary notwithstanding (emphasis added).

As a passionate believer in the Constitution and long committed to its supremacy over state law, Marshall still had to find some way to make a plausible and logical argument on behalf of his clients. He knew that this case was to be a test that would not only involve enormous economic interests but would also implicate a major constitutional issue in an emotionally charged conflict between the victorious American colonists and their creditors in the mother country. Southerners, particularly the southern debtors, were very hostile to the 1783 treaty, feeling that the treaty had not adequately protected the rights of debtors in the United States. Why, Virginians and others asked, should our late-enemy creditors get better treatment than our fellow-American creditors? This was a good question, and an especially good political question. The problem for those who asked it was that the Treaty of Paris, which had ended the war, required such treatment for British creditors, and the Treaty Clause of the Constitution made treaties and federal laws "the supreme Law of the Land."

The ever-resourceful Marshall was able to be faithful not only to his duty to his clients but also to his duty to the Court to which he had just been admitted as an advocate. His best argument was that the debts in question had been contracted before the adoption of the Constitution; the Virginia law had also been enacted prior to the Constitution, when, as Marshall put it, Virginia "was an independent nation." As one of thirteen sovereigns, Virginia had engaged independently in a war with England along with twelve other sovereigns. "Property," Marshall argued, "is the creature of civil society, and subject, in all respects, to the disposition and controul of civil institutions." In other words, since state law had created the obligation to repay the debts, state law should control the extent of the obligation. From that, he argued that because these transactions preceded the ratification of the Constitution and the making of the treaty, the debtor-creditor relations were governed by state law and were not subject to the treaty provisions of the Constitution. Only transactions occurring after the Constitution and the treaty had become effective, he urged, should be so subject. Mar-

shall's approach to the case was analytical, not emotional. In a day
when oratory flourished and when most of the leaders of the bar were
great public speakers who relied on verbal flourishes in argument, Marshall's style was singular. It was long after Marshall's day that people
talked about going for "the jugular" in a great argument, but from all
accounts that is just what Marshall did. Marshall's oratory went for the
jugular of his opponent's theory while exploiting his own strength.
The core of his argument was the only one that he could conscien-
tiously make, consistent with his dedication to the supremacy of the
Constitution over any legislative action.

But in this case even that logic was unsuccessful: a unanimous
Court rejected Marshall's argument. The Court held that the jugular
was protected by the shield of the Constitution embodied in the Treaty
Clause. It was the conclusion Marshall almost certainly would have
reached had he been sitting as a justice in the case, namely, that the
Virginians' obligation to repay the British creditors was governed by
a valid treaty, which under the Constitution was the "supreme Law
of the Land," notwithstanding the Virginia state law to the contrary.
Treaties ending a state of war are not always pleasing to all constituents
of the parties involved—even, as in this case, to the winners.

Even though he lost this case, Marshall's argument made a favorable impression on the justices and on the Federalist leaders he met in
Philadelphia. His reputation now reached a national level and led to a
number of tendered appointments by President Washington, including
the offer of an appointment as attorney general of the United States.
Marshall, however, was not ready to leave his native Virginia. Unlike
wealthy men such as Washington and Jefferson, Marshall lacked the
means to give up the law practice that throve with his growing reputation. Marshall instead became an attorney for Robert Morris—a
prominent participant in the Constitutional Convention—at a time
when Morris was one of the wealthiest men in the United States.
Among other property, Morris owned vast undeveloped acreage in
Virginia and in the new western lands. Even though he lost his only
Supreme Court case, Marshall's contacts during the weeks in Philadelphia were professionally and politically profitable.

The Court's decision was also good for the country. The new nation created by the Constitution was merely an upstart compared to

other countries with histories of hundreds if not thousands of years. It was essential to the standing of the United States in the Western world that it be known to honor its treaty and commercial obligations. By a decision of its highest court, the United States took a position of responsibility that unquestionably enhanced America's standing with other nations. It encouraged the world trade long denied to the colonies under British rule. After the Supreme Court's ruling in this case, the businessmen of other nations would have more confidence in dealing with this new creation forged out of thirteen British colonies in a distant wilderness.

Little has been written about the implications of this case for the Supremacy Clause of the Constitution, which provides that the federal Constitution and federal laws are, like treaties, "supreme" over contrary state constitutions and state laws. Yet *Ware* v. *Hylton* was the first Supreme Court case striking down the action of a legislative body as contrary to a clause of the federal Constitution. That fact did not entirely escape the public's notice. At the time, when states were still clinging to the idea of sovereignty, public reaction to the *Ware* case was largely negative. People were more likely to accept judicial restraint on action by the new national legislature than on state legislative action. As we will see in a later chapter, Chief Justice Marshall's famous opinion, in a landmark case of *Marbury* v. *Madison*, extended the doctrine of judicial review to acts of Congress as well as to those of the state legislatures.

CHAPTER FOUR

MR. JEFFERSON,
MR. MARSHALL,
AND MR. BURR

....

*[N]othing in the Constitution has given [judges] the right to decide for the
Executive, more than to the Executive to decide for them. Both magistrates
are equally independent in the sphere of action assigned to them.*
—President Thomas Jefferson, in
a letter to Abigail Adams, 1804

A T TEN O'CLOCK on the morning of March 4, 1801, the Senate
met in the half-completed Capitol building for the inauguration of a new president. It was the first inauguration to be held
in the new capital, Washington, D.C. John Marshall, the fourth Chief
Justice of the United States, stood ready to administer the constitutional oath of office to Thomas Jefferson at noon. Upon taking the
oath, Jefferson would become the third president of the United States.
With Marshall on the dais of the Senate chamber was Aaron Burr, who
earlier that day had taken the oath of office as vice president. Only by
the narrowest of margins had Burr failed to be elected president, and
under the Constitution at the time, the runner-up became vice president. When Jefferson arrived, the three men stood together before the
Senate. It must have presented an odd sight, for the animosity among

the three was well known. As Henry Adams put it in his masterful history of the period, "the assembled senators looked up at three men who profoundly disliked and distrusted each other."

To understand great events in our history, one must look at the circumstances and the personalities involved. As we watch the rivalries and the intense competition among our contemporary political leaders, figures of bygone days may sometimes seem to be men who sat down in harmony to draft documents like the Declaration of Independence, the Constitution, and the Bill of Rights. Perhaps that image is one we learned as schoolchildren, but from records still available, we know that it is unfounded. The leaders of our first one hundred years included some tough politicians involved in harsh political battles.

Inauguration Day, 1801, provides an apt setting to consider the important conflicts among Jefferson, Marshall, and Burr that have indelibly marked our history and our Constitution. Each of the three men had played a significant political role in the young Republic. President Jefferson had been the primary author of the Declaration of Independence, minister to France, governor of Virginia, secretary of state, and vice president. Both Vice President Burr and Chief Justice Marshall had been soldiers under George Washington. Burr had served as attorney general of New York and as a United States senator. Of the three, Marshall was the relative novice to national politics. It should be remembered that only thirteen years before Chief Justice Marshall swore in Jefferson as president, Jefferson as governor of Virginia had handed young Marshall his certificate of admission to practice law. Although Marshall had been a successful lawyer in Virginia and had been active in state politics—as we have seen, he distinguished himself at the ratification convention in Virginia in 1788—he had not served in the national government until he was chosen as a special envoy to France in 1797. After that temporary duty, it took George Washington, who urged him to run for Congress in 1799, to draw him back to national politics. His service, as special envoy to France, as a member of Congress, and as secretary of state for the last year of John Adams' expiring administration, was solid but unspectacular; he was drafted for those offices. Marshall's national public career really began when Adams appointed him Chief Justice in 1801—just a month before Jefferson's inauguration. Jefferson, on the other hand, had a spectacular career beginning twenty-five years earlier with the drafting of the Declaration. With Marshall's distinguished service as Chief Justice for thirty-four years, however, his influence on the American polity was, as many lawyers and historians agree, equal to, if not greater than, Jefferson's.

The origins and early environments of Thomas Jefferson and John Marshall were very different, yet these two remarkable men arrived at the same high level in the branches they served, one Chief Executive, the other Chief Justice of the United States. They were as different as their origins, while sharing more perhaps than either of them acknowledged. Jefferson was born to aristocracy, social and economic. He was educated in the classics and the law and was a student of languages, music, and science. He had a creative and probing mind. He was, along with Benjamin Franklin, one of our closest approximations to a Renaissance man. Jefferson was also an architect of buildings and of governmental concepts, but more an architect than a builder of government. He was so many things that possibly few really know the whole man. He was seemingly determined to let no one know the whole Thomas Jefferson. He was controlled and at times as methodical as a research scientist, yet capable of rages and intemperate utterances. Still, when necessary, Jefferson was capable of shedding his hostility toward another if it served his objectives. One biographer calls him "the most approachable and the most impenetrable of men, easy and delightful of acquaintance, impossible" to know. Another sees him as a man with a "hard-glazed surface . . . so difficult to penetrate" and "all things to all men." Dumas Malone's lifetime study of Jefferson led him to conclude that no one can truly comprehend this labyrinthine being—surely one of the most personally aloof of all our presidents, rivaled possibly by Coolidge, who had none of Jefferson's color and little of his genius. All in all, Jefferson was one of the most complex men in our history.

One student of Jefferson suggests that on many major issues of his day Jefferson can be found on both sides. Jefferson's talent for rhetoric entrapped him at times in the passion of the moment. Surely his eloquence on the dignity of every human being and his public statements in opposition to slavery are difficult to reconcile with the fact that he used slaves to work his fields. A passage of his draft of the Declaration of Independence, which the Continental Congress deleted, accused King George III of

> wag[ing] cruel war against human nature itself, violating it's [*sic*] most sacred rights of life [and] liberty in the persons of a distant people who never offended him, captivating [and] carrying them into slavery in another hemisphere, or to incur miserable death in their transportation thither.

Yet Jefferson himself was a full participant in that "execrable commerce," the slave trade. In fairness, however, he had much company in the slave business and at times it is clear he felt trapped on the issue.

Disciplined in keeping detailed accounts and records of his plantation, he wrote and kept records as few public men have done. One of the most interesting features of Jefferson is the fact that he was one of America's most prolific and eloquent letter writers. Some observers believe that he intended his vast store of letters, more than fifteen thousand, to tell his life story as he wanted it told rather than having his story told by others. As with all humans, Jefferson's actions and internal conflicts do not always reflect as favorably on him as do his writings. Carefully concealing some aspects of his private life, he destroyed hundreds of letters, including letters to his wife and children. What, if anything, he ever recorded or said about the widely discussed relationship with his household slave Sally Hemings is not known. There remains a letter of apology to the husband of a neighboring plantation owner written by Jefferson after being challenged to a duel by the husband. Jefferson explained that his only interest in the neighbor's attractive wife was to be helpful as a neighbor during the husband's prolonged absences. That episode has the earmarks of mudslinging by Jefferson's political adversaries. Even if we grant some truth to these negative stories, they do not detract from Jefferson as one of the great men among the Founders. But it may help to reveal the human side he sought to conceal.

John Marshall is far less known today than Thomas Jefferson. In retrospect, Marshall was not as good a public relations man as was Jefferson. Unlike Jefferson, Marshall did not leave behind a vast correspondence or memoirs to enlighten, confuse, or build an image. He must be judged largely on what he wrote in the opinions of the Supreme Court, and in the few surviving transcripts of his debates and arguments as a lawyer. But surely Marshall was as great a man as Jefferson.

In John Marshall, we find a very different kind of person. As Jefferson was complex, Marshall was simple in all his tastes, especially in putting the law and the Constitution above all. He was practical where Jefferson was more theoretical. Marshall came from modest means but built a comfortable living, whereas Jefferson had substantial wealth, but later in life struggled financially. Perhaps Jefferson's preoccupation with other interests kept him on the edge of bankruptcy. Marshall was gregarious where Jefferson was reserved. Marshall was at home and at ease with the ordinary folk who were his neighbors, pitching quoits (horseshoes) and drinking port—a bit too much, some said. He was careless and casual about his clothes to the point that there was public comment on it in his later life. Classic stories survive of his carrying a large turkey home from a market in his arm with no wrappings, and of looking to the sky near the close of a conference of the Court and commenting that somewhere in the Court's large jurisdiction it had to be time for a drink. Another story is told that having torn his buckskin breeches mounting or dismounting his horse on the way from Richmond to a session of the Supreme Court, he sent them to a tailor to be mended. They were not returned in time, so he simply donned his long black robe to cover the want of breeches and held Court.

But although common in some respects, Marshall was equally at home with the greatest minds of his time. The sheer brilliance of his mind is revealed in the compelling logic and force of his opinions for the Supreme Court. All show the extraordinary clarity and concreteness that characterize his speaking, his writing, and his debates with Patrick Henry and George Mason in 1788 on the jurisdiction of the proposed federal courts.

John Marshall was the oldest of fifteen children raised in the backwoods of western Virginia. His father, Thomas Marshall, was a boyhood friend of George Washington, and like Washington was a farmer and surveyor. The elder Marshall was also a justice of the peace and a delegate to the Virginia House of Burgesses. In the Marshall household, the names of George Washington, James Madison, Patrick Henry, and of course, Thomas Jefferson, Thomas Marshall's cousin, were all well known even though the Marshall family's social contacts with affluent plantation owners were limited. John Marshall was educated by private tutoring and by home study under the guidance of literate parents, who had more books than most of their backwoods neighbors. At his boyhood home, young John Marshall read Sir William Blackstone's *Commentaries on the Laws of England*, along with books in Latin and Greek. Marshall also loved poetry and often spent evenings reading with others the great English poets of the day. As Lincoln's prose reflected his early Bible reading, Marshall's opinions were to reflect not only his concreteness and his mastery of logic but also his love of words that convey images.

In his youth he spent a year in residence with a clergyman-teacher, where one of his schoolmates was James Monroe, later to become a Marshall adversary both as an anti-Federalist and as president. That was, however, the extent of Marshall's formal education, except for a few weeks of legal study after the Revolutionary War at the College of William and Mary in Williamsburg. He began study there under the great teacher-jurist George Wythe—who had taught Jefferson a dozen years earlier—only to return home, at age twenty-six, to pursue the practice of law in earnest, to marry Polly Ambler, and to enter public life.

It was the intervening war years, however, that did much to shape Marshall's views toward government. In 1775, when relations with England became increasingly strained and war was approaching, John Marshall joined the Virginia militia. By the end of the year, he, his father, and his neighbors had fought against British troops in the Battle of Great Bridge, the first battle between colonists and British soldiers after Bunker Hill. They fought under the state flag, which shows a snake with Virginia as its head and fangs and twelve rattles for the other colonies. This was not just local arrogance; Virginia was the largest, the richest, and the most heavily populated of the thirteen colonies and thought of itself—as the other colonies did at the time—as a sovereign nation. Under the Virginia flag John Marshall and his friends learned about guerrilla warfare. The battle at Great Bridge was a small engage-

ment, but it effectively ended the British effort to divide the thirteen
states in two. Young John Marshall there saw the compelling need to
have unity among the thirteen sovereign states.

In 1775 many colonists were not ready to declare independence
from England. Although they had heard about a distant Continental
Congress, some Americans still wanted to remain under their king, if
only he would give them their rights as Englishmen. The Marshalls,
however, were not among them. After the Battle of Great Bridge,
Thomas Marshall joined the Continental Army. His son went back to
work on the farm, but only for a short time. By the next July, after the
Declaration of Independence had been signed, John Marshall followed
his father into the Continental Army as a lieutenant under General
George Washington. It would be six long, bloody years before another
battle in Virginia, at Yorktown, would end the war.

The strong nationalist in John Marshall may have been born during the winter of 1777–1778 at Valley Forge, where Marshall served
first as lieutenant and then as captain under Washington. There Marshall met Alexander Hamilton, who was senior to him. He saw Hamilton struggle with the fragile finances of the Confederation Congress
that came into existence in 1778. As Washington's aides, Hamilton,
and probably Marshall as well, came to understand what was needed to
make a nation out of thirteen sovereign, independent states joined only
in "a firm league of friendship" under the Articles of Confederation. At
Valley Forge Marshall saw comrades die for want of adequate shelter
and clothing, weakened by malnutrition. There was no power in the
distant Congress of the confederated states—wherever it was sitting—
to compel the states to send what was needed to care for the troops or
even to send troops at all. The words of the Declaration of Independence were inspiring, but where were the boots, the meat, the blan-
kets, the medicine, and the bullets? The Declaration did not provide
supplies, nor did the Congress. George Washington had to depend on
voluntary help and volunteer soldiers.

The men who saw hundreds of their compatriots die that winter
were bitter, but for the most part remained loyal, though some de-
serted and others would not remain after their brief enlistments ran out.
Unity was fragile. Through Washington's example, Marshall learned
that only time and leadership could bring the states together. Later

events surely demonstrated the soundness of Washington's and Hamilton's conviction that a strong central government was imperative for long-range development, if not survival itself.

Jefferson's experience during the war was dramatically different. As a member of the Second Continental Congress, Jefferson led the cause of independence and gave his eloquence to its great Declaration. Later in the war, however, he returned to the Virginia legislature. There, to be sure, he pressed many important political and legal reforms. Yet General Washington expressed frustration that the best and brightest of his fellow Virginians devoted their energy to their state, rather than to the greater interests of America as a whole. "[I]n the present situation of things," Washington wrote at the time, "I cannot help asking: Where is Mason, Wythe, Jefferson . . . ." After years of war, of course, Washington prevailed, despite his difficulties with an ineffective Congress. The British discovered what the United States would learn two centuries later in Vietnam: that locals, fighting on their own turf, sometimes "win" by avoiding superior enemy forces. Washington was able to do at least that with his meager, mainly guerrilla forces, and finally to defeat the British outright with the well-timed help of the French army and navy at Yorktown. Nevertheless, the war years for Marshall drove home the need for a strong central government.

The third fascinating figure in our story is Aaron Burr. Burr was not only one of the most puzzling figures among the Founders, he was also perhaps one of the more brilliant, albeit eccentric. Due largely to Burr's trial for treason—he was acquitted—and Jefferson's highly inflammatory pretrial statements as to his guilt, the name of Burr has become almost an expletive in American history: he is known as a political Benedict Arnold. The reputation, however, is undeserved. Like Marshall, Burr served under Washington in the Continental Army. As an effective young officer he achieved the rank of colonel at an early age. Aaron Burr's talents and standing in the Jeffersonian party were confirmed in the election of 1800. In reality, Burr was, and is recognized by many historians as, one of the very able men of the period. Some of his thinking was surprisingly progressive for the era. One letter Burr wrote to his wife, Theodosia, would earn him respect from the contemporary feminist movement. He wrote:

It was a knowledge of your mind which first inspired me with a respect for that of your sex, and with some regret, I confess, that the ideas which you have often heard me express in favour of female intellectual powers are founded on what I have imagined, more than what I have seen, except in you. I have endeavoured to trace the causes of this *rare* display of genius in women, and find them in the errors of education, of prejudice, and of habit. I admit that men are equally, nay more, much more to blame than women. Boys and girls are generally educated much in the same way till they are eight or nine years of age, and it is admitted that girls make at least equal progress with the boys; generally, indeed, they make better. Why, then, has it never been thought worth the attempt to discover, by fair experiment, the particular age at which the male superiority becomes so evident?

Burr later put his views on the education of women into effect. He saw to it that his daughter, also named Theodosia, received an education well beyond the usual for a young woman of that day. She became in her own right one of the unusual women of her time, knowledgeable in Latin and Greek, fluent in French, and well trained in music.

During Burr's Revolutionary War service, a rivalry began to develop between him and Alexander Hamilton that would ultimately be Burr's undoing. Both men were brilliant, but Hamilton was more stable than Burr. They became, or at least thought they were, rivals for the attention of their commander, General George Washington. Each of them moved to high places very early. Since both were from New York, their rivalry continued after the war, until their duel in 1804 left Hamilton dead and Burr on the road to political ruin. Burr was a lawyer of the first rank with a solid background in the classics. But he was not a patient man. He had a reputation as an ambitious, unscrupulous politician.

The interplay among these three men—Jefferson, Marshall, and Burr—is probably without parallel in the history of our nation. The administration of President John Adams set the stage for the conflicts among them. As they stood together in the Senate for Jefferson's inauguration, Adams was nowhere to be seen. Bitter over his defeat for reelection and the "disloyalty" of former supporters—including some of his Cabinet members—Adams rose early on March 4, 1801, and departed Washington by carriage for Boston. His long friendship with Jefferson would lie dormant for many years. During his presidency, John Adams did not have a very happy time. Anyone succeeding George Washington certainly had a hard act to follow. At the time of Adams' election there was no institutional memory of how things should be done. George Washington's eight years were unique and remain so to this day, even though he had many problems. Most were overcome simply because Washington had such enormous support among the people and the members of Congress. Adams lacked the great prestige of George Washington, and he had not built support at the grass-roots level.

Apart from that, however, Adams also had difficulties dealing with many of the Federalists who had helped elect him. Adams did not get along well with Alexander Hamilton, who did much to undermine Adams' political standing and popularity. Three members of his Cabinet—Timothy Pickering, secretary of state; Oliver Wolcott, secretary of the treasury; and James McHenry, secretary of war—were aligned with Hamilton. None of them was highly regarded for his competency. Hamilton's influence was also stronger among the Federalist members of Congress than was that of President Adams.

Hamilton and the Cabinet, horrified at the official terror following the French Revolution, had wished to pursue a foreign policy favorable to England, France's enemy. Thus, they had bitterly opposed Adams' efforts to make peace with France. Adams also faced pressures from extreme factions within his own party—much as modern presidents do—on domestic issues. The aftermath of the Whiskey Rebellion provides one example. In 1794 hundreds of men in western Pennsylvania took up arms against federal tax collectors in opposition to a federal excise tax on whiskey. The rebels desisted in the face of an army of militia drawn by President Washington from other states. Some of the leaders of the rebellion were tried and convicted of treason. The adamant right wing of the Federalist party demanded that the "rebels" be executed as a warning to other potential lawbreakers. Instead, Adams pardoned them because, he said, it would do no good to execute three or four of these misguided people to "make examples."

Compounding Adams' difficulties, some people, including some members of his own Cabinet, held the mistaken view that the executive power was not vested in the president alone but in the Cabinet as a whole. This was so, they said, even though Cabinet members were appointed by the president to serve "at the pleasure of the president." Indeed, Adams called attention to his own "judgment" that a change was required at the State Department in a curt letter to Secretary of State Timothy Pickering, dismissing him from the Cabinet after Pickering had refused Adams' formal request for his resignation. Later, speaking of his presidency and alluding to the metaphor of the "Ship of State" with the president at the helm, Adams said: "I had all the officers and half of the crew always ready to throw me overboard."

Against this background, it is no wonder that Adams, who was not a very good politician in the sense of knowing how to deal with people and with attacks on himself, left Washington, D.C., in a sour mood and declined even to be present at the inauguration of his successor. Adams might have taken some solace in the fact that John Marshall, the greatest legacy of his presidency, stood with Jefferson on the dais of the Senate chamber and administered the constitutional oath to the new president. Marshall, as we will see, was to be a stalwart defender of the Federalist principles he and Adams shared, and he was thus a constant thorn in Jefferson's side.

Political parties, as we know them now, had only recently begun to take form and shape. Washington's first Cabinet resembled a twentieth-century coalition government with persons of opposing ideologies serving together: Hamilton, a proponent of a strong central government, as secretary of the treasury; and Jefferson, inclined toward state sovereignty and states' rights, as secretary of state. It was an unrealistic hope, of course, that these "factions" would not solidify and become political parties. And although it greatly troubled George Washington, this process had indeed commenced before 1800. The party favoring a strong national government had adroitly adopted the name "Federalists" from the popular essays titled *The Federalist Papers*, written by John Jay, James Madison, and Alexander Hamilton during the battle over ratification of the Constitution in New York. By one means or another, they had characterized those who did not support ratification as "anti-Federalists," that is, anti-nationalists. This label stuck for a while, but those opposing the Federalist party soon realized that there were disadvantages in being an "anti." In time, therefore, the Federalists' opponents—of which Jefferson and Burr became two major leaders—adopted the name "Republicans," or "Democratic Republicans." Although this party was the precursor to the Democratic party we know today, its hybrid name was appropriate: the Democratic Republicans resembled modern Democrats such as Franklin D. Roosevelt because they catered more to the popular will than did their opponents; yet they also resembled modern Republicans such as Ronald Reagan because they desired strict limits on federal power.

As a farsighted and very astute politician, Jefferson wanted his own man as Chief Justice. He hoped that he would be able to appoint a successor to Oliver Ellsworth, who was known to be in declining health, but Adams, after his electoral defeat, prevented that. Although Jefferson had no admiration for, and may have even hated, the British, he admired the English political system in which the High Court of Parliament was supreme, with no "lifetime" judges to tell elected legislators and presidents what they could or could not constitutionally do. At first glance, it is difficult to understand why he should have been concerned about the federal courts because at that time there were only thirteen federal district judges and six Supreme Court justices, and from 1790 to 1800 these federal judges had decided only a handful of cases. One of them, *Ware* v. *Hylton*, was, as we have seen, a harbinger of what was to come in 1803 in *Marbury* v. *Madison*. All of the justices in 1800 were lawyers of known Federalist leanings and Jefferson probably sensed what might come from the strong nationalist-minded judges. Jefferson was beginning to have some concerns about the Supreme Court.

The point was not lost on the Federalists either. As a "lame duck," Adams, together with the Federalist-controlled Senate, wanted to cement the hold of the "right thinking" Federalists on the Supreme Court because he was beginning to have some apprehension about his friend Jefferson's eighteenth-century populism. When Chief Justice Ellsworth retired in late 1800, just before the end of Adams' term, the Federalist senators clamored for the elevation of Associate Justice William Paterson to Chief Justice. Indeed, even Marshall recommended Paterson for the post. Adams rejected those pressures, however, and asked John Jay, who had just declined renomination for governor of New York, to return to the Court. In fact, Adams nominated Jay, and the Senate quickly confirmed him. Jay, however, preferring retirement to his farm in New York, declined the appointment, and Adams was forced to look elsewhere. It is often forgotten that John Marshall was not only a lame-duck appointment, but actually Adams' second choice for Chief Justice.

Among all of his troubles, Adams found a man who was not only loyal to him but who was consistently right on all the issues—John Marshall. When Adams had dismissed McHenry as secretary of war, he nominated John Marshall for the post. Marshall declined, but within days Adams dismissed Pickering as secretary of state, and again turned to Marshall. Marshall's experience as a special envoy to France during what became famous as the XYZ Affair probably made him one of the best-qualified people for the job. Marshall had been one of three envoys sent to Paris in 1797 to negotiate over French interference with American shipping. (It was on this diplomatic assignment that Marshall and his colleagues penned the great endorsement of the liberty of the press quoted at the head of Chapter Thirteen.) The French foreign minister, Talleyrand, refused to receive the American delegation officially, and instead sent three agents, designated X, Y, and Z in dispatches, to solicit a bribe for Talleyrand and a large loan for France as a precondition of negotiations. The Americans refused. When reported in the United States, the events stirred anti-French passions, and Marshall and the other envoys were treated as heroes.

Marshall accepted the appointment as secretary of state. His tenure was brief but was notable for the role he played in Adams' appointment of William Marbury as a justice of the peace, which set the stage for Marshall's most famous opinion, discussed in the next chapter. In need of a nominee for Chief Justice in the last days of his administration, Adams again turned to John Marshall. Although Marshall had declined an appointment as associate justice two years before, at the age of forty-five he accepted the appointment as Chief Justice of the United States.

Even though there had been no judicial opinions to disturb Jefferson, and no need as yet to curb the federal judicial branch, he plainly was annoyed at John Adams' appointment of Marshall. Ironically, despite his resentment and the personal dislike between the two men, Jefferson asked Marshall to administer the oath of office. Since in 1801 it was not yet traditional that the Chief Justice administer the oath of office to the incoming president, Jefferson's gesture demonstrated his awareness of the need for conciliation after the close election he had won.

The election of 1800 remains the closest for the presidency in the history of the United States. Adams sought reelection, and his two principal opponents were Jefferson and Burr, both anti-Federalist Republicans. The votes for president that count under the Constitution are those of the Electoral College, people chosen specifically to elect the president. The Constitution gives each state one elector for each of its senators and representatives. The election of 1800 was carried on under constitutional provisions that have since been changed. At that time each elector cast two votes for president; the candidate prevailing in the Electoral College became president, and the runner-up became vice president. In 1787 that seemed sensible. With two major political parties rapidly evolving, however, it no longer fit the times. The Twelfth Amendment, ratified in 1804 in response to the events of 1800–1801, changed the system so each elector now votes separately for president and vice president. In the election of 1800, the Electoral College produced no one to succeed John Adams: Jefferson and Burr, the Republican candidates, tied with the highest number of votes; Adams came in third. Because no candidate received the required "Majority of the whole Number of Electors appointed," the Constitution left the election to the House of Representatives—a body still controlled, until Inauguration Day, by the Federalists.

Some of those opposed to Jefferson felt that if Burr had done a little campaigning with Congress he would have won the election. Representative William Cooper of New York, a Federalist who did not like Jefferson, later said that had "Burr done anything for himself, he would long ere this have been president." Surprisingly, Burr and his friends based Burr's inaction on the principle that men should not electioneer their political peers for the high office of president. It was a novel and naive idea, especially for a notoriously unscrupulous political operator like Burr. Some writers have felt that Burr's statement that there should be no campaigning for the presidency was merely a cover for his own purposes. In December 1800, however, Burr wrote a letter to General Samuel Smith of Maryland, then a member of the Congress that was soon to choose a president. That letter showed Burr's insight into the thinking of the members of the Electoral College:

> It is highly improbable that I shall have an equal number of Votes with Mr. Jefferson; but if such should be the result every Man who knows me ought to know that I should utterly disclaim all competition— Be assured that the federal[ist] party can entertain no wish for such an exchange. As to my friends—they would dishonor my Views and insult my feelings by harbouring a suspicion that I could submit to be instrumental in Counteracting the Wishes [and] expectations of the [United States]— And I now constitute you my proxy to declare these sentiments if the occasion shall require—

Where, except to other members of the House of Representatives about to elect a president, would Congressman Smith "declare these sentiments"? How much is legend and how much is fact is not clear, but historians acknowledge that in the election of 1800 Aaron Burr remained in New York and declined to campaign for support among House members during the contest for the presidency. Burr very much wanted the office but he may have been reluctant to declare openly against Jefferson, the acknowledged leader of the Republicans and a politician who was Burr's senior.

Thomas Jefferson, on the other hand, vigorously sought support, and was helped by unlikely allies. One curious manifestation of "nonpartisanship" in the contest for president was the role of Alexander Hamilton. His lot in the election was an unhappy one. He considered John Adams to have been an incompetent president, but he distrusted and disliked both Jefferson and Burr. Having undermined Adams' presidency, Hamilton, the brilliant genius of finance, our first national "economist," and a major author of *The Federalist Papers*, urged his friends, including John Marshall, at that time Adams' secretary of state, to support Jefferson over Burr as "the lesser of two evils." Although this was several years before the duel between Hamilton and Burr, their rivalry since the Revolutionary War must have colored Hamilton's assessment. Marshall parried with no clear answer, saying he had no acquaintance with Burr. He did know his distant cousin Jefferson; he did not want either Jefferson or Burr to be president.

As it turned out, Burr obtained the support of a significant number of Federalists. With that support for Burr, Jefferson's dominant position among his own Republicans was not enough to secure immediately a majority in the House. Each state delegation had one vote. It took an astonishing thirty-six ballots before Jefferson prevailed—with the vote of only one state to spare! A bronze plaque in the room of the Capitol where the voting took place memorializes the event.

Jefferson, well aware of the bitter atmosphere of the election and his narrow victory, read a conciliatory inaugural address. "We are all republicans—we are all federalists," he said. It was a plea for unity, not a statement of fact. Ultimately, the plea failed. In the succeeding years Jefferson was in constant conflict with Burr and Marshall. For Aaron Burr this was to be the beginning of four years of frustrating isolation, except for a brief "courting" by Jefferson when the president needed Burr's support for his assault on the judiciary and, indirectly, on Marshall. That assault reached its climax in the Senate impeachment trial of Justice Samuel Chase, the only Supreme Court justice ever so charged. In his second term, of course, Jefferson was to have Burr, his former vice president, indicted for treason and other crimes. The stories of the impeachment of Justice Chase and Burr's trial, as well as their impact on the Constitution, follow in subsequent chapters.

For Marshall, this was the beginning of thirty-four years as the fourth and greatest Chief Justice of the United States. Indeed, when we speak of "The Great Chief Justice," lawyers, judges, and historians alike know we are speaking of John Marshall. He towers over all who have served on the Court, not simply as a jurist but more accurately as a judicial statesman in a time when such a statesman was terribly needed. Marshall was also a splendid teacher of law and government. And he had the great advantage of writing on an almost clean slate. When he became Chief Justice the Court had decided only a handful of cases and few of any great moment. He would fill the slate and the volumes of Supreme Court opinions with words and concepts that will guide us as long as the Republic stands. He saw the future needs of the new nation as none before or since. The first of those needs, as we will see in the next chapter, was an independent judiciary with the power to strike down legislative acts contrary to the Constitution.

CHAPTER FIVE

MR. MARBURY WANTS HIS JOB

....

Marbury v. Madison, 1803

To what quarter will you look for protection from an infringement on the Constitution, if you will not give the power to the Judiciary?
— John Marshall, in the Virginia
ratification convention, 1788

It is a proposition too plain to be contested, that the constitution controls any legislative act repugnant to it . . . .
It is emphatically the province and the duty of the judicial department to say what the law is.
— Chief Justice John Marshall,
in *Marbury* v. *Madison*, 1803

T HE DEBATE OVER "judicial review"—the courts' power to strike down unconstitutional legislative acts—had a long pedigree by 1803. In 1788 Virginia called delegates to a convention to consider the new Constitution drafted in Philadelphia in 1787. George Mason, the prime author of the Virginia Declaration of Rights, railed at the proposed Constitution. He stated simply: "I abominate and detest the idea of a Government, where there is a standing army." Joining him was the great and eloquent patriot Patrick Henry, who a year earlier had declined to be a delegate to the Philadelphia Convention because, he said, "I smelt a rat." So he stayed home. Mason was one of the most respected men in Virginia. As for Henry, every Virginia school boy and girl had learned his eloquent cry: "Give me liberty or give me death!" Those men and their followers feared a strong central government; it looked too much like the British monarchy they had rejected. The "rat" Henry thought he smelled was just what fifty-five delegates then proceeded to draft between May and September of 1787—the Constitution of the United States. Thirty-nine delegates signed it on September 17, 1787. Three who were present, including Mason, refrained from signing because, among other reasons, they first wanted a bill of rights adopted as part of the Constitution. Mason also objected to the power of the federal judiciary, which he claimed would swallow up the judiciaries of the states.

At the Virginia ratification convention, Mason and Henry bitterly attacked the powers granted by Article III of the Constitution to the proposed federal judiciary, especially the Supreme Court, to decide cases and controversies arising under the Constitution, laws, and treaties of the United States. By their very arguments against the Constitution, the two men recognized that Article III vested broad powers of judicial review of legislative action. They contended that to give such power to unelected officials was contrary to all concepts of democracy. These critics argued that creating a separate court system under a federal Constitution would destroy the state courts on which the people had long relied.

A rising young lawyer, John Marshall, age thirty-two, responded to those attacks on the Article III judicial powers, pointing out that all of the state courts were very much overworked and that the federal courts would help in the administration of justice. Furthermore, Marshall emphasized the need for a federal judiciary to decide federal questions:

> Is it not necessary that the Federal Courts should have cognizance of cases arising under the Constitution, and the laws of the United States? What is the service or purpose of a Judiciary, but to execute the laws in a peaceable orderly manner, without shedding blood, or creating a contest, or availing yourselves of force? If this be the case, where can its jurisdiction be more necessary than here?

In the final quarter of the eighteenth century, references in the course of debates to "shedding blood" were not mere oratory. These men remembered Shays' armed rebellion in 1786 and the occasions when states had called up troops in disputes over boundaries and commercial matters. And they remembered Lexington and Valley Forge.

Marshall ultimately proposed the stark question that remains a valid challenge to all those who are broadly critical of judicial power:

> To what quarter will you look for protection from an infringe-ment on the Constitution, if you will not give the power to the Judiciary?

Neither Henry nor Mason could answer Marshall's position head-on. Once it was conceded that the judiciary, and the Supreme Court in particular, should be the ultimate protector of constitutional rights, Marshall was well on his way to winning the debate over the need to have broad powers vested in the federal judiciary. The lessons Marshall learned while debating at the Virginia ratification convention would serve him well in one of the most difficult and important cases he would later decide as the fourth Chief Justice of the United States: *Marbury* v. *Madison*.

The *Marbury* case arose from events that occurred in the final days of John Adams' lame-duck presidency. After his defeat, the outgoing president tried to place as many Federalists as possible in the judiciary before Thomas Jefferson took office in March 1801. At Adams' urging, the Federalist-controlled Congress enacted the Judiciary Act of 1801 less than three weeks before Adams left office. The Act created new judgeships to staff the circuit courts, for which no judges had been pro-vided by the Judiciary Act of 1789. And Adams wasted no time in filling the positions with men of his own party.

Political considerations were undoubtedly a factor in the Federal-ists' move to create those new judgeships, but in reality they were badly needed. Ten years before, Chief Justice Jay, supported by Presi-dent Washington, had urged that such judgeships be created. Under then existing law, the burden was on two Supreme Court justices to join a district judge to make up each of the three circuit courts, which heard appeals from the district courts in addition to conducting trials of their own. We can scarcely imagine today the burden of travel in those days. Requiring Supreme Court justices to "ride circuit," hearing appeals and presiding over trials under the great hardships of housing and primitive travel of that day, was vigorously opposed by all of the justices. Some lawyers even declined appointments to the Supreme Court because of this travel burden. And the very idea of justices sitting in a case on circuit and then taking part in reviewing it on appeal in the Supreme Court made little sense. Marshall and at least one other justice had refused to take part in such a case when it later came before the Supreme Court.

The Judiciary Act of 1801 was one of thirty-two statutes enacted by the lame-duck Congress between December 1800 and March 1801. Another of these statutes—enacted less than one week before Adams left office—created an undefined number of positions as federal justice of the peace for the territory of Maryland and Virginia that was to become the District of Columbia. William Marbury, a ward-level political figure, was one of forty-two individuals nominated by Adams to fill those positions. The Senate confirmed Marbury and President Adams signed his commission. Ironically, John Marshall, still serving as Adams' secretary of state although he had already been commissioned and had assumed the duties of Chief Justice, attested Adams' signature. By some happenstance the commission was not delivered before Adams' last day in office. The new secretary of state, James Madison, did not deliver it after he arrived. Jefferson later acknowledged that he had ordered destruction of all undelivered commissions signed by President Adams.

Marbury was a fellow who did not like to be pushed around, not even by President Thomas Jefferson. Marbury began a lawsuit against Madison to require delivery of the commission. The action he brought was for a writ of mandamus in the Supreme Court of the United States. A mandamus action asks the court to "command" a public official to perform an act required by law, such as, in this case, the purely ministerial act of delivering Marbury's commission. Section 13 of the Judiciary Act of 1789 expressly authorized a mandamus action to be brought in the Supreme Court as an original action—that is, directly in the Supreme Court, rather than in the district court with an eventual appeal to the Supreme Court. Had Marbury brought his mandamus action in the district court—the trial court, where most lawsuits are initially filed—a district judge might have appropriately ordered that the commission be delivered. Even if the commission had been destroyed, the district court might well have ordered that another commission be prepared and delivered. But because Marbury began his action in the Supreme Court, Marshall and his colleagues had to deal with an additional jurisdictional problem as the case came to them. Did the Constitution give authority to Congress to create an "original" action in the Supreme Court for this purpose?

Section 2 of Article III of the Constitution allows some cases to begin in the Supreme Court, but the range of such original actions is very narrow and explicitly defined:

> In all Cases affecting Ambassadors, other public Ministers and Consuls, and those in which a State shall be Party, the supreme court shall have original Jurisdiction. *In all the other Cases . . . ,* the supreme Court shall have appellate Jurisdiction, . . . with such Exceptions, and under such Regulations as the Congress shall make (emphasis added).

The case Marbury attempted to bring did not fall within the Constitution's category of original actions in the Supreme Court. The Constitution makes plain that "[i]n all the other Cases" the Supreme Court is only an appellate court. Marbury's lawyers may have been misled because a few years earlier the Supreme Court had not seen a problem with Section 13. Marshall moved to exploit the weakness in Marbury's argument. There can be no question about the correctness of Marshall's position; it was really very simple: Section 13 of the Judiciary Act of 1789 purported to give the Supreme Court a power beyond that authorized by Section 2 of Article III, which defines the Court's original jurisdiction.

The "Exceptions" Clause—which actually concerns the power of Congress to regulate the Court's *appellate* jurisdiction—had perhaps led Marbury's lawyer to take a "short cut" by going directly to the highest court. That is, Section 13 seemed to make an "exception" to the Constitution's limited grant of original jurisdiction by plainly authorizing a mandamus action directly in the Supreme Court. But if the Act of 1789 had intended to make such an exception, and if the Court had held that the exception was consistent with the Constitution, and if the Court had accordingly issued a mandamus—a command to Madison and Jefferson to deliver a commission to Marbury—how would that command have been enforced? A contempt order? To a president? A judgment that Marbury was in fact and in law a justice of the peace? That might have been an empty victory for Marbury if the government refused to pay him any compensation, forcing him to begin another lawsuit for his salary. Then what?

Had the Court ruled in Marbury's favor, a confrontation would have arisen between the president of the United States and the Supreme Court of the United States. Where would such a conflict have led in the fifteenth year of our existence as a nation, while powers of government were still being sorted out? If the president and the secretary of state ignored the judgment of the Court, how would such a confrontation have affected the prestige of the Court so early in its official life? In a case to come in later years, when the Supreme Court entered a judgment not to his liking, President Andrew Jackson ignored it, reportedly saying: "John Marshall has made his decision; now let him enforce it." But when Jackson flouted the Court it was clear that he was rejecting the Court's power to review the actions of other branches of government long after such power was widely accepted, and Jackson's words were a partisan political gesture.

Marshall's adroit handling of the issue in *Marbury* avoided a confrontation between the judicial and executive branches. The Court ruled against Marbury: the decision was simply that Section 13 was not authorized by Article III of the Constitution, and therefore the court had no choice but to hold it unconstitutional. The Court said that Mr. Marbury was right on his claim, but he was in the wrong court. Had television been with us in 1803, an evening news anchorman might have announced on the day the opinion was delivered: "Jefferson won his case in the Supreme Court." The next day's newspaper might have displayed a similar headline. But although Jefferson did win over Marbury, much more was decided by this historic case than whether Marbury would obtain his commission and become a federal justice of the peace.

Whatever guided the subtle legal mind of Marshall on that day in 1803, he avoided the worst by letting Madison and Jefferson win the "battle," but the Court—and the Constitution—won the "war." Most lawyers of the day had accepted the authority of judicial review that

Marshall had stated at the Virginia ratification convention in 1788. Even Jefferson's close ally and friend Judge Spencer Roane of Virginia's highest court had decided at the state level that an act of the Virginia legislature contrary to the state's constitution was void. Jefferson had not acknowledged that authority when Marshall used it against him in Marbury's case.

How did Marshall reach his result? Marshall's opinion for the Court opens by reciting that the Supreme Court had ordered Madison to "show cause" why a writ of mandamus, a judicial command, should not be issued directing him to deliver Marbury's commission. Madison did not "show cause"; he simply ignored the Court's order. The Court's opinion points out:

> No cause has been shewn [by Madison] . . . . The peculiar delicacy of this case, the novelty of some of its circumstances, and the real difficulty attending the points which occur in it, require a complete exposition of the principles, on which the opinion to be given by the court, is founded.

Marshall's opinion for the Court takes the questions step by step:

> 1st. Has the applicant a right to the commission he demands?
> 2dly. If he has a right, and that right has been violated, do the laws of his country afford him a remedy?
> 3dly. If they do afford him a remedy, is it a *mandamus* issuing from this court?

Addressed in this order, an affirmative answer to questions one and two would not have resolved the case. Marshall thus made the answer to question three—a question of "jurisdiction," the power of a court to decide a case—the central basis of his opinion. Today, with the issue of judicial review firmly settled, the Supreme Court would not take up the questions as Marshall ordered them. The Court would likely first address the question of jurisdiction and, if it found that it lacked jurisdiction—as Marshall finally found—would then dismiss the case. But now, nearly two hundred years later, judges have in mind the words of the master teacher. By reciting the whole story in the order he

did, Marshall set the stage for his historic discussion of judicial review
—and revealed the petty political manipulation of a president of the
United States with respect to an insignificant office—before concluding that, in any event, the Court could not grant Marbury the remedy
he sought.

Marshall answered the first question in the affirmative:

> It is therefore decidedly the opinion of the court, that when a
> commission has been signed by the President, the appointment is
> made; and that the commission is complete, when the seal of the
> United States has been affixed to it by the secretary of state. . . .
>
> To withhold his commission, therefore, is an act deemed by
> the court not warranted by law, but violative of a vested legal
> right.

Marshall also concluded—unnecessarily in light of the third conclusion
below—that not only was Marbury entitled to his commission, but
that the law provided him with a remedy:

> This brings us to the second enquiry, which is,
> 2dly. If he has a right, and that right has been violated, do the
> laws of his country afford him a remedy?
>
> The very essence of civil liberty certainly consists in the right
> of every individual to claim protection of the laws, whenever he
> receives an injury. One of the first duties of government is to af-
> ford that protection. In Great Britain the King himself . . . never
> fails to comply with the judgment of his court.

After deciding that Marbury was entitled to a remedy, Marshall
took up the third question—whether Marbury could get his remedy
directly from the Supreme Court in an original action. Section 13 of
the Judiciary Act of 1789 said he could, but was that provision consistent with Article III, Section 2, of the Constitution? If it was not,
which should the Court apply to the case—the statute or the Constitution? Marshall declared, in ringing sentences still often quoted by
lawyers, teachers, and judges, that the judiciary has the power to re-

view legislative acts, such as Section 13, to determine whether they violate the Constitution:

> It is a proposition too plain to be contested, that the constitution controls any legislative act repugnant to it . . . .
> It is emphatically the province and the duty of the judicial department to say what the law is.

Marshall made sure the point was clear:

> If then the courts are to [consider] the constitution; and [if] the constitution is superior to any ordinary act of the legislature; the constitution, and not such ordinary act, must govern the case to which they both apply.
> Those then who controvert the principle that the constitution is to be considered, in court, as paramount law . . . must close their eyes on the constitution, and see only the law.
> This doctrine would subvert the very foundation of all written constitutions.

Although the Court's treatment of the case runs to more than five thousand words, one must not be too critical of its verbosity. Marshall was not just a judge; he was a great teacher. Great teachers, like great advocates, often repeat and restate to drive a point home. Because so much of what he had to say would be new, Marshall wanted to make it clear.

Why should there have been any doubt about the authority—indeed, duty—of the Supreme Court to pass on the constitutionality of an act of Congress or the president? Suppose Congress, in the mood prevailing at the time of the passage of the infamous Alien and Sedition Acts in 1798, had passed a statute requiring a license for all newspapers or other printed material moving in interstate commerce, with a regulatory structure to enforce it and a power to cancel the license of a newspaper or publisher of a book or pamphlet that printed "false" information. Or a power to deny newspapers and publishers use of the mails. Would Jefferson—that great defender of civil liberties—have

said then what he later stated about judges exercising the power of judicial review: that they were "working like gravity by night and by
day, gaining a little to-day and a little to-morrow, and advancing [with]
noiseless step like a thief"?

There is an easy answer to that question. Marshall and his colleagues were unanimous in making it clear, when the nation was still in
its infancy, that Congress and the president were controlled by the
Constitution, and that judges, who were sworn to uphold the Constitution, would declare an act of the Congress or the president void if
they decided it was contrary to the Constitution. If not at least for this
purpose, then for what purpose did the men at Philadelphia provide for
a system of courts headed by "one supreme Court," vesting in them
"judicial Power [which] shall extend to all Cases, in Law and Equity,
arising under this Constitution, [and] the Laws of the United States"?
That is what Marshall meant in 1788 in his debates with Patrick Henry
and George Mason when he asked: "To what quarter will you look"
for protection if Congress violates the Constitution?

Given Marshall's extensive treatment of judicial review, the actual
resolution of Marbury's lawsuit is perhaps the least important aspect of
Marbury v. *Madison*. Marbury's claim to begin his suit in the Supreme
Court under its original jurisdiction had to stand or fall on Section 2 of
Article III. And it had to fall, said Marshall for the Court, because the
Constitution did not give Congress the authority to enlarge the field of
original jurisdiction of the Court. Only an amendment to the Constitution could accomplish that. Had Marbury brought his claim before a
federal trial judge, it is difficult to see how the court could have done
other than order a commission to be delivered to Marbury, taking the
risk that the president and the secretary of state would ignore such an
order. For reasons lost to history, Marbury never did so, even after the
Supreme Court's ruling that he was entitled to his commission.

The opinion in *Marbury* is plainly one of the major "building
block" opinions of the Supreme Court. It is widely accepted that Marshall seized the moment—even stretched the point—to settle the issue
of the Court's power of judicial review early in Jefferson's first term. At
the same time, Marshall accused Jefferson of violating the law by refusing to deliver Marbury's commission. That scolding—and Marshall's
assertion that the judiciary could have ordered Jefferson's secretary of

state to deliver the commission had Marbury brought his case in the right court—probably did as much to enrage Jefferson as the assertion of the power of judicial review. The five-year office of justice of the peace was an insignificant factor, as Jefferson was beginning eight successful years as president. But Marshall's view that the judiciary had the power to review the actions of the other two branches of the government, a view first articulated at the Virginia ratification convention in 1788 in its debate over the meaning of Article III of the Constitution, had become the law of the land.

That the result in *Marbury*, and Marshall's scolding, rankled Jefferson for a long time afterward is revealed in an 1823 letter Jefferson wrote to Justice William Johnson, his first appointee to the Supreme Court:

> This practice of Judge Marshall, of travelling out of his case to prescribe what the law would be in a moot case not before the court, is very irregular and very censurable. I recollect another instance, and the more particularly, perhaps, because it in some measure bore on myself. Among the midnight appointments of Mr. Adams, were commissions to some federal justices of the peace for Alexandria [in the District of Columbia]. These were signed and sealed by him, but not delivered. I found them on the table of the Department of State, on my entrance into office, and I forbade their delivery. Marbury, named in one of them, applied to the Supreme Court for a mandamus to the Secretary of State, (Mr. Madison) to deliver the commission intended for him. The Court determined at once, that being an original process, they had no cognizance of it; and therefore the question before them was ended. But the Chief Justice went on to lay down what the law would be, had they jurisdiction of the case, to wit: that they should command the delivery. The object was clearly to instruct any other court having the jurisdiction, what they should do if Marbury should apply to them.

Jefferson also described the opinion in *Marbury* v. *Madison* as "being merely an *obiter* dissertation of the Chief Justice." "Obiter dicta"— which literally means "things said in passing"—is a phrase that lawyers use to refer to parts of an opinion not necessary to the court's decision, and therefore not binding on later courts. In truth, Jefferson perhaps had some basis for his objections to Marshall's "obiter," for, as has been noted earlier, the first question for the Court was whether it had jurisdiction. If not, the case was over. But Marshall the teacher needed to make a point—a point now undisputed in law.

Curiously, Marshall did not in the *Marbury* opinion cite *Ware* v. *Hylton*, which afforded abundant authority for the basic constitutional holdings Marshall articulated in *Marbury*. Was that because *Ware* was a case he lost? one might ask. Or was it because he wanted a great holding on judicial supremacy to come only from his own pen? The answer to both of those questions must be a resounding no. Marshall was not a petty or egotistical man. But could it have been because Marbury's case gave an opportunity to frame the issue in terms of a sharp conflict with what he knew was Jefferson's hostility toward the Supreme Court and its power to set aside an act of Congress? Was Marshall influenced by the fact that Marbury's case gave him an opening to frame the issue of judicial supremacy over acts of Congress in both a constitutional and a political framework? The answers to these questions are not so clear. In any event, history credits John Marshall with a great stroke in *Marbury* v. *Madison*, yet a significant measure of credit must be given to the authors of *Ware* v. *Hylton* (discussed in Chapter Three). Jefferson may not have missed the connection, for one of the justices who had decided *Ware*, Samuel Chase of Maryland, became a primary target in Jefferson's assault on judicial independence. To that story I now turn.

CHAPTER SIX

THE IMPEACHMENT OF JUSTICE SAMUEL CHASE

....

[T]he Constitution ought to be so altered as that the President, on application of Congress should have authority to remove any Judge from office.
     —President Thomas Jefferson,
      in a conversation with
      Senator William Plumer, 1803

[I]f the Judges of the Supreme Court should dare, AS THEY HAD DONE [in Marbury v. Madison], to declare an act of the Congress unconstitutional, or to send a mandamus to the Secretary of State, AS THEY HAD DONE, it was the undoubted right of the House of Representatives to impeach them, and of the Senate to remove them, for giving such opinions, however honest or sincere they may have been in entertaining them.
     —Senator William Branch Giles,
      in a conversation recorded
      by John Quincy Adams, 1804

IN AN ERA when the true role of the Supreme Court was not yet widely understood and was still being developed, Chief Justice John Marshall never overlooked an occasion to press home his profound conviction that Article III of the Constitution created a power of judicial review authorizing—indeed, commanding—federal courts

to invalidate a legislative or executive act that they found to be contrary
to the Constitution. There was, however, a significant event that could
have prevented Marshall's vision from ever becoming a reality: President Jefferson's attack on the federal judiciary, beginning with the impeachment of District Judge John Pickering of New Hampshire and
followed by the impeachment trial of Associate Justice Samuel Chase
of Maryland. As will be seen, the impeachment of Chase failed. Had it
succeeded, the federal judiciary and the Supreme Court in particular,
might not have gained the independence necessary to repudiate unconstitutional acts of Congress or the president.

Marshall's view of Article III powers was widely held by lawyers of
the day. But Marshall took his stance at a time when the political ideas
and political parties of our country were evolving. As we have seen,
many of the Founding Fathers who fought shoulder to shoulder for independence from the mother country became fierce adversaries after
freedom was won and the time arrived to establish the political course
of the new Union. In 1801, when Jefferson assumed office, the Federalists controlled the federal judiciary.

Jefferson soon came to realize that the federal judiciary could, if
controlled by his nationalist-minded adversaries such as John Marshall,
pose a significant threat to his power as president. And Jefferson was
not alone in his hostility toward Marshall and the federal judiciary. It
was a reflection of a major difference in the philosophy of the two
emerging national political parties: the nationalist Federalists, on the
one hand, and the states' rights Jeffersonian Republicans, on the other.
The hostility also reflected a fundamentally different approach, at least
theoretically, to the Constitution. Jefferson and his adherents saw the
federal government as constitutionally endowed with strictly limited
powers.

Jefferson's hostility toward the judiciary arose principally from his
opinion that the Federalist-staffed courts opposed him by promoting
the power of the national government. Years later, Jefferson would
aptly but bitterly summarize the ideological differences:

The judiciary of the United States is the subtle corps of sappers
and miners constantly working underground to undermine the

foundations of our confederated fabric. They are construing our Constitution from a co-ordination of a general and special government to a general and supreme one alone.

He placed much of the blame squarely on Chief Justice Marshall:

An opinion is huddled up in conclave, perhaps by a majority of one, delivered as if unanimous, and with the silent acquiescence of lazy or timid associates, by a crafty chief judge [John Marshall] who sophisticates the law to his mind, by the turn of his own reasoning.

Marshall and his colleagues were able to deliver their opinions without fear of political reprisal, Jefferson noted, only because they had "found, from experience, that impeachment is an impracticable thing" and they therefore "consider themselves secure for life." Jefferson did not acknowledge that life tenure—or more precisely, tenure "during good Behaviour"—for judges was intended to do precisely that: to make judges independent of all political ties.

After 1800, however, the judiciary was not so secure. Adams' lame-duck appointments led Jefferson and his party to take steps to repeal the Judiciary Act of 1801 and to launch a broader assault on the judiciary. The new Jeffersonian-controlled Congress did repeal that Act in March 1802, thereby abolishing all circuit judgeships and in effect removing a number of tenured circuit judges from office. Aware that these removals were constitutionally dubious, the very next month Congress also suspended the Supreme Court's sittings for more than a year. The object of this truly extraordinary exercise of raw political power was to avoid a challenge to the constitutionality of the repeal by preventing the Supreme Court from sitting to hear a constitutional challenge to the removal of the circuit judges newly appointed under the Judiciary Act of 1801. Chief Justice Marshall and Associate Justice Chase had suggested to their colleagues that riding circuit—that is, staffing the circuit courts in place of the removed circuit judges—would recognize the validity of the 1802 repealing act and that they should therefore refuse to ride. But the justices did not

folow this suggestion and proceeded to fulfill their duties on the circuit courts. Given Marshall's views, it is ironic that the only reported
case in which the 1802 repealing act was challenged as unconstitutional was decided by none other than Marshall himself while riding
circuit in Virginia. Marshall ruled in favor of the law's validity, and
when the case of *Stuart* v. *Laird* came to the Supreme Court on appeal
from the circuit court, Marshall's brethren affirmed his ruling without
a single dissenting vote. *Stuart* was decided just days after *Marbury* v.
Madison, which had been delayed by the Jeffersonians' suspension of
the Court's session: although *Marbury* was argued before the Court in
December of 1801, the Court did not sit to give its judgment until
February of 1803.

Although they were decided within a week of each other, the *Marbury* case and the *Stuart* case shared little else in common. As we have
seen, *Marbury* was a direct—and very personal—challenge to the legality of Jefferson's refusal to deliver a commission. *Stuart*, on the other
hand, was a dispute between two private litigants in which the legality
of the Jeffersonians' abolishing the circuit judgeships was challenged
only incidentally; the affected circuit judges did not participate in the
case. It is puzzling that William Marbury—who had been denied his
commission as one of forty-two justices of the peace in the new District of Columbia, a minor judicial office with a term of five years and
no fixed salary—saw fit to challenge Jefferson by filing a lawsuit, while
none of the men who had been removed from the sixteen circuit
judgeships throughout the entire United States—a judicial office with
secure tenure and second in rank only to that of a justice of the
Supreme Court—mounted any kind of a similar legal challenge.

What did the circuit judges do? As Albert Beveridge describes it in
his biography of John Marshall, certain of the "deposed" judges had
"taken steps" to bring the 1802 repealing act before the Supreme
Court, "but their energies flagged, their hearts failed, and their only action was a futile and foolish protest to the very Congress that had
wrested their judicial seats from under them." Charles Warren, in his
history of the Supreme Court, reports in a footnote that one of the circuit judges from New Jersey did institute a lawsuit challenging the repealing act, but Warren does not report the outcome of the suit, and

one must conclude that it was abandoned on account of flagging energy and a failing heart. And as for the judges' protest to Congress, in the words of one scholar, it "fell on largely deaf ears."

In any case, the Supreme Court's decision in *Marbury* v. *Madison* intensified Jefferson's overt hostility and bitterness toward the federal judiciary. In February of 1803, the same month *Marbury* was decided, Jefferson launched a campaign to intimidate federal judges with the threat of impeachment if they opposed him. This is not historical conjecture; it is an aspect of a great man on a little-known subject of crucial importance to our political development as a country. Jefferson's own letters and public utterances make this clear, as do the utterances and acts of his closest political allies, particularly Representative William Branch Giles of Virginia. Giles was widely recognized as Jefferson's spokesman in the Congress. As early as 1801, immediately after Jefferson's inauguration and two years before Marshall's opinion in *Marbury* v. *Madison*, Representative Giles wrote Jefferson, stating:

> It appears to me that the only check upon the judiciary system as it is now organized and filled, is the removal of all its executive officers [judges] indiscriminately.

Later, after Giles came to the Senate in 1804, he was recorded by a new young Federalist senator, John Quincy Adams, as saying: "*We want your offices,* for the purpose of giving them to men who will fill them better." There was nothing unusual about that desire in a politician, except that Giles was talking about the "offices" of federal judges, and impeachment was the means he had in mind.

Article II, Section 4, of the Constitution provides that all civil officers of the United States, including judges, may be removed from office "on Impeachment for, and Conviction of, Treason, Bribery, or other high Crimes and Misdemeanors." For judges, that is the only method of removal. Under the Constitution, judges "hold their Offices during good Behaviour," that is, for life absent misbehavior. The House of Representatives has the sole power to impeach an official, and the trial is conducted in the Senate. Notwithstanding the Constitution's reference to impeachment for "high Crimes and Misde-

meanors," the Jeffersonian Republicans viewed impeachment as a political tool. Giles candidly described impeachment proceedings as, in
his view, "nothing more than an enquiry, by the two Houses of Congress, whether the office of any public man might not be better filled
by another." He knew he had President Jefferson's support.

In a shot across Marshall's bow, just days before the Court sat in
February 1803, after the fourteen-month hiatus imposed by Congress,
Jefferson transmitted a formal message to Congress seeking the impeachment of District Judge John Pickering of New Hampshire. This
would be the first impeachment of a federal judge. Judge Pickering's
virtues and shortcomings were not really at issue. He was a sick man
who today would likely be diagnosed as having Alzheimer's disease,
along with acute alcoholism, making it impossible for him to perform
his duties. His friends and judicial colleagues should first have tried to
persuade him to retire, and he should have ceased serving on the
bench. There was no provision, however, for removal of a judge who
had become physically or mentally disabled as had Judge Pickering, although since that time a statute has been enacted authorizing a disabled
judge to take "senior status." Pickering was in no sense guilty of the
"high Crimes and Misdemeanors" necessary under the Constitution
for impeachment, but the Jeffersonians wanted to use his case to make
the point that federal judges were not invulnerable. Pickering was sin-
gled out by the Jeffersonians in order to get Congress—and the people—accustomed to the idea of removing federal judges.

Pickering's humiliating impeachment trial in the Senate was a
complete farce. Because few were willing to oppose Jefferson openly,
it was a summary, one-day affair. Pickering did not appear in person or
by counsel. In truth, he had no defense and he became a convenient
example for the Republicans. That Jefferson and his congressional supporters were establishing a precedent for impeachment of their judicial
adversaries, rather than attacking Pickering for allegedly breaking the
law, is evidenced by the fact that the floor managers at his trial initially
refused to permit evidence of his illnesses to be introduced. The Senate swiftly voted on the impeachment and Pickering was removed.

The next federal judge targeted for impeachment was Associate
Justice Samuel Chase. This time, Jefferson did not publicly seek the
impeachment. After encouraging Representative Joseph Nicholson of

Maryland to proceed, Jefferson added: "[As] for myself it is better that I should not interfere." Jefferson kept out of sight during this overtly political attack on the judiciary, but his correspondence shows that he was stimulating members of Congress and others to act. Chase's trial, unlike Pickering's, was anything but a summary affair. Giles, now in the Senate, was a leading supporter of Jefferson's direct attack on the Court. Giles had said that the idea of the independence claimed by federal judges was "nothing more nor less than an attempt to establish an aristocratic despotism in themselves." He went on:

> [I]f the Judges of the Supreme Court should dare, AS THEY HAD DONE [in *Marbury* v. *Madison*], to declare an act of the Congress unconstitutional, or to send a mandamus to the Secretary of State, AS THEY HAD DONE, it was the undoubted right of the House of Representatives to impeach them, and of the Senate to remove them . . . .

On the same occasion Giles is quoted by John Quincy Adams as saying:

> [A] removal by impeachment was nothing more than a declaration by Congress to this effect: You hold dangerous opinions, and if you are suffered to carry them into effect you will work the destruction of the nation.

Justice Chase was a likely target for the Jeffersonians. He was a very able jurist, but his lack of judicial temperament was apparent, especially when he rode circuit as an appellate judge and when he presided over trials as a trial judge. He was intemperate and explosive on the bench. In addition, Chase, a signer of the Declaration of Independence and a freedom fighter in every sense of the word, was a staunch supporter of the Federalists' views and was not shy about sharing his beliefs with lawyers and juries. He was never known to back down from a challenge, political or otherwise, and he was constantly being challenged by the Jeffersonians for his conduct on the bench. His tendency to impose upon and sometimes quarrel with juries was evident as early as 1794, two years prior to his appointment to the Supreme Court, when, as chief justice of the General Court in Baltimore, he had a skirmish with a grand jury. The jury felt so strongly about his conduct that it eventually charged him with abuse of authority. Chase scolded the jury for challenging his authority, accusations flew back and forth, but nothing significant ever came of that event.

In 1800 Justice Chase presided over three controversial trials that evoked the ire of Jeffersonians and gave them the fuel to institute Chase's impeachment trial. The trial of John Fries is the most well documented of the three. Fries was tried for treason arising out of his participation in the "Hot Water" uprising of 1799. The Hot Water Rebellion was another case of armed resistance to taxes imposed by the new federal government. The tax in question was imposed on houses based on the number and size of their windows. The revolt derives its name from the protestors' tactic of pouring scalding water on tax assessors when they tried to measure the windows. Fries was eventually arrested and convicted of treason. A new trial was granted due to juror misconduct. Prior to the original trial Chase had mentioned that he thought troops should have been sent to quash the Hot Water insurrection. Chase presided over the second trial in 1800, and it was almost a foregone conclusion that the result would be the same as in the first trial since Fries presented no new evidence and called no new witnesses. The only irregularity claimed was that Chase issued a written opinion, based on his own judicially pronounced views, on the meaning of "treason" prior to the oral argument of counsel. Chase later explained that he issued the written opinion before oral argument because he wanted to make it clear that the legal meaning of the word was settled.

The other two trials came as a result of the Alien and Sedition Acts of 1798. The Acts were so broadly worded that they could be interpreted to prohibit most oral or written utterances against the president or Congress. Some felt the Acts were passed at the prompting of President Adams not in response to any wartime threat but as a tool to be used against political adversaries. They were almost certainly contrary to the First Amendment's guarantee of freedom of speech. The legislatures of Kentucky and Virginia—relying on texts supplied by Jefferson and Madison, respectively—adopted famous resolutions declaring the

Acts to be unconstitutional and declaring that those states would enforce them only on the states' own terms. When riding circuit, however, Justice Chase strictly enforced the laws from their inception. The Jeffersonian Republicans took note.

Thomas Cooper and James T. Callender, both political writers, were charged with sedition. Cooper attacked the law itself, which quickly led to charges against him. Although Justice Chase respected Cooper and was generally fair and deliberate throughout Cooper's trial, he made it clear to the jury that he thought Cooper was guilty of sedition. In that day a trial judge was free, as in England, to convey to the jurors his own views about the weight of the evidence as to guilt. After the trial the Jeffersonians cried foul in the press, and Chase responded publicly with indignation, making it appear as though there might be some merit to the Jeffersonian charges.

Unlike Cooper, Callender was a scandalous character. He came to America in the 1790s to escape charges of sedition pending against him in his native Scotland. The Jeffersonians saw that Callender was a gifted writer who was not reserved in his abuse of government officials. Several Jeffersonians, including Thomas Jefferson himself, befriended Callender shortly after he arrived in this country and enlisted him to write several articles fervently criticizing the Federalists, and John Adams in particular. These writings did more than just upset faithful Federalists, including, undoubtedly, Justice Chase; they eventually led to Callender's arrest under the sedition laws.

Chase must have known that Callender's trial would not be pleasant, especially after Chase had been so viciously attacked after the Cooper and Fries trials. The trial was to take place in Richmond, Virginia, and tensions between the Federalist-dominated judiciary and the Jeffersonians were mounting. What Chase did not know was that his conduct at the trial would become part of the primary charges against him in an impeachment trial in the Senate.

The mood at Callender's trial was much as Chase suspected it would be. Callender's attorneys, who probably assumed Callender was guilty under the sedition law as it was written, attempted to challenge the law on constitutional grounds. But Justice Chase refused to allow the attorneys to discuss the constitutionality of the law, requiring instead that they focus their attack on the substantive aspects of the statute. The attorneys apparently became so frustrated that they withdrew from the case. Some have speculated that their resignation was a tactic aimed at persuading the jury that Chase was a tyrant and that it should acquit Callender. Chase, however, undertook to explain carefully to the jury that his actions in the case, and his instructions to the jury in particular, were based on his interpretation of the sedition laws and not on his political convictions. All the same, as in Cooper's trial, Chase's comments made clear that he thought Callender was guilty under the law. Callender was ultimately convicted by the jury, but he was subsequently pardoned by Jefferson in March 1801. Chase's adversaries paid no attention to detail and publicly claimed that Chase's conduct and his comments at trial were politically motivated.

These events formed the basis of many of the charges against Justice Chase, but the event that precipitated his impeachment occurred in 1803, coincidentally just two months after the Supreme Court decided *Marbury*. Addressing a grand jury in Baltimore, Chase criticized the Republicans' repeal of the Judiciary Act of 1801 and complained:

> The independence of the National Judiciary is already shaken to its foundation; and the virtue of the people alone can restore it. . . . [O]ur Republican Constitution will sink into a *Mobocracy*, the worst of all possible Governments.

Justice Chase was a conservative who was skeptical of such things as granting the right to vote without any requirement of property ownership. He went on to tell the jury:

> [T]he *modern* Doctrines, by our late *reformers*, that all men in a State of *Society* are entitled to enjoy *equal Liberty*, and *equal Rights*, have brought this mighty mischief upon us: And I fear that it will rapidly progress, until peace [and] order, freedom and property, shall be destroyed.

Jefferson and his partisans took those words as an attack on the principles of the Constitution itself. In order to conceal the political nature of their attack, however, they encouraged the Republican press to exploit Chase's lack of judicial temperament and to develop public opinion that Chase was guilty of criminal conduct. The incidents leading to the impeachment trial, however, suggest how the campaign of vilification of Chase was but a stage in the Jeffersonian campaign to destroy judicial independence. Justice Chase was not charged with bribery or corruption, as has been the case in the impeachment trials of federal judges in recent years. The intensely partisan House of Representatives did not even claim that Chase had violated any law, but only that he was biased, intemperate, and, in general, guilty of conduct unbecoming a judge. The House framed eight impeachment charges against Chase, dealing with the conduct described above and other incidents. All of the charges, whether true or not, fell well short of impeachable conduct, and could be applied more or less to other members of the Supreme Court. As Senator John Quincy Adams wrote to his father, former President John Adams:

> These articles [of impeachment] contained in themselves a virtual impeachment not only of Mr. Chase, but of all the judges of the Supreme Court from the first establishment of the national judiciary.

The Republican-controlled Senate required Chase to appear within a month after the charges were approved in the House. There were seventeen states at the time of Chase's trial, and consequently thirty-four senators participated in the impeachment proceedings. The Constitution required that two thirds, twenty-three senators, vote to convict in order to remove Justice Chase from office. Special seating was provided for various notables, including members of Jefferson's Cabinet, members of the House of Representatives, and others. The spectacle of the affair was heightened by the fact that Aaron Burr, president of the Senate by virtue of his position as vice president, presided over the trial. The previous year, he had killed Alexander Hamilton in a duel—to settle a dispute arising out of some alleged attacks by Hamilton on Burr's character. Although the duel had occurred in New Jersey, Burr's political enemies in New York had procured an indictment in New York and compelled Burr to absent himself from the state. At the time of the trial, Burr had also been indicted in New Jersey. The awkwardness of having Burr preside over the trial, and the bitter feelings of the time, were revealed in a letter written by Senator Plumer of New Hampshire, a Federalist, on November 7, 1804, in which he said:

> We are indeed fallen on evil times. . . . The high office of President is filled by an *infidel;* that of Vice-President by a *murderer.*

Burr, who had been continually ignored as vice president, was now much sought out by Jefferson and his friends. A look at correspondence from that time reveals that everybody in Washington knew what was going on. The witnesses against Judge Pickering had all been rewarded by political appointments. One of them, John Sherburne, was later appointed to fill the vacancy created by Pickering's ouster. Even Burr, who was then near the end of his term as vice president, was suddenly given a great deal of favorable attention; three of his relatives were appointed to federal political offices by Jefferson. Burr found himself at the center of attention—invited to dinners at the White House and dinners with members of the Cabinet. Senator Giles went out of his way to write to the governor of New Jersey urging dismissal of the murder charges against Burr.

Luther Martin of Maryland, one of the great advocates of the time, headed the team of lawyers defending Justice Chase. All of Chase's counsel were outstanding lawyers. Martin was the director of his exceptional defense at the Senate trial and Robert Goodloe Harper joined in to help plan defense strategy. On the other side, several members of the House of Representatives, the impeaching body, conducted, or "managed," the prosecution. John Randolph was the primary "manager" for the House. Although he was one of the best and most flamboyant orators of his time, Randolph was not a lawyer, and his prosecution of Chase was ineffective. His lack of understanding of the Constitution and of the law in general was apparent, and his prosecution was largely political in nature. His ostentatious attacks on Chase often provided Luther Martin with numerous opportunities to dissect the prosecution's arguments and expose their weaknesses.

John Marshall, the Chief Justice, was present in the Senate for the trial, waiting to be called as a witness on behalf of Chase. Notwithstanding the effectiveness of Chase's overall defense strategy, Chief Justice Marshall's testimony was a disappointment. Marshall seemed profoundly disturbed, even frightened. He was well aware that he might be the next target. His apprehension is revealed in a letter where, in a strange retreat from the *Marbury* opinion, he wrote:

> I think the modern doctrine of impeachment should yield to an appellate jurisdiction in the legislature. A reversal of those legal opinions deemed unsound by the legislature would certainly better comport with the mildness of our character than [would] a removal of the Judge who has rendered them unknowing of his fault.

This was an uncharacteristic retreat by Marshall from his position in *Marbury* v. *Madison*, but it reveals his concern about Jefferson's chances of success. One can imagine that a lawyer or even a judge might write an article suggesting that alternative. But for the Chief Justice of the United States to express these thoughts while an impeachment was pending against his colleague demonstrates the deep apprehension the Chase impeachment had created. Was his testimony a strategic maneuver? A "bargaining chip"? Marshall's own friends, including his brother, remarked that the Chief Justice's testimony left much to be desired. It was the one occasion in Marshall's career that revealed a lack of firmness.

In his closing argument for the defense, Luther Martin emphasized the importance of the case to the future of the country under the Constitution. It would, he said, "establish a most important precedent as to future cases of impeachment." Martin argued that impeachment under the Constitution could not rest on anything less than conduct that constituted an indictable offense against the United States. Anything less, he argued, would place judges "at the mercy of the prevailing party." Of course, that was exactly what William Branch Giles had advocated, and what President Jefferson wanted. But after Martin's argument, even Republican senators must have understood that if the vote was to expel Chase, one day the tables would be turned and Federalist-controlled Congresses would attack Republican judges on the same basis. The implications were far-reaching.

The Senate's verdict was in favor of Justice Chase on all eight articles of impeachment. At best, on the charge relating to Chase's statements to the Baltimore grand jury, the prosecution obtained only nineteen votes to convict out of a total of thirty-four. That was a majority, but it was four votes short of the two thirds the Constitution requires. The impeachment had failed, and with it the attempt to force federal judges out of office for purely political reasons.

The likes of Jefferson's assault on judicial independence were not seen again for nearly a century and a half, until President Franklin D. Roosevelt, frustrated and angry at what he saw as an activist "conservative" Supreme Court, tried to curb judicial power by a quite different route. Roosevelt's chief "adversaries" on the Court were justices over age seventy. His Court-packing plan was to have Congress authorize him to appoint a new justice for each "old man" who failed to retire at age seventy. This aroused a great debate throughout the country, one that crossed party lines with Montana's Democratic senator, Burton Wheeler, leading the opposition to the plan. Every bar association in the country had committees, conferences, and forums debating the subject. It was democracy in action. Roosevelt, popular and powerful as he was, gradually found the tide turning against him. Many lawyers who agreed with his criticisms of the Court backed away from destroying the tradition of judicial independence simply because of some transitory misuse, or even abuse, of that power. Much as bipartisan opposition had defeated Jefferson's attack, so too it stopped Roosevelt's Court-packing plan.

Roosevelt's attack was the most recent, and perhaps the final, attempt to destroy the independence of the federal judiciary. However, the fact that two powerful presidents have attempted and failed to assert control over the Supreme Court is evidence that our system of separation of powers does in fact guarantee the independence of the three branches as the Founding Fathers plainly intended. Our system of divided, separated powers does not produce a tidy system of government, nor was it expected to do so. There is, as history reveals, the risk that the absolute powers of the Court can be abused; the decisions in the *Dred Scott* and *Plessy* cases discussed in later chapters provide examples. But those tragic mistakes have been relatively few, given the exercise of reasoned judgment by the Court, working within the framework of judicial self-restraint.

CHAPTER SEVEN

PRESIDENT JEFFERSON'S PAPERS ARE SUBPOENAED BY JOHN MARSHALL

....

United States v. *Aaron Burr*, 1807

Some time in the latter part of September [1806], I received intimations that designs were in agitation in the western country, unlawful and unfriendly to the peace of the Union; and that the prime mover in these was Aaron Burr, heretofore distinguished by the favor of his country.

—President Thomas Jefferson, in
a message to Congress on the
alleged Burr Conspiracy, 1807

What loophole [Marshall] will find in [Aaron Burr's] case, when it comes to trial, we cannot foresee.

—President Thomas Jefferson, in a letter
to Senator William Branch Giles, 1807

WITHIN TWO YEARS of the impeachment of Justice Chase, Aaron Burr again found himself in the middle of a confrontation between Jefferson and Marshall. This time, however, Burr had considerably more at stake—he was on trial for treason and other crimes. In less than two years Burr had gone from being vice president of the United States to being faced with the prospect of a trial that could lead to the gallows or a firing squad—all sponsored by the man under whom he had served as vice president. In the course of the government's prosecution of Burr, Chief Justice Marshall would set a key precedent in the relationship between the president and the judiciary.

Jefferson did not relish his near defeat by Burr in the election of 1800, and very likely he did not fancy the ambitious Burr being his vice president. Older political leaders tend to be very suspicious of younger party members who show too much strength. But in that day, and indeed until President Eisenhower's administration, the office of the vice president had not taken on any particular definition, except as the presiding officer of the Senate and the figure waiting in the wings in case of the death or resignation of the president. During the election of 1800, before the vote in the House of Representatives was taken, Burr had written to Jefferson that if elected vice president, he would be glad to give up that office if Jefferson, as president, thought he could be more useful in some other position. The story of this "paper dueling" between Jefferson and Burr before the results were final has been told by Milton Lomask in his *Life of Aaron Burr*. Under the circumstances, Jefferson was apparently content to have Burr remain in the sterile vice presidency, where he would be under constant scrutiny.

Burr, a dynamic and activist politician, was heading into four frustrating years during which he was ignored by the president except for the brief occasion when, as we have seen, Jefferson sought his support in the impeachment of Justice Samuel Chase. Burr was still a relatively young man, in his forties, and if Jefferson adhered to President Washington's voluntary two-term limit, Burr would be only fifty-three when Jefferson retired. What kind of a president would Aaron Burr have made? Perhaps a very good one. He understood the Constitution. He was a very able lawyer. He understood the political process. He was tough. He had served in the Senate and his presence and personality fitted him for leadership. But Burr was not a patient man; he lacked the willingness to wait and try again as have some others, notably Grover Cleveland and Richard Nixon, who would not accept setbacks or defeats.

By the end of Jefferson's first term, Jefferson wanted no part of

Burr. Even before his duel with Hamilton, Burr had been passed over for renomination as vice president in favor of one of his toughest rivals in New York, Governor George Clinton. Clinton led the Republicans in New York and could count on Jefferson's support in any conflict with Burr.

The coolness between Thomas Jefferson and Aaron Burr became icy after Burr's vice presidency terminated in 1805. Burr left public life, returned to the practice of law, and traveled to Europe seeking financial and political support for his undefined plans in the western territories of the United States. No doubt Jefferson was glad to have Burr depart on his travels to Europe—or anywhere else for that matter. But word from Europe about Burr's activities gave rise to suspicion concerning his efforts to contact leaders abroad.

Although Burr's political career was in a precipitous decline, he was still a threat. Burr's killing of Hamilton destroyed any political future Burr had in New York, and the hostility toward dueling in the Puritan-influenced northern states seriously undermined Burr's national status. But in the South Burr retained some following, and he was very popular in the new, sparsely populated areas of the West. The westerners wanted support for development of the vast wilderness area. Many believed that Burr could be elected to the Senate from whichever western state he chose for his new residence. And Jefferson well knew how ambitious Burr was.

Burr's party rivals were quick to place the worst interpretations on his European adventures. Although no chiefs of state received Burr, the naturally suspicious Jefferson was worried. Burr's travels took place long before the twentieth-century custom of congressional junkets around the world. In those days travel was slow and expensive and Congress was not financing foreign travel by congressmen or bureaucrats. On return to the United States, Burr began adventuresome moves in the West that aggravated Jefferson even more. Jefferson must have wondered what his former vice president was up to.

Historians have speculated for nearly two centuries as to Burr's true objectives. Events between 1805 and 1807 leave little doubt that Burr had some kind of grand plan, however vague, concerning the region west of the Appalachians, the territories in and adjacent to the Mississippi River Valley. At worst, some believed he meant to set up a nation of his own, perhaps including Mexico, with himself as "Emperor." At best it was an effort to speed up development of the West, exploiting the great asset of the Mississippi River to serve settlers on the agriculturally rich western frontier.

Burr was not alone in wanting to press westward. Curiously, Jefferson and Burr held similar views about the importance of developing the western territories and shared concerns about the presence of France and Spain in North America. These concerns originated when the region west of the Appalachians had opened up to settlement after the Revolutionary War. Americans living on the frontier, especially farmers, needed access to the Mississippi River for shipping their produce to eastern markets through New Orleans, as transportation of grain was enormously difficult by land, even when the grain was "liquefied" into whiskey. Accordingly, Americans were deeply concerned about French and Spanish control of the river and the port of New Orleans. Responding to this significant political problem, Jefferson himself had consummated the Louisiana Purchase in 1803. But even after Jefferson had secured exclusive American control of the Mississippi and its gateway, Spanish territory still hemmed in the United States—Florida and the Gulf Coast to the south and Mexico to the west. As president, Jefferson therefore needed to proceed cautiously in dealing with Spain, still a world power at that time. As a private citizen, Burr, on the other hand, could act without inhibition or consideration of the national interest.

Burr's enemies, Jefferson included, suggested that Burr intended to use force to set up a new country in the western territories. Burr had indeed organized a number of men—perhaps one hundred as it turned out—all armed and provisioned for river travel. But few, if any, men traveling between Pittsburgh and New Orleans in that day—or even between Richmond and Washington—would be without rifles and pistols. In the sparsely inhabited western territories along the Ohio and Mississippi Rivers, travelers would need guns to provide daily food and to deal with the hostile Indians. And Burr's "navy" was a cluster of river flatboats.

Burr was obviously up to something that bordered, if carried out, on illegality. But was it treason? It is reasonable to assume that, opportunist that he was, Burr had no concrete plans but was looking for al-

ternatives that would have put him in action if a war with Spain ensued. His critics accused him of trying to promote a conflict with
Spain. Leonard Baker's excellent biography on Marshall, *John Marshall:
A Life in Law*, quotes Charles Biddle of Philadelphia as stating that Burr
told him that he was gathering settlers for the lower Mississippi River
Valley who would be available in the event a conflict developed with
Spain. Similarly, Thomas Truxton, naval hero in the war with England, stated that Burr asked him to command a sea expedition if an attack in Vera Cruz developed into a war with Spain. Truxton declined.
Nevertheless, reports from the British minister to the United States discovered years later reveal that even while Burr was vice president, he
discussed possible plans for separating from the United States the entire
region west of the Appalachians. Even if this was only talk, not a real
plan, Jefferson would have had reason to be disturbed.

Jefferson finally ordered his military commander in the West, one
General James Wilkinson, a dubious character, to track Burr's activities. Wilkinson had been a friend of Burr's. As the son of a Princeton
University president, Burr had helped get the general's sons admitted
to that university, where both Burr and James Madison had studied. In
fact, Jefferson made Wilkinson governor of the Louisiana Territory as
part of his efforts to curry favor with Burr during the impeachment trial
of Justice Chase. When Burr went west, he not surprisingly met with
the general. Based on these visits and on the general's correspondence,
Burr had no reason to think of the general as an adversary. But in November 1806, largely as a result of General Wilkinson's reports, Jefferson issued a proclamation concerning the mysterious activities in the
West.

The proclamation informed Congress and the public that "sundry
persons," all of them citizens or residents of the United States, were
"conspiring and confederating together" for the purpose of an expedition "against the dominions of Spain" and were building support for
their "criminal enterprises." The proclamation continued in sweeping
terms:

> I hereby enjoin and require all officers, civil and military, of the
> United States, or of any of the States or Territories, and especially
> all Governors, and other Executive authorities, all judges, justices,

and other officers of the peace, [and] all military officers . . . to be vigilant . . . in searching out, and bringing to condign punishment, all persons engaged or concerned in such enterprise . . . .

Within sixty days Jefferson followed with a special message to Congress, this time specifically naming Aaron Burr as the "prime mover" in an "unlawful enterprise" involving "armies and navies," and describing Burr as the "principal actor, *whose guilt is placed beyond question*" (emphasis added). The president went on to state that three of Burr's "principal emissaries" had been arrested, but one "had been liberated by *habeas corpus*"—a legal action by which prisoners can challenge the legality of their confinement—while two others had been removed to the Atlantic seaboard. Jefferson was suggesting that his plea to "judges" and "justices" had been ignored in dealing with the "criminals"—the term he sprinkled throughout his proclamations and messages to Congress. In one sense Jefferson was correct, for several weeks after his message to Congress, the Supreme Court, in an opinion by Chief Justice Marshall, ordered the other two arrested "co-conspirators" released because of the absence of proof that they had committed treason.

As several historians have noted, Jefferson's statements basically told the American people and the Congress that Aaron Burr was guilty of treason. It is difficult to recall any statement ever made by another president, especially regarding a national political figure, that so clearly pronounced guilt before trial. Surprisingly for a great libertarian and humanist, Jefferson's campaign against Burr rivals anything undertaken by the late Senator Joseph McCarthy. The White House, even before the day of electronic communications, was a "bully pulpit" for both constructive and destructive rhetoric. Naturally, Jefferson's pronouncements were carried by every newspaper in the country.

Jefferson also released affidavits of Wilkinson and others, along with copies of purported letters from Burr, some in code. These affidavits recited that Burr had made statements about planning to "dismember the union." When this material reached the press, a great hue and cry followed. "Burr is a traitor and should be hanged" was the prevailing attitude that Jefferson's propaganda had inspired.

After the massive campaign of rumors, speculation, and exaggeration, Jefferson ordered his attorney general to secure indictments of Burr and his associates for treason. Two grand juries, after hearing the evidence Jefferson presented, declined to return indictments. But finally General Wilkinson's troops arrested Burr in what is now Alabama and brought him to Richmond, Virginia, in chains and under armed military escort for a third try at an indictment.

One cannot read what Jefferson told Congress and the press without a smile at the irony. It compares so directly with some of the partisan media messages of today—exceeding all but the worst. Jefferson's utterances shock some who do not know the details of the "brass knuckle" political combat of that day or of Jefferson's harsh manner of dealing with his political adversaries. Far away and having neither General Wilkinson's military couriers nor the ability to issue White House proclamations, Burr could hardly answer Jefferson's public campaign against him.

Brought to Richmond in March of 1807 by Jefferson's command, Burr became the catalyst that again brought together three historic antagonists—Jefferson, Marshall, and himself. Marshall could have avoided taking part, although as circuit justice for the federal circuit that included Virginia, it was not unusual for him to preside over trials there. As we have seen, it was then common for Supreme Court justices regularly to preside over both grand juries and criminal trials on circuit, a practice Congress forced on justices for the first hundred years of our history. Moreover, Richmond was Marshall's hometown. Perhaps he feared that his old friend Judge Cyrus Griffin, district judge for Virginia, could not stand up to Jefferson's onslaughts. Although he said nothing publicly against Jefferson, from the beginning Marshall took note of the wild publicity induced by the president, and he warned against "any attempt which may be made to prejudice the public judgment, and to try any person, not by the laws of his country and the testimony exhibited against him, but by public feelings, which may be and often are artificially excited against the innocent as well as the guilty."

Once Burr arrived in Richmond, a grand jury was assembled. The hype Jefferson had launched, however, made it impossible to find jurors who had not heard something of the rumors and the news stories, regularly laced with hysterical rhetoric about "Aaron Burr's Conspiracy," "Treason," and "General Wilkinson's Reports." Burr's alleged treasonous role dominated the news and, of course, the gossip and the rumors enlarged on this.

Once the difficult task of finding qualified jurors was accomplished, Marshall's next task was to preside over a grand jury, beginning in May 1807. Chief Justice Marshall analyzed the prosecution's charges, the evidence, and the nature of the crime of treason Jefferson had proclaimed. Here was Marshall the teacher-jurist. Marshall was prudent, moving slowly and deliberately, knowing that by taking any steps or results favorable to Burr he would necessarily have to cope with Jefferson's anger. Jefferson was convinced that Marshall was biased in favor of Burr. That feeling was intensified by one unfortunate incident outside of the courtroom. An old friend of Marshall's, who was one of Burr's lawyers, held a dinner in Richmond while Marshall was presiding over the grand jury considering an indictment of Burr. Historians have not been able to determine with any assurance the details of the dinner, but we do know that both Marshall and Burr were in attendance. Marshall wisely never undertook to explain; his friends, somewhat lamely, said that Marshall did not know that Aaron Burr would be attending the dinner and that he left early to avoid embarrassment. He did not succeed in avoiding embarrassment, but the event probably stands out because historians can find so little negative on Marshall. In fairness, we must remember that John Marshall, although a formal man on the bench, was a casual, gregarious fellow. His stag dinners with other leaders of the day at his house in Richmond were famous at the time and have been well documented.

Burr could not—safely at least—assume that Marshall would favor him in any way. After all, Burr had killed Marshall's good friend and confidant Alexander Hamilton just three years before, and it was known that Marshall had no regard for Burr. This might have been enough to support a request by Burr that Marshall recuse himself, but Burr never did make such a request. Burr was well aware of the tension that existed between Marshall and Jefferson.

Although represented by some of the ablest lawyers in America, including the famous Luther Martin of Maryland, Burr took an active personal part in the proceedings. Many believed that anyone who assisted Burr was also a traitor, but Burr's counsel were not men to be intimidated. As with Marshall, to them this was more than the trial of Burr: it was a test of our system. Perhaps to some observers Burr was merely an incidental player. Burr's conduct in Richmond was exemplary. He seemed almost to relish being a martyr, a role he had flirted with since his youth.

While waiting for Wilkinson to arrive in Richmond to testify before the grand jury, Burr became concerned about the prosecution's evidence based on General Wilkinson's reports to Jefferson. Burr wanted to see all of Wilkinson's reports, not just those portions Jefferson saw fit to release to Congress and the public. What Burr wanted to know was what his erstwhile friend Wilkinson had reported to Jefferson about the "armies" and "navies" and warlike plans mentioned in the president's proclamations, messages to Congress, and press releases. He requested Marshall to issue a subpoena to require the president to produce *all* of the Wilkinson letters. A judge ordering a president to produce records? Unheard of! No occasion for such a demand had ever arisen in the courts from 1790 to 1807.

On Burr's motion Marshall directed that a subpoena duces tecum—an order to produce documents—be issued to Jefferson. The power of a mere judge to command a president of the United States to appear and to produce his official records called forth concepts that had their roots in the Declaration of Independence and the Constitution—indeed, even in the Magna Carta of 1215. Was the president above the law? Most of the lawyers knew of Lord Edward Coke's reply to King James I that "the King should not be under man, but under God and the Laws." Lord Coke had thrown himself on the floor to dramatize that he was below the king just as the king was below the law. What value would there be in the presumption of innocence and other safeguards if a defendant, accused by the president and publicly denounced as a traitor to the United States, could not compel the government— the accuser—to disclose any papers or records that would aid the defense? Would Jefferson, an author of the Declaration, a passionately eloquent advocate of the rights of individuals, become Jefferson the scheming politician in a contest with an adversary?

Marshall's careful opinion began by noting that the Constitution entitled every accused person to legal process to compel the attendance of witnesses, and he then asked whether the president was exempt from those provisions of the Constitution. He concluded that as to the issuance of a subpoena to testify, "the law does not discriminate between the president and a private citizen." He then turned to the more immediate issue of the production of documents, and found no basis to treat them differently from testimony. The requirement of disclosure is not necessarily absolute, Marshall acknowledged:

> There is certainly nothing before the court which shows that the letter in question contains any matter the disclosure of which would endanger the public safety. If it does contain such matter, the fact may appear before the disclosure is made.

That question, Marshall's opinion made clear, would be answered when the documents were provided to the court.

Jefferson initially resisted the subpoena. His concerns for the rights and dignity of an accused individual did not extend to Aaron Burr, a "treasonous conspirator." But Jefferson had to contend with Chief Justice Marshall. In his opinion, Marshall had referred to a trial the previous year, *United States* v. *Smith and Ogden*, in which Jefferson had instructed his Cabinet members to defy subpoenas on the ground that obedience would interfere with their official duties. Marshall cited the case for a different point, but the message was clear. Jefferson, good lawyer that he was, knew that Marshall could dismiss the indictment if the subpoena was ignored. Although Jefferson asserted that the president "must be the sole judge of which of them the public interests will permit publication," he sent the documents to the prosecutor with instructions to withhold any portions that disclosed matters vital to the public interest. At this point Burr did not press for the omitted materials, but Marshall had made clear that not even a president could withhold evidence—unless disclosure would jeopardize national security. And Marshall's opinion conveyed the clear implication that it was for the court, not the president, to decide that question.

While the debate raged over the subpoena, General Wilkinson arrived in Richmond and attention quickly turned back to the alleged crimes at hand. The details of the complex moves, maneuvers, and procedures are not relevant to the story. It is enough to state that after the difficulty of securing minimally unbiased grand jurors, these jurors held the evidence sufficient to put Burr to trial and thus indicted Burr for treason and other crimes. Marshall set bail at $10,000, which was immediately put up by Burr's indignant friends.

Selecting a trial jury from an area with only a few thousand eligible jurors was as difficult as selecting the grand jury. Finally, twelve men were sworn in a jury box in a courtroom in the Old State House in Richmond, which still stands today. Marshall had prepared the ground by his extended discussions with the grand jury in a series of opinions on interlocutory procedural matters. This deliberately stately pace—and Marshall's "lectures" on the Constitution—may well have served to abate some of the passionate hostility toward Burr.

As it turned out, some of the documents, reports, letters, and even the testimony of General Wilkinson—when Burr's counsel forced the prosecution to produce him—cast serious doubt on the integrity of the general and his motives. The events at the trial in Richmond virtually destroyed the already dubious reputation of this manipulative general. His labyrinthine story, replete with contradictions and confusion, ultimately reflected far more damage on himself than on Burr, and surely no credit on Jefferson, whose entire case rested on Wilkinson. Was Jefferson misled by Wilkinson's "reports," or was he just too eager to believe anything negative about Burr? Some biographers have been too willing to ignore or minimize Jefferson's conduct in the Burr case.

The drawn-out trial ended with a jury verdict acquitting Burr of the treason charge. Jefferson claimed that Marshall had virtually directed a verdict in favor of Burr. Not so. Marshall's instructions to the jury came straight from Article III, Section 3, of the Constitution:

> Treason against the United States, shall consist only in levy-
> ing War against them, or in adhering to their Enemies, giving

them Aid and Comfort. No person shall be convicted of Treason unless on the Testimony of two Witnesses to the same overt Act, or on Confession in open Court.

Marshall patiently, and at great length, had explained to the jurors the history, meaning, and purpose of this clause. Of course, there was no evidence of "levying War," no evidence of "adhering to the[] Enemies" of the United States, no evidence of "giving . . . Aid," no "two Witnesses to the same overt Act" of treason, and no "Confession in open Court." Indeed, no solid evidence of any "army" or any "ships"—only a few dozen men and some riverboats on Harman Blennerhassett's Island, in the Ohio River near Marietta, Ohio.

The evidence produced by the government in the case arguably would have justified a judge in directing a verdict of not guilty on the treason charge, given the stringent requirements of the Constitution. But Marshall the teacher took the risk of a guilty verdict, which he could have then set aside in a judgment notwithstanding the verdict, if necessary. Marshall realized that a verdict from a jury of twelve would do much more to vindicate Burr than would the judgment of a Federalist judge. The jury acquitted Burr. Jefferson was enraged.

President Jefferson's public campaign to destroy Burr before his trial was totally indefensible conduct. But the question whether Burr was an opportunist "con man" or just an overeager braggart is still unclear. When an intriguer like Burr mixes with a scoundrel like General Wilkinson, the results are difficult to interpret. Thomas Jefferson's tactics had not produced the result he sought. But Aaron Burr never lived down the impact of Jefferson's campaign or the revelations of his own strange conduct. Upon completion of his one term as Jefferson's vice president, Burr was never again to hold public office. His youthful predictions of a dismal future for himself became self-fulfilling prophecies, and whether he perhaps suffered by unconsciously comparing himself with his successful father and his famous grandfather, Jonathan Edwards, we shall never know.

As the participants in the trial recognized, however, the consequences for Jefferson and Burr were only part of the story, and not the most important part. Chief Justice Marshall once again established an important precedent for the new nation—that the president was not above the law and the legal process. His decision to subpoena Jefferson's papers, and to assert the judicial power to determine whether they should be disclosed, set a precedent for the powers of the courts and the presidency that lasts to this day. While the rulings in Aaron Burr's case were made by a trial judge, that judge was John Marshall, and later decisions of the Supreme Court have confirmed the correctness of his rulings.

CHAPTER EIGHT

DARTMOUTH COLLEGE AND THE CONTRACT CLAUSE

....

Trustees of Dartmouth College v. *Woodward*, 1819

No State shall . . . pass any . . . Law impairing the Obligation of Contracts . . . .

—Article I, Section 10, U.S. Constitution

"It is, Sir, as I have said, a small college. And yet there are those who love it!"

—Daniel Webster, in the oral
argument of the *Dartmouth
College* case, 1818

IN 1787, WHEN THE DELEGATES at Philadelphia were debating the Contract Clause of the Constitution, they were not focusing on the question that was to emerge in the *Dartmouth College* case— whether a state legislature could convert a royally chartered college into a state university. Their minds were focused primarily on commercial contracts, not royal charters, and the imperative need for commercial stability in the new nation.

The Convention in Philadelphia was inspired in large part, as discussed earlier, by commercial disputes among the states. The delegates knew that the new Union of thirteen states, each independent and sovereign since 1776, could never develop as a true nation if there were thirteen sovereigns legislating on commercial matters to fit the needs and desires of their own constituencies. To see the wisdom in such reasoning, we need only to look to the history of Europe for centuries before the advent of the European Common Market and the difficulties Europeans have faced as they have attempted to develop unity and to promote trade among themselves. Relieved of the onerous manufacturing and trade restraints imposed by the British Parliament to keep the colonies subservient, Americans could now fabricate and sell any lawful product. Under the Commerce Clause, no state could place arbitrary limits on goods coming from outside its borders, as was possible under the Articles of Confederation. In 1787, without giving it a name, we invented our own common market under the Commerce Clause.

But merely precluding barriers to trade among the states was not enough. In 1787 insolvent debtors were a harsh fact of life in the venturesome, free society that was being developed in America. In those early years the new nation had an abundance of debtors. And as Mr. Shays demonstrated in 1786, these hard-pressed debtors were militant enough in their calls for debt relief to give Shays' name to the "rebellion" that had to be put down by military force and resulted in a death sentence—that was never carried out—for Shays himself. As all bankers know, borrowers are critical constituents for lenders, and both are needed to stimulate manufacturing, trade, and commerce. As practical men—lawyers, tradesmen, and agriculturists—the delegates knew that at times, through the vagaries of weather and markets, some people would be overcome by debt and would need relief. The framers frowned on the ancient concept of imprisonment for debt that was still being practiced. The delegates were firm in their belief that bankruptcy laws must be the same for all states if trade and commerce among the states were to prosper, and so they decided that Congress, not the states, should be the exclusive regulator of bankruptcies. The delegates in Philadelphia wanted to be sure that trade and commerce would not be burdened by thirteen separate sets of "bankruptcy laws." Uniformity of debtor-creditor relationships would be imperative to make this new "common market" work.

The solution the delegates settled upon was twofold. First, the Constitution authorized Congress to enact "uniform Laws on the subject of Bankruptcies throughout the United States." Second, the Contract Clause of the Constitution forbade the states to "impair[] the Obligation of Contracts," as they might otherwise do to give debtors in their states relief, especially from creditors in other states. The second of these clauses was at the center of a dispute over control of Dartmouth College, a dispute which became the vehicle for another significant building block in the nation's constitutional jurisprudence from the pen of Chief Justice Marshall.

A long-standing internal power conflict had raged in New Hampshire over the control of Dartmouth, a "small college" chartered by the Crown. In 1715 Dartmouth, like the College of William and Mary in Virginia and Princeton in New Jersey, had received its original charter and support from the king of England. In the case of Dartmouth, its charter had come from the monarch's royal surrogate in the colony of New Hampshire. The college was run by a self-perpetuating Board of Trustees, whose authority derived from that royal charter.

Even after the Revolutionary War, the college continued to operate under the royal charter, although the college's support from London had long since ceased. It was not until a quarter of a century after the Constitution became operative that the state of New Hampshire attempted to change Dartmouth's governing structure. In 1816 the New Hampshire legislature decided that because the original charter "emanated from royalty," it was incompatible with the concepts of a free people. The Dartmouth College charter was thus amended by the legislature to make the college a state institution. This was the crucial step in a controversy that had spanned two generations. This one statute gave rise to issues that the Supreme Court would ultimately be asked to resolve. In doing so, the Court resolved more than the future of a small college in New Hampshire.

Not surprisingly, the incumbent trustees objected to the legislature's action. Among other things, the new charter increased the number of trustees and subjected them to control by a board of overseers. The old trustees claimed that their offices and rights were vested by the previous action of a valid government—the British Crown—that had authorized the charter and appointed them. For the trustees the char-

ter entailed something essentially in the nature of a contractual commitment. The courts would be required to decide whether it was a
contractual obligation protected by the Constitution.

William H. Woodward, a New Hampshire state court judge, ordered all of the college's records removed from the control of the
trustees. The trustees, acting in the name of the college, sued for their
return. The trustees importuned Daniel Webster, himself a Dartmouth
graduate, to act for them. Webster, who was in his thirties at the time,
had already established a solid reputation as a Supreme Court advocate.
His task was to defend the original charter and the powers of the incumbent trustees. William Wirt was enlisted to defend the New
Hampshire legislature's action. Wirt, also a leader of the Supreme
Court bar, was then attorney general of the United States. In that day,
government lawyers—like members of Congress—continued to engage in private practice. As a young lawyer, Wirt had been part of the
defense team in the treason trial of Aaron Burr in 1807.

On the surface Wirt's case on behalf of the state looked strong. In
light of long-standing American skepticism about monarchy, especially
the British monarchy, it seemed sensible, even logical, to those who
had fought and won a war against England to sever all residual relations
with the mother country and reject its appointees, the trustees. Why
should a college tracing its origins to an act of the defeated monarch
continue to function under its original royal charter when New
Hampshire was prepared to take it over as a state university?

But that reasoning went too far. Could property and rights granted
by the authority of the king while he was the acknowledged governing
authority of the colonies be expropriated by a state government? If so,
some land titles would be in jeopardy. Should Dartmouth's charter be
treated like a land grant from the Crown? Was it a contract? Would
commercial contracts be subject to legislative revision? These were
probably the common speculations in the newspapers, taverns, and
courthouses in New Hampshire. Outside the state, colleges, churches,
and other institutions whose origins derived from royal charters were
disturbed.

Oratorical court arguments were often the order of the day. Webster charged that the state legislature had violated New Hampshire's

own constitution by overstepping the bounds that separated the legislative from the judicial branch. Webster said:

> If the [separation of powers] has any meaning, it is, that the legislature shall pass no act directly and manifestly impairing private property, and private privileges. It shall not judge, by [legislative] *act*. It shall not decide, by *act*. It shall not deprive, by *act*. It shall leave all these things to be tried and adjudged by the law of the land.

But along with flashes of eloquence Webster presented hard analysis and solid logic. To bring the Dartmouth case within the reach of several other cases decided by the Supreme Court, he had to persuade at least four of the seven justices that the original royal charter of the college was a contract, valid when made. Once there, Webster had to persuade them that the New Hampshire legislature's amendment to the charter violated the Contract Clause of Article I of the Constitution.

The New Hampshire legislature, said Webster, had arbitrarily infringed on contract rights when it removed the trustees appointed by royal authority and seized control of the college; in so doing, it violated the Contract Clause. The Court had already plainly marked the way for that argument in a case involving a royal land grant to the Episcopal Church, *Terrett* v. *Taylor*, decided in 1815.

In *Terrett*, the Court, in an opinion by the able Justice Joseph Story, recognized the validity of a royal land grant made by the king to the Episcopal Church in this country. The principles guiding the Court in that earlier case would seem to call for a decision contrary to the act of the New Hampshire legislature in the *Dartmouth College* case. But with a Court that had existed less than thirty years, precedents were not as firmly rooted as they would be a century later. Clear as Justice Story's opinion was, the political fallout of the Court's *Terrett* decision had been more fodder for the debate between the Jeffersonian proponents of states' rights and the Federalists pressing for national power in order to make the former colonies a true nation.

At that time, moreover, not all lawyers paid attention to the

Supreme Court's decisions, few as they were. The Court's opinions were not printed promptly when cases were decided and often were not available until many months later. And only a few lawyers argued cases in the High Court. Although Marshall was one of the leading advocates of his time, he had argued only one case in the Supreme Court during the decade before he assumed the bench. Daniel Webster, however, was one of the lawyers who followed Supreme Court opinions closely. Webster reminded the Court of its opinion in *Terrett*, sustaining a royal land grant under the Contract Clause.

Webster's argument reflected John Marshall's and Joseph Story's concepts of the Constitution. In framing a new government under a written constitution, we had "chosen to take the risk of occasional inconvenience from the want of power, in order that there might be a settled limit to its exercise, and a permanent security against its abuse." Politically, Webster shared Marshall's views on the need for predictability in the law and the need for a strong national government.

Webster closed his argument by emphasizing the broader significance of the issues at hand. Important as the case was to the Dartmouth trustees, and to other royally chartered institutions, it was vastly more so to Americans trying to develop trade and commerce here and abroad based on enforceable contracts. By itself, Dartmouth's future was irrelevant to the future of the emerging nation. All of the royally chartered colleges could have been taken over as state universities without impeding the development of commerce, but if a charter was a contract, then the power of a state legislature to interfere with it would have major significance for the commercial and economic future of the new nation.

No records of oral arguments were made during the *Dartmouth College* case, but reasonably reliable notes were taken, usually by the newspapers. One of these has Webster concluding as follows:

It is the case not merely of that humble institution [Dartmouth], it is the case of every college in our Land! It is more! It is the case of every eleemosynary institution throughout our country—of all those great charities founded by the piety of our ancestors to alleviate human misery, and scatter blessings along the pathway of life! It is more! It is, in some sense, the case of every man among us who has property of which he may be stripped, for the question is simply this, "Shall our State Legislatures be allowed to take *that which is not their own,* to turn it from its original use, and apply it to such ends and purposes as they in their discretion shall see fit."

Webster's plea prevailed with the Court. All but one of the participating justices voted to reverse the New Hampshire court and to sustain the Dartmouth College trustees. Chief Justice Marshall delivered the opinion of the Court. In typical fashion, he posed two questions:

1. Is this contract protected by the constitution of the United States?
2. Is it impaired by the acts [of the New Hampshire legislature]?

The answer to the first was clear. The charter "is plainly a contract to which the donors, the trustees, and the crown, (to whose rights and obligations New-Hampshire succeeds,) were the original parties." Significantly, Marshall flatly rejected the argument that the Contract Clause did not extend to such a contract because it was not the sort that the delegates in Philadelphia had had in mind:

It is not enough to say, that this particular case was not in the mind of the Convention, when the article was framed, nor of the American people, when it was adopted. It is necessary to go farther, and to say that, had this particular case been suggested, the language would have been so varied, as to exclude it, or it would have been made a special exception. The case being within the words of the rule, must be within its operation likewise, unless there be something in the literal construction so obviously absurd, or mischievous, or repugnant to the general spirit of the instru-

ment, as to justify those who expound the constitution in making
it an exception.

That conclusion tells us a great deal about Marshall's general interpre-
tative approach to the Constitution. Proceeding to his second question, Marshall concluded that the state legislature's act impermissibly
impaired the obligations of the royal charter.

But by sustaining the college's position under the Contract Clause,
the Court was treading on dangerous waters. Under the Articles of
Confederation the thirteen separate, independent sovereigns had
joined in "a firm league of friendship" and their strong feeling about
liberty and states' rights abounded; they did not want any part of a national government that acted like George III. The *people* could control
the state legislatures; state government was close at hand. But a monster distant national government in New York, Philadelphia, or Washington was another matter.

As a result, although the Court did sustain Dartmouth's position,
a distinct and sensitive deference to state autonomy emerges in the
opinions of the justices. Two justices, Joseph Story and Bushrod
Washington, wrote separate concurring opinions. Story's opinion, in
particular, reflected the delicacy of the state-federal aspects of the case.
He wrote:

> I entertain great respect for the legislature, whose acts are in ques-
> tion. I entertain no less respect for the enlightened tribunal whose
> decision we are called upon to review. In the examination, I have
> endeavored to keep my steps *super antiquas vias* of the law, under
> the guidance of authority and principle. It is not for judges to lis-
> ten to the voice of persuasive eloquence or popular appeal. We
> have nothing to do but to pronounce the law as we find it; and
> having done this, our justification must be left to the impartial
> judgment of our country.

Notwithstanding the apparent deference to state autonomy, the
highest court in the land firmly declared in concrete terms that the
original charter was a contract and that the Constitution meant what it
said: "No State shall . . . pass any . . . Law impairing the Obligation of

Contracts . . . ." At the same time, the Court carried the meaning of the Constitution to situations that the delegates in Philadelphia probably had not thought about. In so doing, the Court established the Constitution as a document that could meet the rapidly changing needs of the nation. All this for "a small college" and, as Daniel Webster put it, "those who love[d] it."

CHAPTER NINE

THE LIVING CONSTITUTION

....

M'Culloch v. Maryland, 1819

The Congress shall have Power . . . To make all Laws which shall be necessary and proper for carrying into Execution the foregoing Powers, and all other Powers vested by this Constitution in the Government of the United States . . . .

—Article I, Section 8, U.S. Constitution

Let the end be legitimate, let it be within the scope of the constitution, and all means which are appropriate, which are plainly adapted to that end, which are not prohibited, but consist with the letter and spirit of the constitution, are constitutional.

—Chief Justice John Marshall,
in *M'Culloch* v. *Maryland*, 1819

O NE OF THE MOST SIGNIFICANT constitutional controversies in the early years of the nation was the extent of Congress's authority under the Necessary and Proper Clause, quoted above, to exercise powers not expressly recited in the Constitution. As was the situation when Marbury sued for his position as justice of the peace, the case that brought the issue to the Supreme Court involved relatively unimportant amounts of money that the state of Maryland claimed was owed in taxes by the second Bank of the United States. M'Culloch, who was an officer at the Baltimore branch of the bank, was hauled into the Maryland courts for refusing to pay the tax. As is more often than not the case, however, in this lawsuit the political philosophies of the contending forces were at the base of the dispute. Thus, Maryland's challenge to Congress's constitutional authority to establish a central bank became the latest stage in a battle that had raged since George Washington's first administration.

In 1791 Alexander Hamilton, the first secretary of the treasury, proposed the creation of a national bank. "Strict constructionists" such as James Madison, then a member of Congress, and Thomas Jefferson, then secretary of state, opposed the plan because the Constitution nowhere made reference to the creation of "banks" or "corporations."

Jefferson looked at the issue as a states' rights lawyer. This strict constructionist approach suggests that Jefferson was not as profound an economist as he was a political science generalist. Jefferson's vision of a nation of "sturdy yeomen" farmers did not require a national bank. Surely, if someone had proposed an eighteenth- or nineteenth-century version of the twentieth-century Federal Reserve Board or National Labor Relations Act, Jefferson would have been opposed. His acknowledged grasp of large political concepts exceeded his grasp of economic and fiscal realities.

Hamilton—economist, political scientist, and often Jefferson's intellectual adversary—led the fight for the bank. Hamilton had used his experience as a fiscal manager of the meager resources of the Confederation during the Revolutionary War to lay the foundations for the economic stability of the new Republic. He grasped the idea of a "common market" before people used that term, and he foresaw the need for a strong federal hand in the new nation's financial structure. He saw a bank as imperative for economic development under the Commerce Clause and the expansion of trade and industry that would derive from the Constitution's new concepts of patents and copyrights. On the importance of patents and copyrights, Jefferson was fully in accord with Hamilton. That was Jefferson, the creative man. Both of them knew the history of patents and copyrights in Europe, where the only way to get protection for creative works was to know a powerful lord.

When Congress passed the bill creating the first Bank of the United States over the anti-Federalists' constitutional objections, President

Washington felt it his duty, before signing the bill into law, to determine whether it was constitutional. Because he was not a lawyer, he sought the opinions of members of his Cabinet, including Hamilton and Jefferson. Hamilton argued that the Necessary and Proper Clause provided ample authority for a national bank. In words that would later be echoed by Chief Justice Marshall, Hamilton argued that the Constitution granted broad general powers that Congress could use to meet national needs:

> If the end be clearly comprehended within any of the specified powers, [and] if the measure have an obvious relation to that end, and is not forbidden by any particular provision of the constitution—it may safely be deemed to come within the compass of the national authority.

Jefferson disagreed, but Washington was persuaded by Hamilton and the act creating the first Bank of the United States became law. Political opposition to a national bank by the Jeffersonian Republicans continued, and after a few years, when they gained control of Congress, the authorization for the bank was allowed to expire.

The War of 1812 with England left the American economy in a shambles and changed the minds of some regarding a national bank. In 1816, halfway through Marshall's remarkable career as Chief Justice, it was proposed that Congress for the second time create a Bank of the United States. Jefferson was out of office, but he and many other Republicans, including James Madison, remained as opposed to any national bank then as they had been to the first national bank more than twenty years before.

Jefferson was perhaps more adamant than Madison in arguing that the Constitution gave Congress no power to create a bank or any kind of corporation. When Congress enacted a new National Bank Act, President Madison relented in his opposition and signed the bill. Madison later explained that although he still thought the Constitution did not authorize a national bank, he would not allow his private opinion to override the fact that the public and Congress had for twenty years accepted the existence of the first Bank of the United States.

The National Bank Act of 1816 gave voice again to the economic genius of the departed Alexander Hamilton and the imperative of national fiscal policies and practices. It was, in a sense, a concrete implementation of the idea that held thirteen independent states together from 1776 to 1781, as expressed in the slogan "united we stand, divided we fall." Americans were beginning, but only vaguely beginning, to grasp the reality that this concept governed economic and commercial matters as well as political ones. Everyone favored more roads and canals to enhance travel and commerce—even great believers in limited government such as Jefferson himself—but regional rivalry and squabbling stymied most efforts, as did a belief on the part of some that the Constitution did not give the distant national government such expansive powers. Again, there would be a test between the Hamilton-Marshall nationalist view of the Constitution and Jefferson's narrower view of constitutional powers.

It was true, as Jefferson argued, that the Constitution said not a word about "corporations" or "banks." Here was Thomas Jefferson the "strict constructionist," who ironically criticized Marshall for niggling over words. Jefferson might as well have contended that Congress could not authorize a national capitol building, or the White House as the official residence of the president, because the Constitution did not mention such structures.

Yet in common with others, Jefferson could find what he wanted in the Constitution and could ignore that with which he disagreed. The act of Jefferson that best illustrates this phenomenon, and which shrewd proponents of the national bank used against him, was the Louisiana Purchase. That act, one of the most extraordinary of Jefferson's career, was ironically one directly contrary to Jefferson's professed strict standards of constitutional interpretation. Writing privately to a proponent of the purchase, Senator Wilson C. Nicholas of Virginia, Jefferson stated his view that the purchase was beyond the authority of the federal government—and beyond his authority as president—because the Constitution did not grant the power to expand the territory of the United States:

> [W]hen I consider that the limits of the United States are precisely fixed by the treaty of 1783, that the Constitution expressly declares itself made for the United States, . . . I do not believe it was

meant that [Congress] might receive England, Ireland, Holland, etc. into it, which would be the case on your construction [of the Constitution]. . . . Our peculiar security is in the possession of a written Constitution. Let us not make it a blank paper by construction.

Yet "receive" new territory is ultimately what Jefferson did. Some years later Jefferson explained his move to his friend John B. Colvin as a necessity:

A strict observance of the written laws is doubtless *one* of the high duties of a good citizen, but it is not *the highest*. The laws of necessity, of self-preservation, of saving our country when in danger, are of higher obligation. To lose our country by a scrupulous adherence to written law, would be to lose the law itself, with life, liberty, property and all those who are enjoying them with us; thus absurdly sacrificing the end to the means. . . .
. . . [There is] a law of necessity and self-preservation, [which] render[s] the *salus populi* supreme over the written law. The officer who is called to act on this superior ground, does indeed risk himself on the justice of the controlling powers of the Constitution, and his station makes it his duty to incur that risk. But those controlling powers, and his fellow citizens generally, are bound to judge according to the circumstances under which he acted.

In those first years of nationhood there was the constant possibility that either France or Spain might move in and occupy the territory. Beyond the Louisiana Territory was a vast land stretching west to the Pacific. To have lost the Louisiana Territory would have been not only a barrier to the expansion of the country but a constant threat from a great power literally on our doorstep. A war to secure it would have been the likely result had Jefferson failed to act as he did.

The Louisiana Purchase was one of Jefferson's lasting contributions to his country, but it was possible only by abandoning the strict standards of interpretation he claimed to apply to the Constitution. Jefferson chose to adhere to those strict standards, however, in the debate over the second Bank of the United States. In his opposition to a national bank, Jefferson sounded more like Patrick Henry than like Madison, the Grand Architect of the Republic, as many historians depict him. Jefferson surely was an architect of government in certain respects, but not nearly so much as his contemporaries Hamilton and Marshall.

Chief Justice Marshall's private views about a national bank were reflected in his ownership of some of its stock, which he disposed of before the national bank case, *M'Culloch* v. *Maryland*, was argued in 1819. Marshall's caution was uncommon in a day when few questions were raised about a judge's private investments or extrajudicial activities. Justice Joseph Story was president of a bank in Salem, Massachusetts, during most of his tenure on the Supreme Court, a fact memorialized by an eighteenth-century banjo clock, now hanging in the justices' formal dining room in the Supreme Court building, that bears an inscription thanking Justice Story for "his most distinguished services as President of this Corporation from January 3, 1815 until until [*sic*] his resignation, August 22, 1835." In such a climate, Marshall's stock ownership would not have provoked attention. But he perhaps anticipated controversies over conflicts of interest that would occur later in the Court's history.

Two basic issues came before the Supreme Court in the bank case. One issue was the power of the state of Maryland to impose a tax on an instrumentality of the federal government, either directly or indirectly. Perhaps conscious that a direct tax on a national bank would be vulnerable, the Maryland tax was indirect. State law required that all currency issued by the bank be printed on paper that could be secured only from the state of Maryland—at a price. The other, and central, question was the underlying challenge to the power of Congress to create such a bank.

Daniel Webster argued the case for the Bank of the United States. He urged that creation of the bank was well within Congress' power to "make all Laws which shall be necessary and proper for carrying into Execution" its other powers. "Necessary and proper," he argued, encompassed all powers usual and suitable, and not specifically prohibited. He was no doubt aware that his argument tracked what Marshall had written and thought over the years. Marshall had recorded, in his biography of George Washington, a work widely read by leaders of

that day, that proponents of the first Bank of the United States had argued that "when a power is delegated to effect particular objects, all
known and usual means of effecting them must pass as incidental to it."
Making this principle the "supreme Law of the Land" was what the
Marshall Court was about to do.

Supporting Webster was William Wirt, who had argued against
him in the *Dartmouth College* case. Wirt contended that the Court
should

> compare the law in question with the powers it is intended to
> carry into execution; not in order to ascertain whether other or
> better means might have been selected, for that is the legislative
> province, but to see whether those [powers] which have been
> chosen have a natural connection with any specific power; . . .
> whether they are appropriate means to an end.

Marshall delivered the opinion of the Court upholding the national bank and rejecting Maryland's power to tax it. He first dealt with
a question which today seems somewhat remote: whether the Constitution was the voice of the people, as the Preamble declared, or the
voice of the states. The attorneys for Maryland had argued that the
Constitution was adopted by sovereign states and the powers granted
by it to the federal government must be subordinate to the powers of
the states. Marshall's opinion acknowledged that those who drafted
the Constitution were delegates sent to Philadelphia by the states and
that the final draft was sent back to the states for consideration. But
as he pointed out, the Constitution left to the people of each of the
states in state conventions, not to state legislatures, the authority to say
whether they wanted the new Constitution in place of the Articles of
Confederation.

From there Marshall went on to point out that when it was ratified
by the people the Constitution became the act of the people. While the
ratification conventions were held state by state, "measures they adopt
do not, on that account, cease to be the measures of the people themselves, or become measures of the State governments." The Constitution that the delegates drafted was specifically meant to be the voice of
the people, as its Preamble declared: "We the People of the United

States . . . do ordain and establish this Constitution for the United States of America." Its purpose was plainly declared—"to form a more perfect Union." In other words, to grant new national powers that were not available to the Congress established by inadequate Articles of Confederation. The delegates who assembled in Philadelphia wanted something better and stronger. The *M'Culloch* case demonstrated the inseparability of commercial and political problems.

Marshall then moved on to the crux of the case: whether the Constitution authorized creation of a national bank. That question depended on interpretation of Section 8 of Article I of the Constitution, which undertakes to describe the "legislative Powers" of the federal government.

One of the singular aspects of our Constitution is its brevity. The entire original document is readily reproduced on sixteen pages of a pocket-sized pamphlet. It was not intended to be a code of laws. When it is compared with the constitutions of other countries, including some using ours as a model, it is evident that its genius lies in part in its brevity. Indeed, it is probably the shortest comprehensive organic document in history. Marshall's *M'Culloch* opinion pointed out the obvious—that, as Webster and Wirt had argued, such a document could not conceivably define in detail all of the powers vested in each of the branches of the government it created: "Its nature, therefore, requires, that only its great outlines should be marked, its important objects designated . . . ." This is what Chief Justice Marshall meant when he made his often quoted and much misused statement that "we must never forget, that it is a *constitution* we are expounding." Because in many ways it marks only the "great outlines," the Constitution does not define, in very careful and precise terms, the limits on federal power—the outer boundaries.

Section 8 of Article I describes Congress' powers in both general and specific terms. It specifically gives Congress authority to borrow money, to regulate commerce, to coin money, to establish post offices and post roads, and to grant patents and copyrights. It also gives Congress power to create courts, without spelling out the detail of their structure or jurisdiction, to define some federal crimes, to declare war, and to raise and support armies and navies.

But at the conclusion of Section 8 is that sweeping provision—the

Necessary and Proper Clause—a "catchall" clause, which, to Marshall, made the document a "living Constitution." That clause is broad: Congress has the power

> To make all Laws which shall be necessary and proper for carry-
> ing into Execution the foregoing Powers, and all other Powers
> vested by this Constitution in the Government of the United
> States, or in any Department or Officer thereof.

As already noted, Jefferson and the Republicans read this clause narrowly, to encompass only powers *strictly* necessary.

The 1805 case of *United States* v. *Fisher* construing the Necessary
and Proper Clause had already alienated the Jeffersonians. It considered
whether the United States was a preferred creditor of someone who
had been declared bankrupt under the Bankruptcy Act of 1800. The
Constitution authorizes Congress to enact "uniform Laws on the subject of Bankruptcies throughout the United States." The Federalist
Congress in 1800 had done so, and had given the federal government's
claims against the bankrupt estate priority over the claims of the states
and all other creditors. The statute was attacked as unconstitutional.
Chief Justice Marshall rebuffed this argument, relying on the Necessary
and Proper Clause. His opinion for the Court rejected a narrow view
of the Clause:

> In construing this clause it would be incorrect, and would
> produce endless difficulties, if the opinion should be maintained
> that no law was authorized which was not indispensably necessary
> to give effect to a specified power.
> . . . Congress must possess the choice of means, and must be
> empowered to use any means which are in fact conducive to the
> exercise of a power granted by the constitution.

From the Jeffersonian point of view, such language was more of the
Federalist dogma.

In *M'Culloch* Marshall and the Court again relied on the Necessary
and Proper Clause in upholding creation of the national bank chal-

lenged by the Jeffersonian Republicans. With respect to the power to create a corporation for a national bank, Marshall's opinion answered in a brief sentence: "The power of creating a corporation is never used for its own sake, but for the purpose of effecting something else." In short, the power to create the bank was incidental to the general powers vested in the Congress by the Constitution. Curiously, some of Jefferson's rhetoric was consistent with this concept even if his position on specific issues of national power was not.

After readily conceding that the powers of the national government are limited by the Constitution and that those limits are not to be exceeded, Marshall's opinion concluded:

> [W]e think the sound construction of the constitution must allow to the national legislature that discretion, with respect to the means by which the powers it confers are to be carried into execution, which will enable that body to perform the high duties assigned to it, in the manner most beneficial to the people.

With his usual restrained eloquence, Marshall continued in words that will live as long as our nation continues:

> Let the end be legitimate, let it be within the scope of the constitution, and all means which are appropriate, which are plainly adapted to that end, which are not prohibited, but consist with the letter and spirit of the constitution, are constitutional.

This is one of five quotes from Marshall's pen that are engraved in marble and embellished with gold leaf on the wall behind the bronze statue of Marshall in the Lower Great Hall of the Supreme Court of the United States.

Here we see Marshall expressing, in almost the same words, the views he had set out in his debate with Patrick Henry and George Mason in 1788 on the ratification of the Constitution in Virginia. Of course, judges carry with them "baggage"—the content of their past experience—when they go on the bench, and necessarily so. Part of that baggage is the sum of their understanding of the Constitution itself. No little part of Marshall's own baggage derived from his wartime experience fighting against England with only voluntary contributions from the states, experience that Jefferson and Madison lacked.

Having addressed Congress' power to charter the second Bank of the United States, Marshall rather quickly brushed aside the tax issue in the case, that is, the validity of Maryland's tax on the bank:

> If the States may tax one instrument, employed by the government in the execution of its powers, they may tax any and every other instrument. They may tax the mail; they may tax the mint; they may tax patent rights; they may tax the papers of the custom-house; they may tax judicial process; they may tax all the means employed by the [national] government, to an excess which would defeat all the ends of [that] government.

In short, the power to tax carried to the extreme is, as has often been said, the power to destroy. Such a result was not intended by the American people. They did not design their "national" government to be dependent on the goodwill of the states. Clearly, the Constitution never intended that the states had reserved the power to tax—or destroy—the national government.

The Court thus upheld Congress' power to create the bank and rejected the states' power to tax it. Although a majority of the justices in 1819 had been appointed by either Jefferson or Madison, both of whom believed a national bank was unconstitutional, the Court's opinion was unanimous. Jefferson at Monticello, ten years out of office, was again enraged at the judicial "thieves" and at Marshall in particular. Madison was silent.

Madison, although agreeing with Jefferson on the bank issue, had long before recognized the need for a strong national government and a strong judiciary. In a letter to George Washington on the eve of the Constitutional Convention of 1787, he had written: "[T]he national Government should be armed with positive and compleat authority in all cases which require uniformity . . . . [This] national supremacy ought also to be extended . . . to the Judiciary departments."

John Marshall's conception of the Constitution embodied that view. It is a paradox of history that if Jefferson's view of the Constitution and the powers of a national government had prevailed in the 1930s, Franklin D. Roosevelt's New Deal programs would likely have suffered a far worse fate than they experienced at the hands of the Supreme Court of that day. It was FDR's good fortune to have Chief Justice Charles Evans Hughes presiding—a man who knew the Constitution as well as did Marshall and who was as familiar with the political process as was FDR himself. Marshall, seen by some as the arch "conservative" and "property judge," would probably have been far more sympathetic to the need for congressional action in the 1930s than were some of the members of the Court at that time. Had Marshall and the other justices of 1819 sat during the Great Depression, perhaps FDR might not have needed or tried to pack the Court.

Yet Marshall's words in *M'Culloch* about a living Constitution—that the Constitution was "intended to endure for ages to come, and, consequently, to be adapted to the various *crises* of human affairs"—were never intended and are not to be read to mean that judges are free—as some judges like to interpret Marshall's words—to read into the Constitution their individual and political views about the needs of the nation and its people, or to legislate from the bench to satisfy those perceived needs. What Marshall meant was that the political branches—the elected Congress and the president—which have the responsibility for resolving the difficult economic and social problems of the country, should be given wide latitude. In his view, judges should pay appropriate deference to the conclusions of the elected political branches as expressed in legislation. Marshall did that. Jefferson, ironically, would not have done so. Despite his overriding belief in a parliamentary government in which the elected representatives were the supreme law, he opposed a bank that was, after all, the creature of the American "parliament"—the Congress. Ours is a "living Constitution" primarily in the hands of those elected by the people; the Necessary and Proper Clause, as interpreted in *M'Culloch*, is one of the key "building blocks" of our constitutional structure that gives the "living Constitution" its full meaning.

Marshall's opinion for the Supreme Court upholding Congress'

power to create a national bank was another example of Marshall the
great teacher as well as the farsighted statesman and jurist who sensed
what was needed to give meaning to the Constitution. Much of our
basic constitutional jurisprudence comes to us from John Marshall's
"expounding" as he did in this case and in the earlier *Marbury* case.

CHAPTER TEN

THE STEAMBOAT CASE— CREATING THE AMERICAN COMMON MARKET

....

Gibbons v. Ogden, 1824

The Congress shall have Power . . . To regulate Commerce with foreign Nations, and among the several States . . . .
—Article I, Section 8, U.S. Constitution

The power over commerce, including navigation, was one of the primary objects for which the people of America adopted their government . . . .
—Chief Justice John Marshall,
in *Gibbons* v. *Ogden*, 1824

WHILE THE THREE GREAT ANTAGONISTS, Jefferson, Marshall, and Burr, fought out one of the momentous trials in American history in the summer of 1807, another constitutional milestone in our national life was just beginning to evolve. Robert Fulton finished building his steam-propelled riverboat in New York. Although it is widely believed that Fulton invented the steamboat, his invention was actually a hull with a shallow draft usable in our rivers and inland waters. He simply adapted steam power, which had been around for quite a while in Europe, to that design.

Fulton had formed a partnership for a commercial steamboat line in New York with Robert R. Livingston. Among his many accomplishments, Livingston had been chancellor of New York State—the judge who presided over the Court of Chancery and also sat as a member of the state's highest court—when the national government under the Constitution was established. In that capacity—there being no federal judges at the time—he administered the oath to George Washington as the first president on April 30, 1789, at City Hall in New York.

The New York legislature had granted Livingston the exclusive right to license all steam-powered transportation on the navigable waters within New York State. If the state controlled its roads, its land, and the trees upon the land, why not the waters running over the land? In the minds of most people of that day, the grant of such a state license creating a monopoly seemed well within the power of a state. People were anxious to have business develop, and granting such a privilege in the field of navigation would stimulate an economy that had stagnated during the Revolutionary War. Granting exclusive rights to aggressive, imaginative leaders was one way to get things done. These were men with a vision of the future. They were willing to take risks for profit and fame, as well as for the public good. A grant of exclusive control of navigation, like the new federal system of granting patents and copyrights, was thought by some to be a good way to encourage investors to finance business expansion.

Acting under this grant, the partnership of Livingston and Fulton issued a navigation license to Aaron Ogden, a former governor of New York, which gave him a steamboat monopoly on the Hudson River. But along came Mr. Thomas Gibbons, who also had a steamboat and had secured a federal navigation license for the New York area under a statute enacted by the United States Congress in 1793. He demanded that New York State recognize his right to travel on the Hudson River with his steamboat. Livingston, a former jurist, insisted that he, as the surrogate of New York, controlled those waters and that he had already licensed Ogden. Litigation ensued, and the New York courts agreed with Livingston that Gibbons must get a license from Livingston to travel on the Hudson River and thereby stopped Gibbons' steamboat operations.

All this was taking place when our country was on the threshold of expanding commercial activity. Canals and roads were being extended and the availability of patents and copyrights was stimulating the latent creative talents of an ambitious, aggressive people. Competition was encouraged. The world's greatest market economy was about to emerge. The American people had not yet fully accepted—or even fully understood—the new federal system. And, of course, there had been no steamboats to give rise to the kind of legal problems that arose between Gibbons and Ogden until Fulton's *Clermont* was launched. New technologies often create countless new legal problems, as railroads, airlines, radio, and television were to do later. The people, like the legislature and judges of New York State, had seen no problem. State officials still thought of themselves as sovereign over traffic on their own rivers and lakes. The federal government's action in licensing Gibbons' steamboat, however, called that view into question.

Gibbons, the now-stymied steamboat operator, took the case to the Supreme Court of the United States, where it was argued in a room on the ground floor of the United States Capitol, below the chamber then occupied by the Senate.★ The New York press was naturally very interested in the case. What was a federal court doing interfering with New York rivers? This was a state matter. The legislature and the courts of the state of New York had settled it. One reporter, new to Supreme Court sessions, sent his newspaper a detailed story of the setting, describing Chief Justice John Marshall, who was then seventy years old. He depicted Marshall as "a large, thick-set, athletic man, with a grave, substantial complexion, and with no prominent features, his hair is of an iron gray, cut short before and tied in a club behind"— "a solid and substantial man, without an extraordinary share of genius, taste or elegance." The "thick-set" was perhaps wide of the mark—the reporter can be excused because he saw Marshall garbed in his loose black robe—but the description otherwise agrees with other contemporary accounts.

Daniel Webster, who represented Gibbons, was again helping to

---

★This courtroom has now been fully restored, under the direction of lawyer-architect George White, the Architect of the Capitol, and stands as it was when this case was argued.

make constitutional history. In the courtroom, Webster defended a nationalist point of view. He had a hard case. After all, the states ratifying the Constitution had reserved to themselves powers over a range of internal matters. For more than a quarter of a century since the Constitution was adopted the states had controlled their own waters. And, of course, without Fulton's steamboat, there might not have been much water traffic. The Supreme Court had not been previously called upon to say what the Commerce Clause of the Constitution meant except in one case where transportation was not involved.

Webster could no doubt take some comfort in earlier decisions of the Marshall Court that recognized the imperatives of national power to unify the states and the people in a federal system. The lawyers in the courtroom that day should have known that the Court, which had decided *M'Culloch* v. *Maryland* only a few years earlier, would not readily accept New York's parochial states' rights argument.

On the other hand, Webster had Chancellor James Kent's opinion in the New York Court of Chancery to contend with, and Webster knew that Chancellor Kent, who had decided the case in favor of New York's power to control its waterways, was a formidable figure in the law, whose opinions carried great weight. Indeed, Chief Justice Marshall shared the legal profession's high regard for Chancellor Kent. His opinion would open with more than the traditional bow to the judge whose decision was being reviewed:

> "No tribunal can approach the decision of this question, without feeling a just and real respect for that opinion which is sustained by such authority; but . . . the Judges [of the Supreme Court] must exercise, in the examination of the subject, that understanding which Providence has bestowed upon them, with that independence which the people of the United States expect from this department of the government."

Webster began his argument with sixteen crucial words found in Section 8 of Article I of the United States Constitution:

> The Congress shall have Power . . . To regulate Commerce with foreign Nations, and among the several States . . . .

This provision, said Webster, can only mean that "the power of Congress to regulate commerce [is] complete and entire, and . . . that the [state legislative] acts in question [are] regulations of commerce" over which the state had largely surrendered control to the national government. Webster contended that because the congressional statute authorizing navigation on the Hudson River was "the supreme Law of the Land" under Article VI of the Constitution, the conflicting New York law forbidding Gibbons to use the Hudson River must be deemed invalid. Webster's argument had the ring of a John Marshall opinion. This was quite logical because, through his frequent appearances before the Court, Webster knew Marshall's constitutional views and thus he knew the approach to take.

William Wirt was still the attorney general of the United States in 1824 but again he found time to join Webster in representing Gibbons. Although Wirt was appearing before the Court for a private client, his argument was enhanced by the prestige of his official position. Wirt focused on the divisive impact of state laws that placed barriers to the free movement of goods and services. Pointing to the anger already aroused by quarrels between the states over commercial and trade disputes— some involving armed forces—Wirt stressed the potential for political bitterness, even possible violence, that could flow from New York's action barring from its waters all but the vessels with a Livingston license. Wirt concluded:

> It is a momentous decision which this Court is called on to make. Here are three States almost on the eve of war. It is the high province of this Court to interpose its benign mediatorial influence. . . . If you do not impose your friendly hand, you *will* have civil war.

That may seem like overstatement, but it is not really. One need look only to the history of wars in Europe—the Balkans in particular—to see how often commercial conflicts and boundary disputes have led to bloody wars. Perhaps some of the justices remembered the conflict between Maryland and Virginia over control of navigation and fishing rights on the Potomac River and in the Chesapeake Bay—a conflict resolved only through the personal intervention of George Washington.

Thirty-seven years before the argument in *Gibbons*, John Lansing, one of New York's delegates to the Constitutional Convention in Philadelphia, had spoken in opposition to a proposed "national" plan of government. He had predicted: "The states will never sacrifice their essential rights to a national government." But the predictions of Lansing—who left the Convention early and who fought against the ratification of the new Constitution because it gave too much power to Congress at the expense of the states—turned out to be wrong. By ratifying the Constitution, states had indeed sacrificed some of their rights—control of interstate commerce being but one.

Ultimately, the Court decided for the plaintiff, Thomas Gibbons. The case really turned on what the Constitution meant by the word "commerce." Did it include transportation? A definition confined to the buying, selling, and trading of goods while ignoring how articles of commerce got from here to there was not acceptable to the Court. Commerce, said Marshall, was commercial intercourse, trade "between nations, and parts of nations, in all its branches." How could there be "commercial intercourse" without transportation, without the ways and means of carrying goods and merchandise from producer to consumer?

Marshall said, as he had in the Virginia ratification convention in 1788, that political and commercial problems were intertwined and could not be resolved separately:

> The power over commerce, including navigation, was one of the primary objects for which the people of America adopted their government . . . .
>
> The word ["commerce"] used in the constitution, then, comprehends, and has been always understood to comprehend, navigation within its meaning; and a power to regulate navigation, is as expressly granted, as if that term had been added to the word "commerce."
>
> To what commerce does this power extend? . . . [It extends] to commerce "among the several States." The word "among" means intermingled with. A thing which is among others, is intermingled with them. Commerce among the States, cannot stop

at the external boundary line of each State, but may be introduced into the interior.

In other words, although the Constitution does not *explicitly* deal with "the exclusively internal commerce of a State"—intrastate navigation between Albany and New York City, for example—the *implication* of the Commerce Clause meant that a congressional statute regulating any aspect of commerce, including navigation on rivers, preempts a conflicting state law if the activity being regulated "affect[s] other States." Thus, although the commerce at issue in *Gibbons* v. *Ogden* itself was indisputably interstate—Mr. Gibbons ran his steamboats between Elizabethtown, New Jersey, and New York City—the Supreme Court would rely on *Gibbons* half a century later in *The Daniel Ball*, a case that upheld congressional regulation of a steamer that transported goods on the Grand River "entirely within the limits of the State [of Michigan], and [that] did not run in connection with, or in continuation of, any line of vessels or railway leading to other States." Such activity fell within the scope of the Commerce Clause because it affected other states: the steamer "was employed in transporting goods destined for other States, or goods brought from without the limits of Michigan and destined to places within that State."

But this is to jump ahead of our story. The key holding of the Court in *Gibbons* v. *Ogden* was that the Constitution clearly contemplates transportation as an integral part of commerce, for how could goods move in "Commerce . . . among the several States" in that day except by ships or wagons? In short, transportation was part of commerce. Plain and simple? Yes, but only after Marshall explained it.

In his opinion for the Court in *Brown* v. *Maryland*, decided three years after *Gibbons*, John Marshall the teacher would invoke history in support of this conclusion:

> The oppressed and degraded state of commerce previous to the constitution can scarcely be forgotten. . . . It is not, therefore, [a] matter of surprise, that the [Commerce Clause] should be as extensive as the mischief, and should comprehend all foreign commerce and all commerce among the States. To construe the

power so as to impair its efficacy, would tend to defeat an object, in the attainment of which the American public took, and justly took, that strong interest which arose from a full conviction of its necessity.

The Court concluded its opinion in *Gibbons* v. *Ogden* by stating:

This Court is, therefore, of opinion, that the decree of the court of New-York for the Trial of Impeachments and the Correction of Errors, affirming the decree of the Chancellor of that State, which perpetually enjoins the said Thomas Gibbons, the appellant, from navigating the waters of the State of New-York with the steamboats the Stoudinger and the Bellona, by steam or fire, is erroneous, and ought to be reversed, and the same is hereby reversed and annulled: and this Court doth further DIRECT, ORDER, and DECREE, that the [lawsuit] of the said Aaron Ogden be dismissed, and the same is hereby dismissed accordingly.

Marshall's ruling in favor of Gibbons gave a whole new impetus to national commerce, and in later years the reach of the Commerce Clause would be expanded even further.

There was strong criticism of Marshall's opinion for the Court by "states' righters," some of whom had lived under the "multilateral treaty" of the Articles of Confederation for so long that they could not swiftly adjust to the reality that we had grown from a loose confederation into a true nation. The impact of this holding could not be softened much by Marshall's tactful references to the difficulty and sensitivity of the issue or the usual compliments as to how well the contending arguments had been presented. Marshall was well aware that the mind-set of many distinguished lawyers, judges, and political leaders was a problem. There was no escaping the essential point that the highly respected Chancellor Kent's decree was "erroneous, and ought to be reversed." There was no way to mince words and also convey the message. The Court's decision marked a new epoch in American history, and its impact on the economy is difficult to overstate.

The small businessman making saddles, bridles, and horse harness in Virginia who had contented himself with the Virginia market might read about the case of *Gibbons* v. *Ogden* in the Richmond or Norfolk newspapers. Commerce among the several states, including the transportation essential to it, was something with which the states could no longer meddle. Steamboats could go anywhere the water was deep enough. So, the businessman might ask, why not send some saddles and harness up to New York, Boston, or Philadelphia? The expanded market made possible by the elimination of barriers to trade and transportation could drive down unit costs so that the businessman could compete for this new and bigger market. This could in turn stimulate the demand for canals and roads to ship saddles and harness inland.

Marshall and the Court had paved the way for what we can now see was the American common market—a national market open equally to all Americans. Was the idea of allowing no tariffs or other barriers to trade between New York and New Jersey a novel idea? Not to Hamilton, Washington, Madison—and Marshall.

Such views are now advancing in the international arena. Several countries of Europe recognized the imperative of a common market when they met and signed the Treaty of Rome in 1957. The Maastricht Treaty and the European Union it creates continue that trend and promise to bear further fruits of Europe's common market. How long will it be until Poland, Hungary, and other newly freed Eastern European countries are knocking at the door? And what of the several republics of the former Soviet Union? How long before all of Europe is one market like the United States? On this continent, the recently adopted North American Free Trade Agreement between the United States, Canada, and Mexico will create a common market even larger than the European Union—indeed, the largest in the world. The recently ratified amendments to the General Agreement on Tariffs and Trade (GATT) herald a possible worldwide economic integration.

As we acknowledge the benefits of common markets and contemplate expanding our own, should we not remember that this modern concept began with the genius of Hamilton and the vision of Chief Justice Marshall?

CHAPTER ELEVEN

THE GREAT MISTAKE

....

Dred Scott v. Sandford, 1857

[T]he question of slavery or no slavery [should] be decided by the only competent authority that can definitely settle it forever, the authority of the
Supreme Court of the United States . . . . When the question comes before
the Supreme Court of the United States, that tribunal alone will declare what
the law is.

—Senator Henry Clay,
in the debate on the
Compromise of 1850

The words "people of the United States" and "citizens" are synony-
mous terms, and mean the same thing. . . . The question before us is,
whether the class of persons described in the [lawsuit] compose a portion of this
people . . . . We think they [do] not, and that they are not included . . .
under the word "citizens" in the Constitution . . . . On the contrary, they
were at the time considered as a subordinate and inferior class of beings, who
had been subjugated by the dominant race . . . and had no rights or privileges
but such as those who held the power and the Government might choose to
grant them.

—Chief Justice Roger Taney, in
Dred Scott v. Sandford, 1857

114

DRED SCOTT, a black man and a slave, was at the center of a nineteenth-century American legal, political, and constitutional controversy. The conflict occurred eight decades after the Declaration of Independence was signed. The controversy over slavery, that terrible state of degradation of life and liberty, had continued even after states had bills of rights and long after Americans declared that "all Men are created equal." Thousands of human beings whose fathers or earlier ancestors had come to North America from Africa—after surviving the trip in chains on slave ships—would have their future determined in a case in the courts involving Dred Scott.

At least four times Americans had laid aside the question of what to do about the evil institution of slavery. As we have seen in Chapter Four, Thomas Jefferson's draft of the Declaration of Independence condemned King George III for violating the "most sacred rights of life and liberty" by allowing slavery in his realm, but this passage was deleted at the insistence of the southern colonies as the price for making that document the "*unanimous* Declaration of the thirteen United States of America." Eleven years later at the Constitutional Convention of 1787, many of the delegates were opposed to slavery, but they were also aware that if they tried to suppress that institution, the delegates from the plantation states, the economies of which were tied to slavery, would likely walk out. There would then be no new governmental structure to replace the feeble one existing under the Articles of Confederation. The northern delegates were confronted with a hard choice, believing that if they tried to abolish slavery the Convention would be dissolved and the thirteen states would be left to probable balkanization, which would invite intervention by Spain or England— or even France, our onetime ally. The delegates elected to place the need for a new Constitution ahead of the liberty of enslaved blacks. That decision, although indefensible, can be explained. We must remember that the explosive issue divided the country.

But those opposed to slavery did not surrender after the Constitutional Convention. For them, this was not simply a political or economic issue but the great moral problem of their day. Their influence had been felt during the sessions of the Confederation Congress meeting in New York while the delegates in Philadelphia drafted the Constitution in the summer of 1787. In the Northwest Ordinance enacted that year, the Confederation Congress prohibited slavery forever in the Northwest Territory, from which Ohio, Indiana, Illinois, Michigan, Wisconsin, and part of Minnesota were formed.

In the next seventy years the economy of the South remained locked to slavery, and the political conflict between northern and southern leaders in Congress continued. The abolitionist movement pressed for clear-cut solutions, but the political power of the southern slave states blocked dramatic changes. Some of those opposed to slavery saw a real risk of breaking up the Union and this fear deferred positive action outlawing slavery. As countless thousands of Americans moved westward and new states came into being, Congress and political leaders vacillated, and the South forced compromise.

The first major accommodation was the Missouri Compromise of 1820. To offset the admission of Maine as a free state, Missouri was admitted to the Union as a slave state, but slavery was prohibited in the remainder of the Louisiana Territory north of the line drawn by the southern border of Missouri (36° 30′ N latitude). It was also tacitly agreed that free and slave states would be admitted in pairs in order to protect the South's interests. Thus, the United States had avoided a definitive resolution of the slavery issue for the third time.

As late as 1850, less than eleven years before the bloodiest war in history up to that time, Congress continued to avoid the question, forcing another "compromise." The Compromise of 1850 provided for the admission of California as a free state and the suppression of the slave trade in the District of Columbia, in exchange for the establishment of Utah Territory and New Mexico Territory with no prohibition of slavery and the enactment of a tougher fugitive slave law.

Despite efforts at compromise, tensions grew throughout the early 1850s. Congress effectively repealed the Missouri Compromise by passing the Kansas-Nebraska Act in 1854. That law allowed the inhabitants of Kansas and Nebraska to determine whether their states would be slave or free, even though both states were north of the line drawn in the Missouri Compromise.

It became ever more clear that Congress would not solve the problem of slavery. Some in Congress openly chose to leave the question to the judiciary. That famed orator of the Senate, Henry Clay of Kentucky, proclaimed to his colleagues and the nation that Congress ought to apply the principle of non-intervention . . . and to leave the question of slavery or no slavery to be decided by the only competent authority that can definitely settle it forever, the authority of the Supreme Court of the United States . . . . When the question comes before the Supreme Court of the United States, that tribunal alone will declare what the law is.

As they have always done, of course, members of Congress reserved the right to make speeches claiming that the justices of the Supreme Court were "making law" instead of tending to their constitutional duty of simply interpreting the law. As the French observer of America, Alexis de Tocqueville, had predicted, this great political issue of the eighteenth century—like so many other political questions—had been "resolved . . . into a judicial question."

The case in which the Supreme Court tried to succeed where Congress had failed was *Dred Scott* v. *Sandford*. Dred Scott had lived in many places, going where his masters went: Virginia, Missouri, Illinois, and what was to become the State of Minnesota. Those moves were important if the theory advanced by his lawyers was correct, for they argued that if he could show residence in any place where slavery was illegal, the law said he was no longer a slave. Although he ultimately did show such residence, the terrible error of the Supreme Court doomed him to remain in slavery.

Dred Scott's lawyers first sued for his freedom in Missouri state court in 1846. In St. Louis they brought separate cases for himself and his wife, seeking damages for assault and wrongful imprisonment. Scott's first hurdle was to establish that by reason of his residence in free territory—both at Fort Armstrong, in the free state of Illinois, and at Fort Snelling, near the future site of St. Paul, Minnesota, in territory closed to slavery by the Missouri Compromise—he was no longer a slave. In the Missouri state trial court, a jury had returned a verdict that Scott was free. But in 1852 the Missouri Supreme Court reversed that verdict by a 2 to 1 vote. The critical basis of the decision in *Scott* v. *Emerson* was that Missouri was not obliged to enforce the law of another state or territory that conflicted with Missouri's own law. Under Missouri law, the majority held, Scott remained a slave regardless of his residence in a free state or territory. Whatever Scott's status in some

other place, his returning to Missouri, a slave state, made him a slave
again. The majority of the Missouri Supreme Court concluded with
more general observations on the institution of slavery:

> As to the consequences of slavery, they are much more hurt-
> ful to the master than the slave. There is no comparison between
> the slave in the United States and the cruel, uncivilized negro in
> Africa. When the condition of our slaves is contrasted with the
> state of their miserable race in Africa, . . . we are almost per-
> suaded, that the introduction of slavery amongst us was, in the
> providences of God, who makes the evil passions of men sub-
> servient to his own glory[,] a means of placing that unhappy race
> within the pale of civilized nations.

Such attitudes can only astound the modern reader.

Rather than appealing the case to the United States Supreme
Court, Dred Scott's lawyer brought a new lawsuit for assault and
wrongful imprisonment, this time in the federal circuit court in Missouri, against his current slaveholder, John Sanford (whose name was
incorrectly spelled "Sandford" in the official records of the case). Under Article III of the Constitution, federal courts have jurisdiction over
many suits "between citizens of different States." Scott's lawyer based
his claim of federal jurisdiction on the "diversity of citizenship" between Scott, who lived in Missouri, and Sanford, who was a citizen of
New York. Sanford answered that because Scott was "a negro of
African descent" whose ancestors were slaves, he was not a "citizen"
who could sue in federal court under Article III of the Constitution.

The circuit court ruled against Sanford on this jurisdictional issue,
and proceeded to the merits of the case. Again, the issue of Scott's residence in free territory was determinative of his slave status: if such residence had emancipated him once and for all, Scott was a free man; if
not, he was still Sanford's slave. In reliance on an earlier Supreme
Court decision, *Strader* v. *Graham*, and on the Missouri Supreme
Court's decision in Scott's state case, the federal trial judge instructed
the jury that the law of Missouri controlled and that prior residence in
free territory was of no consequence. Thus, Scott remained a slave.
Two weeks later, on May 30, 1854, Congress enacted the Kansas-

Nebraska Act, which repealed the Missouri Compromise of 1820 with respect to those two territories.

In February 1856, the case was argued in the Supreme Court on appeal. At that time, a majority of the justices came from slave states. For twenty-one years, since the death of Chief Justice Marshall, the center chair on the Court had been occupied by Roger Taney (pronounced "Tawney") of Maryland. That Taney was pro-slavery was not in doubt. Over a period of four days, Montgomery Blair of St. Louis argued the case for Dred Scott, and Henry G. Geyer, a United States senator from Missouri, and Reverdy Johnson of Maryland, a former attorney general of the United States, argued for Sanford. In addition to reiterating arguments put forth in the trial court, Geyer and Johnson advanced a new argument on behalf of their client, an argument with great political implications: Scott's residence in territory in which slavery was prohibited by the Missouri Compromise did not make him free because Congress lacked the power to exclude slavery from the territories; in other words, the Missouri Compromise was unconstitutional.

Taney had originally assigned Justice Samuel Nelson to write the opinion in the case, but when extensive conferences produced no definite result because of the Court's internal conflicts, the case was set for reargument the following term in December. The litigants were directed to advise the Court on two issues: first, whether the Supreme Court could properly review the trial court's ruling that it had jurisdiction on the ground that Scott was a "citizen" who could sue in federal court; and second, if so, was Scott indeed a "citizen" of Missouri within the meaning of the Constitution. Meanwhile, leaks concerning the Court's confidential conferences, indiscreet conversations of justices, and the political implications had drawn public attention to the case. The press was filled with stories, some built on rumor and some traceable to "leaks" from the justices. The reports fueled rumors about the goings-on inside the Court and about the views of particular justices.

Many political leaders of the day were almost resigned to the idea that the South would secede from the Union on the slavery issue. Some abolitionists in New England believed that in the long run such a separation would be a good thing. The justices were well aware of the political passions that dominated every political gathering from precinct caucuses to state party conventions. Chief Justice Taney was a Jacksonian-Jeffersonian Democrat. Like Taney, James Buchanan, the president-elect in 1856, was a southern, pro-slavery sympathizer. Buchanan opposed secession but also opposed the use of force to prevent it.

Horace Greeley, the crusading editor, was almost fanatical in his abolitionist views and in his hostility to Buchanan. For some of Buchanan's friends, the feeling was mutual. During the previous presidential campaign Jeremiah S. Black, a justice on the Pennsylvania Supreme Court and later Buchanan's attorney general, wrote:

> No greater service could be rendered to the cause of truth . . . than by putting Greeley where he ought to be. He is a liar and the truth is not in him. He is a mush toad spotted traitor to the Constitution. And he is a knave beyond the lowest reach of any comparison I can make. Shall this political turkey buzzard be permitted to vomit the filthy contents of his stomach on every decent man in the country without having his neck twisted?

It was clear that the *Dred Scott* decision would stir the political passions of the day.

The reargument of the case was heard by the Court in December 1856. The same attorneys, with the addition of George Ticknor Curtis, brother of Associate Justice Benjamin Curtis, argued for Scott. The enormous political implications of the case were apparent and rumors continued to dominate the news. James Buchanan would take office on March 4, 1857.

On February 3, President-elect Buchanan wrote to Justice John Catron asking when the case would be decided. Buchanan, of course, wanted to know just how to deal in his inaugural address with the burning issue of Congress' power over slavery in the territories. No president-elect or president would dare write such a letter in modern times, and no justice so addressed would respond. But this was 1857, and the status of Dred Scott had become wrapped up in the major political issue of the day. Justice Catron wrote Buchanan:

It rests entirely with the Chief Justice to move in the matter. So far he has not said anything to me on the subject of Scott's case. It was before the judges in conference on two several [*sic*] occasions about a year ago, when the judges expressed their views pretty much at large. All our opinions were published in the N.Y. *Tribune*, the next day after the opinions were expressed. This was of course a gross breach of confidence, as the information could only come from a judge who was present. That circumstance I think, has made the Chief more wary than usual.

Justice Catron accommodatingly added that he would keep Buchanan "posted."

This cozy correspondence, highly inappropriate by present standards, continued. Justice Catron wrote again to Buchanan four days later to advise him that the case would be discussed at the Court's next conference on Saturday, February 14, but that the opinion would not be announced before the end of the month. And even if the opinion were announced before March 4, it would not be of much help for Buchanan's inaugural address because, Catron predicted—incorrectly, as it turned out—the Court probably would not decide the question of the power of Congress over slavery in the territories. Again, this was a gross breach of judicial standards.

At the conference of the justices set for February 14, the decision would rest on the basis of the arguments two months earlier. Today, the Supreme Court discusses the cases argued on Monday two days later at the Wednesday conference, and those argued on Tuesday and Wednesday are discussed at the Friday conference the same week. Sometimes, but not often, a case is put over and discussed at a later conference. But in that day, the justices did not all reside in the Washington area and conferences were scheduled accordingly. And the long delay after the *Dred Scott* reargument resulted in part from health problems of Chief Justice Taney, then in his eightieth year.

Although the February 14 conference produced a determination that Justice Nelson would write an opinion disposing of the case on narrow grounds that would affect only Scott and relatively few other slaves, the Court soon reversed itself and decided to address the power of Congress to prohibit slavery in the territories. On February 19, Justice Catron wrote to Buchanan yet again, informing him that the Court *would* render a decision on the larger issues of slavery and congressional power. In a letter dated four days later, Justice Robert Grier confirmed Catron's prediction, informing Buchanan that six or seven justices would rule against Dred Scott and against the power of Congress.

Buchanan, relying on the advice of Justices Catron and Grier, and possibly other justices, told his inaugural audience that the principle of majority rule should prevail in the territories on the slavery question. He concluded, however, that the ultimate issue of slavery under our system was for the Supreme Court to decide and that he, as president, would abide by its decision. Knowing in advance what the outcome would be, he said he would "cheerfully submit" to the Court's decision.

Chief Justice Taney delivered the opinion of the Court on March 6, 1857, two days after Buchanan's inauguration. When the opinion came down against freedom for Dred Scott, editorial opinion about the Court in the North was scathing. The *New-York Daily Tribune* wrote that Taney's reasoning was "entitled to just so much moral weight as would be the judgment of a majority of those congregated in any Washington bar-room." Going beyond the question of state law upon which the lower courts had relied, the Court announced that the Missouri Compromise enacted by Congress was unconstitutional. The details and nuances of the reasoning in the opinions of the justices are not essential to our story. But it is worth noting that although Taney did not ignore the eloquent language of the Declaration of Independence and its relevance to construction of the Constitution, he wholly misread the Declaration and ignored history. To Taney, the history leading to the Declaration of Independence, as his opinion recites, showed that

> a perpetual and impassable barrier was intended to be erected between the white race and the one which they had reduced to slavery, and governed as subjects with absolute and despotic power, and which they then looked upon as so far below them in the scale of created beings, that intermarriages between white persons

and negroes or mulattoes were regarded as unnatural and immoral, and punished as crimes, not only [as to] the parties, but [as to] the person who joined them in marriage. . . .

We refer to these historical facts . . . in order to determine whether the general terms used in the Constitution of the United States, as to the rights of man and the rights of the people, was [*sic*] intended to include [the African race], or to give to them or their posterity the benefit of any of its provisions.

The language of the Declaration of Independence is equally conclusive . . . .

[After its first sentence, it] then proceeds to say: "We hold these truths to be self-evident: that all men are created equal; that they are endowed by their Creator with certain unalienable rights; that among them is life, liberty, and the pursuit of happiness; that to secure these rights, Governments are instituted, deriving their just powers from the consent of the governed."

The general words above quoted would seem to embrace *the whole human family,* and if they were used in a similar instrument at this day would be so understood. But it is too clear for dispute, that the enslaved African race were not intended to be included, and formed no part of the people who framed and adopted this declaration . . . (emphasis added).

Reading Taney's opinion with all its internal inconsistencies, disjointed sentences, and gross misreading of history, one must strain to recall that this is the work of a judge long regarded as an able and conscientious jurist. But from time beyond memory many men born and bred in the environment he shared had heard this theme. Irrational, illogical—even immoral—this was part of the fabric of their existence. The voice of the slave states, articulated by a majority of the justices, was clear: people, by their votes, not limited by any fundamental fairness or human decency or morality, would decide whether the promise of the Declaration that "all Men are created equal" had any meaning—and whether "all Men" meant only "all *white* Men."

The history of the Constitution is inevitably shaped by the people who "expound" it. It is interesting to consider—though one can do no more than speculate—how a case such as *Dred Scott* might have been had it arisen when John Marshall was Chief Justice. Marshall, curiously, is often contrasted with his successor, Roger Taney; Marshall is frequently described, and was so described throughout his career, as a "property judge," interested chiefly in material rights but not in human, individual, or civil rights. Yet while Marshall was, indeed, a supporter of the rights of property, one of his opinions touching on slavery rebuts any suggestion that he was not concerned about human rights, and reflects a humanity missing from Taney's opinion in *Dred Scott*. *Boyce* v. *Anderson*, decided in 1829, concerned a slave owner's claim for injuries to several slaves sustained while they were being transported by steamboat on the Mississippi River. Marshall's opinion swiftly rejected the claim that liability for injury to a slave was governed by the law of damage to property. Marshall wrote that humanity would forbid treating a slave as a piece of freight:

> A slave has volition, and has feelings . . . . These properties cannot be overlooked in conveying him from place to place. He cannot be stowed away as a common package. Not only does humanity forbid this proceeding, but it might endanger his life or health.

Of course, how much Marshall could prevail on his colleagues would depend on the setting in which the issue was considered. In 1857 perhaps not all the skills and persuasion of John Marshall would have set Dred Scott free.

Some historians suggest that the final verdict on the Supreme Court of 1856–1857 or on Roger Taney has not been rendered. But virtually all historians and lawyers deplore his handling of the case—and the dubious conduct of more than a few of the justices. Of course, in the closing years of the twentieth century it is difficult to grasp the setting of 1856–1857. It is not clear how much, if any, Taney's declining health and his age contributed to his confused, inept handling of Dred Scott's appeal. In 1857, so medical experts say, a man of eighty could well be like a man of ninety or ninety-five today. And we know that the revered Oliver Wendell Holmes, who retired from the Supreme Court at age ninety-one, went to sleep on the bench and in conferences years before he left the Court. Chief Justice Charles Evans

Hughes had the unhappy task of confronting Holmes and requesting that he retire because the time had come. Indeed, the time had come, and Holmes departed. The time had perhaps come for Taney before the *Dred Scott* case.

But another factor played an important role in the Supreme Court's momentous failure to reject slavery. Taney believed that the result he reached—ruling that blacks whose ancestors were slaves were not citizens under the United States Constitution and that Congress could not ban slavery in the territories—would avoid the beginning of armed hostilities between the North and the South. On the eve of the election of 1860, Taney wrote in a private letter:

> My thoughts have been constantly turned to the fearful state of things in which we have been living for months past. . . . I can only pray that [violence] may be averted and that my fears may prove to be nothing more than the timidity of an old man.

Of course, Taney's fears were well founded, though his prayers went unanswered. The violence of the Civil War was likely more terrible than he could possibly imagine. Through various compromises, the North and South had sought desperately, even against morality and reason, to avoid the bloodshed. Political leaders of the day, unable to find a solution, placed the burden of resolving the slavery issue on the members of the Supreme Court. No doubt Taney, conscious of that responsibility, knew that a decision to free Scott might well have precipitated war. Perhaps the thought was too great for an "old man" of failing health. The decision to tolerate slavery in the hopes of avoiding violence failed, however, and a historic opportunity for the Court was lost.

In February 1839, while serving as a representative in Congress after his presidency, John Quincy Adams proposed three amendments to the Constitution that would have totally abolished slavery. Two months later, he spoke at the New-York Historical Society's celebration of the fiftieth anniversary of George Washington's inauguration as the first president of the United States. In his lecture Adams pointed out that the Declaration of Independence had declared the "natural rights of mankind," and he lamented that there were still "philoso-

phers" in this country "who deny the principles asserted in the Declaration as self-evident truths—who deny the natural equality and in-
alienable rights of man." No doubt these so-called philosophers
included the supporters of slavery, given what Adams later called "[t]he
utter and unqualified inconsistency of slavery, in any of its forms, with
the principles of the . . . American Revolution, and the Declaration of
Independence." Adams' anniversary lecture also pointed out that "the
Constitution of the United States was a *return* to the principles of the
Declaration of Independence." In 1857 the Supreme Court failed to
give heed to these simple but significant truths.

CHAPTER TWELVE

"SEPARATE BUT EQUAL" IS NOT EQUAL

....

Plessy v. Ferguson, 1896

No State shall make or enforce any law which shall abridge the privileges or immunities of citizens of the United States; nor shall any State . . . deny to any person within its jurisdiction the equal protection of the laws.
—Amendment XIV (1868), U.S. Constitution

[I]n view of the Constitution, in the eye of the law, there is in this country no superior, dominant, ruling class of citizens. There is no caste here. Our Constitution is color-blind, and neither knows nor tolerates classes among citizens. In respect of civil rights, all citizens are equal before the law.
—Justice John Marshall Harlan,
dissenting in *Plessy v. Ferguson*, 1896

AFTER THE CIVIL WAR, those who had fought long and hard to abolish slavery secured passage of what are known as the Civil War Amendments—the Thirteenth, Fourteenth, and Fifteenth Amendments to the Constitution, ratified in 1865, 1868, and 1870 respectively—as well as enactment of the first Civil Rights Act, which provided additional protection for the rights of the freed slaves. Slavery had been abolished and full citizenship had been granted to former slaves. Notwithstanding these significant improvements in civil rights in America, political and legal equality was a long way off.

The "melting pot" concept of American history has never really included African Americans. They are the only segment of our mixed population who came here not by choice, but in chains. By contrast, the masses of people from Asia, Latin America, and Europe in the nineteenth and twentieth centuries came, like earlier immigrants, freely, joyously, seeking something better than what they had left behind. Whites were not alone responsible for the forced migration of people from Africa—powerful African tribes were in league with European and Arab slave traders and joined them to round up fellow Africans for "export"—but the fact remains that those Africans who came here did not emigrate voluntarily, but were exported and became slaves.

Separation of the races is inherent in any system of race-based slavery. That was true in America from the time of the landing of the first slaves in the seventeenth century up through the Civil War. No laws were needed to carry out the separation that existed. It was simply the natural result of centuries of demeaned status for the slaves and the resulting attitude of whites toward a slave class that became fixed from generation to generation. Before the Civil War, very few blacks ever traveled anywhere, although they were sometimes "shipped" from point to point, and even fewer had any educational opportunities.

Not until after Lincoln's Proclamation and postwar Reconstruction, when people began to recognize the rights of the former slaves, did the issue of equal treatment for all Americans come into focus on a national level. For some time after emancipation, the economic status of blacks remained in a state that did not bring many of them into frequent contact with whites in terms of transportation, housing, or employment. But as blacks' economic condition improved slowly, painfully, minimally, problems of segregation began to evolve. The development of public transportation, together with the very modest improvement in the economic situation of blacks as the twentieth century approached, brought the two races into more frequent contact. Segregation laws were promulgated to keep blacks in an inferior position.

In this environment, twenty-five years after the end of the Civil War, the legislature of the state of Louisiana passed a law providing for separate railway carriages for the "white and colored races." Such "sep-

arate but equal" state statutes were common at the time, and among
the southern states, travel accommodations, restaurants, and schools
were almost universally segregated. In fact, it was not uncommon in
some parts of the South, well into the twentieth century, for blacks to
be compelled to walk on one side of the street and whites on the other.
The Louisiana statute provided another lost opportunity for the Supreme Court to advance the principles embodied in the Constitution
and the Declaration of Independence.

The first section of the infamous Louisiana statute, enacted in
1890, provided that

> all railway companies carrying passengers in their coaches in this
> State, shall provide equal but separate accommodations for the
> white, and colored races, by providing two or more passenger
> coaches for each passenger train, or by dividing the passenger
> coaches by a partition so as to secure separate accommodations:
> *Provided,* That this section shall not be construed to apply to street
> railroads. No person or persons, shall be admitted to occupy seats
> in coaches, other than, the ones, assigned, to them on account of
> the race they belong to.

The second section of the law set forth the manner in which the statute
was to be enforced and laid down penalties for violations:

> [T]he officers of such passenger trains shall have power and are
> hereby required to assign each passenger to the coach or com-
> partment used for the race to which such passenger belongs; any
> passenger insisting on going into a coach or compartment to
> which by race he does not belong, shall be liable to a fine of
> twenty-five dollars, or in lieu thereof to imprisonment for a pe-
> riod of not more than twenty days in the parish prison . . . .

The Louisiana law also made clear that railway officials could eject any
passenger who refused to occupy the compartment to which he or she
was assigned on the basis of race, and that railways were not liable for
damages resulting from such action. Railway employees were also subject to a fine or imprisonment if they refused or neglected to enforce

the statute. The legislature made an exception, however, for nurses caring for children of the other race; they were exempt from the law probably because the legislature wanted to ensure that black nurses and nannies could continue to attend to white children while traveling.

Homer Adolph Plessy, who was one-eighth black and a former slave, was living in Louisiana at the time. He purchased a railroad ticket "between two stations within the State of Louisiana," and proceeded to ignore the segregation law. When Plessy entered the train, the conductor assigned him to a coach set aside for black passengers. But Plessy courageously insisted upon taking possession of a vacant seat in a coach assigned to white passengers. When ordered to vacate the seat, Plessy refused and was forcibly ejected by railroad officials with the aid of a police officer. He was not asked to pay a fine, one of the alternative penalties under the statute, but rather was sent directly to the parish jail.

In the case that followed, no question was raised in the courts as to whether the accommodations offered Plessy were in fact of equal quality. Instead, Plessy argued that segregation in and of itself violated both the Thirteenth and the Fourteenth Amendments. The Thirteenth Amendment abolished "slavery [and] involuntary servitude." The Fourteenth Amendment provided, among other things, that "[a]ll persons born or naturalized in the United States . . . are citizens of the United States," thus correcting the error of *Dred Scott*, and that "[n]o state shall make or enforce any law which shall abridge the privileges or immunities of citizens of the United States, . . . nor deny to any person . . . the equal protection of the laws." This case was only one of many that required the Supreme Court to determine what those phrases meant.

The Louisiana courts held that the statute segregating rail accommodations according to race was a constitutional exercise of the state's "police power" so long as the accommodations were "equal," which the statute specifically required. The case then went to the United States Supreme Court, where the question was posed in terms of whether requiring equal public accommodations with mandated separation—"separate but equal"—was a valid exercise of state police power in the face of the Thirteenth and Fourteenth Amendments. Plessy's counsel again argued that the real question was not *equality* of the facilities but *difference of treatment* of passengers based solely on race.

The analogy of the railroad car to public highways was plain. If the Louisiana statute was constitutional, Plessy argued, separate streets or separate sides of streets could be mandated based on race, since railroads and streets were both public highways.

On Monday, May 18, 1896, the Supreme Court convened to announce its decision in Homer Plessy's case. It declared against him by a vote of 7 to 1. (Justice David Brewer did not participate in the decision of the case.) The Court blandly overlooked the pronouncement of one hundred and twenty years earlier in the Declaration of Independence that "all Men are created equal," sharing the same rights to "Life, Liberty, and the Pursuit of Happiness," and gave a cramped reading to the provisions of the Thirteenth and Fourteenth Amendments. As terrible as the *Dred Scott* holding had been, *Plessy* was arguably more condemnable inasmuch as the country had fought a Civil War over the issue of slavery and had had many years to contemplate the conclusions arrived at by the Court in 1857 in *Dred Scott*. In that sense, Homer Plessy's defeat was even more racist than Dred Scott's. But the opinion in Plessy's case had one merit that could not be found in the 1857 case. It was the ringing and eloquent dissent of one justice, John Marshall Harlan, that made the difference—and which would ultimately become the law on the issue.

Beginning the Court's opinion, Justice Henry Brown, writing for a seven-person majority, feebly sought to imitate John Marshall's style by declaring that it was "too clear for argument" that the Louisiana law did not violate the Thirteenth Amendment. The majority recognized that the amendment "abolished slavery and involuntary servitude." In the majority's view both slavery and involuntary servitude implied "a state of bondage; the ownership of mankind as a chattel" and "the absence of a legal right to the disposal of his own person, property and services." Relying upon Justice Joseph Bradley's opinion in the *Civil Rights Cases* in 1883, which had—over another lone dissent by Justice Harlan—struck down portions of the federal Civil Rights Act of 1875 prohibiting discrimination in public accommodations, Justice Brown concluded that separating eating and travel accommodations based on one's color "cannot be justly regarded as imposing any badge of slavery or servitude . . . but only as involving an ordinary civil injury." "It would be running the slavery argument into the ground," said Justice

Brown, quoting Justice Bradley again, "to make it apply to every act of discrimination which a person may see fit to make."

As to the Thirteenth Amendment, Justice Brown concluded that

> [a] statute which implies merely a legal distinction between the white and colored races—a distinction which is founded in the color of the two races, and which must always exist so long as white men are distinguished from the other race by color—has no tendency to destroy the legal equality of the two races, or reëstablish a state of involuntary servitude.

Indeed, not a "tendency" but a devastating blow. Nevertheless, the Court claimed it need say nothing more regarding Plessy's Thirteenth Amendment claim.

Turning to the Fourteenth Amendment, Justice Brown reasoned that a proper interpretation of that constitutional provision must begin with the first Supreme Court opinion construing it—what is commonly known as the *Slaughter-House Cases*. In those cases, which did not involve the rights of freed slaves, butchers who were not permitted to operate their own slaughterhouses within the city of New Orleans claimed that their rights under the Fourteenth Amendment were violated. In 1873 the Supreme Court had rejected that claim on the ground that the Fourteenth Amendment provided no federal protection to rights flowing from state citizenship; "privileges or immunities of citizens of the United States," it had reasoned, were distinct from privileges or immunities derived from state law.

In reliance on the *Slaughter-House Cases*, Justice Brown concluded that, although the "main purpose" of the Fourteenth Amendment was "to establish the citizenship of the negro," that case "did not call for any expression of opinion as to the exact rights it was intended to secure to the colored race." Incredibly, the majority opinion in *Plessy* v. *Ferguson* held that the purpose of the Fourteenth Amendment "was undoubtedly to enforce the absolute equality of the two races before the law," but that

> in the nature of things it could not have been intended to abolish distinctions based upon color, or to enforce social, as distin-

guished from political equality, or a commingling of the two races upon terms unsatisfactory to either.

This view obviously ignored the fact that the Fourteenth Amendment gave blacks full citizenship that every state was bound to respect.

Having concluded that absolute equality under the Constitution is required, but "distinctions" based on race are permissible, the majority stated that "permitting, and even requiring" the separation of the white and black races "in places where they are liable to be brought into contact do not necessarily imply the inferiority of either race to the other." The majority justified its conclusion by noting—and it is a sad commentary on the state of affairs in our country in 1896 that it could do so—that many similar segregation statutes "have been generally, if not universally, recognized as within the competency of the state legislatures in the exercise of their police power." Justice Brown further supported the Court's decision by referring to the disgraceful state laws "forbidding the intermarriage of the two races," which "may be said in a technical sense to interfere with the freedom of contract, and yet have been universally recognized as within the police power of the State." The Court's ultimate holding, that Louisiana's segregation statute did not violate the fundamental rights embodied in the Fourteenth Amendment, seems remarkable today. But that is precisely the result the Court reached.

Plessy's counsel had argued to the Court that "the enforced separation of the two races stamps the colored race with a badge of inferiority." The Court responded that such an argument was a "fallacy" and declared that if blacks felt that way, it was "not by reason of anything found in the [Louisiana] act, but solely because the colored race chooses to put that construction upon it." Did the justices forget that only thirty-nine years earlier the Court itself had held that Dred Scott was not even a citizen of the United States because of the color of his skin? Did the Court deliberately choose to ignore the fact that, with few exceptions, blacks came to this country not of their own free choice, but in chains to be sold as slaves? It was to be another six decades before the Court held, in *Brown* v. *Board of Education*, that separating people on the basis of race is tantamount to placing a badge of inferiority upon one race.

The lone dissenter in *Plessy*, Justice John Marshall Harlan, re-minded his colleagues that the Court had previously held that a rail-road was a "public highway" available to all, and that the Thirteenth Amendment had

> not only struck down the institution of slavery . . . but it pre-vent[ed] the imposition of any burdens or disabilities that consti-tute badges of slavery or servitude. It decreed universal civil freedom in this country.

Discussing the Thirteenth, Fourteenth, and Fifteenth Amendments to-gether, Harlan continued:

> These notable additions to the fundamental law were wel-comed by the friends of liberty throughout the world. They re-moved the race line from our governmental systems.

Harlan then proclaimed what some have described as the finest words of his distinguished career on the Supreme Court:

> [I]n view of the Constitution, in the eye of the law, there is in this country no superior, dominant, ruling class of citizens. There is no caste here. Our Constitution is color-blind, and neither knows nor tolerates classes among citizens. In respect of civil rights, all citizens are equal before the law.

Prophetically, Harlan added:

> In my opinion, the judgment this day rendered will, in time, prove to be quite as pernicious as the decision made by this tri-bunal in the *Dred Scott case*.

More than halfway through the first two hundred years of our his-tory as a free people, most Americans were sadly unaware of Harlan's eloquent utterance or of the opinion of the nation's highest court. Har-lan's dissent foreshadowed what was to come from the Supreme Court in opinions from 1954 through the 1990s. Neither the *Plessy* holding nor the Harlan dissent produced the reaction it deserved, particularly since the dissent had charted the way that was ultimately to be adopted by the Court in 1954. Many legal scholars and historians of that era tended to ignore this extraordinary case, which is astonishing because in many respects it was a more damaging holding than *Dred Scott*. It had a gloss of equality—a filmy, false gloss to be sure—but that cloak led to its being more or less forgotten for more than a half century. Just why this remarkable case was relegated to something like footnote status by some of the foremost historians in that period defies explanation. Today it must seem to most Americans incredible that a century ago Justice Harlan's opinion was a *dissent*—a protest—not a holding of the Supreme Court, and that he was the only justice to challenge the Court's misreading of our history and misinterpretation of our Constitution's commitment to freedom.

The lopsided decision in *Plessy*, in light of the low public standing of the Supreme Court after its opinion in the *Dred Scott* case in 1857, suggests that the Court in 1896 had not learned—and worse yet, that only one justice understood—what the Constitution really meant in terms of true human freedom. The views of this one dissenter are truly seminal expressions that must rank with the most eloquent utterances in the pages of opinions of the Supreme Court. His indignation was eloquent but restrained, yet his outrage was unmistakable. More than thirty years after Lincoln had signed the Emancipation Proclamation and the nation had ratified the Thirteenth Amendment, the Supreme Court had not awakened.

The *Plessy* decision had a profound influence on more than just public transportation. In the South and elsewhere, education was also segregated—to the extent black children were educated at all. "Separate but equal" was a myth. The unspoken purpose of the system was to deny blacks educational opportunities and, with that, employment opportunities. Lacking both political and economic power, blacks had little choice but to submit to segregation. But one hundred and sixty-seven years after the signing of the Constitution, the Supreme Court finally declared that separate was "inherently unequal." The decisive stroke came on May 17, 1954, in the case of *Brown* v. *Board of Education*. By this time there was broad national support—albeit not unanimous—for the idea that segregation in public schools and elsewhere violated the Constitution. Among others, President Eisenhower's Justice Department, under the direction of Attorney General Herbert Brownell, acting as an amicus curiae, or friend of the Court, vigorously asserted that segregation in public schools violated the Constitution. The Court agreed unanimously. The view of the Constitution expounded in Justice Harlan's *Plessy* dissent finally became the law of the land.

As we look back on the development of civil rights in America, from *Dred Scott* and *Plessy* to *Brown* and beyond, it becomes clear that the tasks of a nation whose people sought freedom from the time of its birth are never finished. Countless philosophers could be cited for the point that human progress is terribly slow. One need go no further than this century to find countless wars, with Hitler's and Stalin's bloody suppression of human rights and destruction of human values vividly demonstrating just how treacherous and halting human progress can be. But America stands as an example that progress can be made. It remains our challenge to continue making progress in the area of human rights and to lengthen our stride in doing so.

CHAPTER THIRTEEN

THE FIRST AMENDMENT AND PRIOR RESTRAINTS

....

Near v. Minnesota, 1931

The liberty of the press is indeed essential to the nature of a free state; but this consists in laying no previous restraints upon publications, and not in freedom from censure for criminal matter when published. Every freeman has an undoubted right to lay what sentiments he pleases before the public; to forbid this, is to destroy the freedom of the press . . . .
— Sir William Blackstone, *Commentaries on the Laws of England,* 1765

Among those principles deemed sacred in America . . . there is no one, of which the importance is more deeply impressed on the public mind, than the liberty of the press. That this liberty is often carried to excess, that has sometimes degenerated into licentiousness, is seen and lamented; but the remedy has not yet been discovered. Perhaps it is an evil inseparable from the good to which it is allied; perhaps it is a shoot which cannot be stripped from the stalk, without wounding vitally the plant from which it is torn. However desirable those measures may be, which might correct without enslaving the press, they have never yet been devised in America.
— Charles Cotesworth Pinckney,
John Marshall, and Elbridge Gerry,
in a letter to Talleyrand, 1798

A S WE HAVE ALREADY SEEN, great cases in the history of the Constitution often have humble beginnings. *Near* v. *Minnesota* was the first great censorship case decided by the Supreme Court, yet its stage was set not in one of the large eastern cities with their many vigorous newspapers, but in one of the northernmost regions of the country, Duluth, Minnesota. To understand the setting, however, requires a bit of the history of that place.

The startling discovery, in the closing years of the nineteenth century, of massive ore deposits under the barren wasteland of northern Minnesota—left behind after the rich forests had been converted into lumber—had a marked impact on the development of both the state and the United States as a whole. The Minnesota ore fields were once the land of the Chippewa tribes, the land of the "Sleeping Giant," which in the Native American tongue was *Mesabi,* and they came to be known as the Mesabi or Mesabe Range. Unknown to the Chippewa, a true sleeping giant of enormous wealth lay beneath the land where they once hunted. The swift expansion westward after the Civil War had taxed the sources of iron ore. The steel industry had reached maximum capacity in an economy hungry for more bridges, railroads, cars, and machinery. The demand for steel stimulated an enormous expansion of the economy of northern Minnesota. Removal of the vast supply of rich ore lying just below the surface taxed all existing transportation facilities—ships on the Great Lakes and rails. The Great Lakes that already carried great fleets of ships conveying grain east now carried Mesabe ore to the eastern steel mills as well. Raw ore flowed east and shining steel came west in the form of rails, freight cars, ships, and power shovels.

There were other imports too: labor was scarce, and the stream of immigrants from Europe grew. Minnesota and Wisconsin had always attracted Germans, Swedes, Norwegians, Danes, and Finns, who were used to short, warm summers and long, cold winters. Minnesota and Wisconsin regularly provided both. The poor of Italy, Ireland, and Scotland also came, and before long more than half the people living on the Mesabe Range were first-generation immigrants. As with the 1849 California "gold rush," this "iron rush" also attracted its share of riffraff who exploited the needs of thousands of newly arrived workingmen. Many of these workers had no families but did have payroll cash in their pockets. The natural inclinations of the new residents overflowing in the towns and villages near the mines could not always be held in check by the inadequate local police. Moreover, local governments, rich with new tax revenues, would soon discover that great wealth corrupts as absolute power corrupts.

Contributing to the problems of the day was the Eighteenth Amendment to the Constitution, adopted in 1919. "Prohibition" created a thriving bootlegger industry. Stills in cellars and barns, along with the traditional, but illegal, liquors from Canada a few miles to the north, became commonplace. The Canadian border, extending for thousands of miles across largely wild country, could not be sealed. The Mesabe range was a natural entry point for "Canadian Imports," which were distributed not only to the well-paid mine workers on the range, but also in the cities of Minneapolis, St. Paul, Madison, Chicago, and Des Moines. The Anti-Saloon League had not yet grasped the power of market demand in the post–World War I era. The rapid growth and newfound wealth in Minnesota attracted not only gamblers, pimps, and racketeers, coupled with the variety of illegal activities that come with them, but also the dubious ancestors of the modern-day "investigative reporters."

This setting brings us to the story of this chapter. John Morrison launched a weekly newspaper, the *Duluth Rip-saw*, designed as an "attack" newspaper, or "scandal sheet." It was bent, so he claimed, on exposing illegal and immoral conduct by public officials and other business leaders. Many who saw the rampant corruption welcomed him as a crusading reformer. The victims of Morrison's dubious brand of journalism, however, responded with criminal charges. Prominent political leaders, including a flamboyant lawyer and state senator, George Lommen, testified against Morrison. Morrison was convicted of criminal libel, but by making a public apology, he managed to serve no jail time under his sentence.

Nevertheless, Morrison's victims threatened revenge. In 1925 Lommen, among others, sponsored a public-nuisance bill that swiftly passed the Minnesota legislature. This "gag law" was the subject of *Near* v. *Minnesota*. The public-nuisance law was directed at "obscene, lewd and lascivious" and "malicious, scandalous and defamatory" publications. "Participation" in such activities was deemed to "constitute a commission of . . . nuisance" subject to the penalties of the law. The state attorney general or any county attorney was empowered to institute suit for a permanent injunction against the offending publication. If both of those officials failed or refused to institute such a suit, any citizen could do so.

The public–nuisance law was supported by a strange coalition of business interests, the establishment press, racketeers, and corrupt politicians. All were interested in finding some way, any way, to suppress the "exposé" newspapers. The mainstream press in Minneapolis, St. Paul, and Duluth was strangely silent on the law and its First Amendment implications. Morrison's death the year after the law was enacted put an end to his crusade. For a brief period "yellow journalism" was relatively silent and the new law was unused.

There were other practitioners of Morrison's craft, but they could never enlist the sympathy that even some public leaders had at first expressed toward Morrison's "cleanup campaign." Jay Near had been around as part of the fringe press chiefly in the Twin Cities. With Morrison gone, he and Howard Guilford, another longtime hanger-on in local press politics, formed a partnership in 1927 and published a weekly in Minneapolis called the *Saturday Press*. The *Saturday Press* was patterned along the same lines as Morrison's *Rip-saw*, but did not lay serious claim to the benign objective of reform.

Shortly after Near and Guilford began publication, a car pursued Guilford in Minneapolis, and he was shot in a "Chicago gangster"–style shooting. Guilford survived, but Near reacted in their newspaper by alleging links between organized crime and the mayor of Minneapolis, the chief of police, and the county attorney, Floyd Olson. Olson was a rising young figure in the Farmer-Labor party, which succeeded the Democratic party in Minnesota. He would later serve three terms as governor of the state. The *Saturday Press* charged the named officials with failure to enforce laws and, in particular, failure to pursue the investigation of the gangsters who attempted to murder Guilford. Moreover, the attacks on the officials were blended with Near's and Guilford's own brand of vicious anti-Semitism. One column read:

GIL'S CHATTERBOX

I headed into the city on September 26th, ran across three Jews in a Chevrolet; stopped a lot of lead and won a bed for myself in St. Barnabas Hospital for six weeks. . . .

Whereupon I have withdrawn all allegiance to anything with a hook nose that eats herring. I have adopted the sparrow as my national bird until Davis' law enforcement league or the K.K.K. hammers the eagle's beak out straight. So if I seem to act crazy as I ankle down the street, bear in mind that I am merely saluting MY national emblem.

All of which has nothing to do with the present whereabouts of Big Mose Barnett. Methinks he headed the local delegation to the new Palestine-for-Jews-only. He went ahead of the boys so he could do a little fixing with the Yiddish chief of police and get his twenty-five per cent of the gambling rake-off. Boys will be boys and "ganefs" [crooks] will be ganefs.

GRAND JURIES AND DITTO

There are grand juries, and there are grand juries. The last one was a real grand jury. It acted. The present one is like the scion who is labelled "Junior." That means not so good. There are a few mighty good folks on it—there are some who smell bad. One petty peanut politician whose graft was almost pitiful in its size when he was a public official, has already shot his mouth off in several places. He is establishing his alibi in advance for what he intends to keep from taking place.

But George [the grand juror], we won't bother you. We are aware that the gambling syndicate was waiting for your body to convene before the big crap game opened again. The Yids had your dimensions, apparently, and we always go by the judgment of a dog in appraising people.

We will call for a special grand jury and a special prosecutor within a short time, as soon as half of the staff can navigate to advantage, and then we'll show you what a real grand jury can do.

Up to the present we have been merely tapping on the window.
Very soon we shall start smashing glass.

Olson quickly went to court in Minneapolis to quash the *Saturday Press*
under the 1925 Minnesota public-nuisance law. The state trial court
temporarily enjoined the publication of the weekly. The *Saturday Press*
was gagged for more than a year under the temporary restraining order
while Near waited for a hearing in the state supreme court, although
Near did write a series of columns for another local paper, the *Beacon*,
even while the restraint order was outstanding.

The prior restraint on the *Saturday Press* provoked no outcry or
protest from the "establishment press." Near was widely known as an
anti-Semite, an anti-Catholic, and a racist. He found little sympathy in
Minnesota, where he had long been a headache to the establishment
press, including those who ordinarily would have supported a claim to
freedom of the press. Perhaps too few Minnesota lawyers and government officials, however, remembered what both Sir William Blackstone and three American ministers to France—Charles Cotesworth
Pinckney, John Marshall, and Elbridge Gerry—had written regarding
the dangers of suppressing freedom of expression and freedom of the
press, even "bad" press.

Near's case was not argued in the Supreme Court of Minnesota
until the spring of 1928. In May of that year Minnesota's highest court
sustained, against a First Amendment challenge, the constitutionality of
both the trial court's temporary injunction and the public-nuisance
law. The court stated that, while the voice of the honest press must always be heard, "malice, scandal, and defamation when untrue or
published with bad motive or *without justifiable ends*" did not enjoy any
constitutional protection.

At this point, distant friends of the free press, including the American Civil Liberties Union (ACLU), took notice. They were concerned that the people of Minnesota, a traditionally populist state with
claims to a liberal tradition, could tolerate such a grave attack on the
First Amendment. Their concern finally brought Near's case to the attention of others in the media, notably the dynamic, arrogant, and eccentric Robert McCormick of the *Chicago Tribune*. He moved in, took

over the appeal, and selected leading Chicago lawyers to carry on the battle in the United States Supreme Court. Surely not a friend of the ACLU, McCormick was despised by the establishment media for traits somewhat like those that brought Near into disrepute. The "Colonel," as he was called, was a nonpracticing lawyer and a nonworking journalist—except that he owned the *Chicago Tribune*. But McCormick's resources, like his zeal, were virtually unlimited. Now Near himself was almost forgotten; the battle centered on the Constitution and the principle of freedom of the press.

The case was argued before the United States Supreme Court on January 30, 1931, in the Old Supreme Court Chamber in the United States Capitol, a room now restored as the Senate chamber of an earlier period. Finally, after an abnormally long time even for an important constitutional case, the Court's opinion was issued on June 1, 1931.

In a 5 to 4 decision striking down the Minnesota public-nuisance law as unconstitutional, Chief Justice Charles Evans Hughes began the analysis in the majority opinion by stating that the Minnesota law was

> unusual, if not unique, and raises questions of grave importance transcending the local interests involved in the particular action. It is no longer open to doubt that the liberty of the press, and of speech, is within the liberty safeguarded by the due process clause of the Fourteenth Amendment from invasions by state action. . . . Liberty of speech, and of the press, is . . . not an absolute right and the State may punish its abuse. . . . Liberty, in each of its phases, has its history and connotation and, in the present instance, the inquiry is as to the historic conception of the liberty of the press and whether the statute under review violates the essential attributes of that liberty.

Chief Justice Hughes then noted that the statute was "not aimed at the redress of individual or private wrongs" by way of monetary damages. Nor was the truth or falsity of the published material at issue. That could be settled by a civil lawsuit for libel. Rather, he noted, the Minnesota Supreme Court had taken the position that "[t]here is no constitutional right to publish a fact merely because it is true," and that the public-nuisance law was intended neither to protect "the person attacked nor to punish the wrongdoer," but to protect "the public welfare." For lawyers concerned with the constitutional values of the First Amendment, the United States Supreme Court's decision was inevitable. For those journalists who truly understood the nature and consequences of the Minnesota Supreme Court's ruling, however, more was needed to relieve their anxiety. This was especially true because four justices—spearheaded by Minnesota's own Justice Pierce Butler—vigorously dissented from Chief Justice Hughes' opinion.

For those in Minnesota, it was a question of which was worse: the rampant corruption in local government or the sleazy press. Accordingly, Chief Justice Hughes needed to say more; he had to draw the lines clearly. The public-nuisance law was clearly designed to crush publishers like Near and Guilford, but could it be so confined? The nuisance law looked like censorship to Hughes, even though he readily conceded the scandalous nature of what Near and Guilford had published:

> [T]he operation and effect of the statute in substance is that public authorities may bring the owner or publisher of a newspaper or periodical before a judge upon a charge of conducting a business of publishing scandalous and defamatory matter—in particular that the matter consists of charges against public officers of official dereliction—and unless the owner or publisher is able and disposed to bring competent evidence to satisfy the judge that the charges [against the officers] are true and are published with good motives and for justifiable ends, his newspaper or periodical is suppressed and further publication is made punishable as a contempt. This is of the essence of censorship.

Hughes reminded his readers that more than a century and a half earlier, Blackstone had written in his *Commentaries on the Laws of England* that

> [t]he liberty of the press is indeed essential to the nature of a free state; but this consists in laying no *previous* restraints upon publi-

cations, and not in freedom from censure for criminal matter when published.

Indeed, in this country, even before our Constitution was adopted, the concept of prior or previous restraint on publication was firmly rejected. In 1774, in a letter to "Inhabitants of Quebec," the Continental Congress stated:

> The last right we shall mention, regards the freedom of the press. The importance of this consists, besides the advancement of truth, science, morality, and arts in general, in its diffusion of liberal sentiments on the administration of Government, its ready communication of thoughts between subjects, and its consequential promotion of union among them, whereby oppressive officers are shamed or intimidated, into more honorable and just modes of conducting affairs.

Hughes also quoted the Court's prior opinion in *Patterson v. Colorado*, authored by Justice Oliver Wendell Holmes in 1907:

> "[T]he main purpose of such constitutional provisions [as the First Amendment] is to prevent all such *previous restraints* upon publications as had been practiced by other governments . . . . The preliminary freedom extends as well to the false as to the true . . ." (emphasis in original).

From Blackstone's time to the present, the freedom of the press from previous or prior restraint has been essential to the protection of a free press—even where false and libelous statements were concerned. Hughes acknowledged, as the Supreme Court did again in the 1970s, that during wartime, publication of material that threatens the national security or that clearly threatens to incite violence might conceivably be "previously restrained." But outside of these very narrow exceptions, the freedom of the press from previous restraint is absolute.

Justice Pierce Butler, whose brother had been a victim of "Near journalism," and who was an able lawyer and jurist not noted for moderation in expression, wrote for the four dissenting justices. He opened his vigorous dissent firmly, stating that the majority opinion

> gives to freedom of the press a meaning and a scope not hereto-
> fore recognized and construes "liberty" in the due process clause
> of the Fourteenth Amendment to put upon the States a federal re-
> striction that is without precedent.

The flaw in Justice Butler's rejection of the history of the rule against previous restraint emerges in his implicit approval of what the Minnesota Supreme Court had said in sustaining the nuisance statute. Butler quoted that court:

> "The constituent elements of the declared nuisance are the
> customary and regular dissemination by means of a newspaper
> which finds its way into families, reaching the young as well as the
> mature, of a selection of scandalous and defamatory articles
> treated in such a way as to excite attention and interest so as to
> command circulation. The statute is not directed at threatened li-
> bel but at an existing business which, generally speaking, involves
> more than libel. The distribution of scandalous matter is detri-
> mental to public morals and to the general welfare. It tends to dis-
> turb the peace of the community. . . . It was never the intention
> of the constitution to afford protection to a publication devoted
> to scandal and defamation."

Justice Butler seemed to accept the Minnesota Supreme Court's appraisal that

> "[i]n Minnesota no agency can hush the sincere and honest voice
> of the press, but our Constitution was never intended to protect
> malice, scandal, and defamation when untrue or published with
> bad motive or without justifiable ends."

Here, perhaps, is the essence of the case for prior restraint: the malicious and defamatory press must be "abated" and subjected to "previous restraint." To Justice Butler, freedom of the press was only for the so-called *responsible* press, for honest reporting and sincere editorial comment. But who is to decide who is responsible? In a free society, that is the overriding question.

Butler interpreted the First Amendment as prohibiting the advance licensing of the press, but also took the position that, even in Blackstone's view, legislation could properly be addressed against "abuse of the right of free press." Butler wrote:

> It is fanciful to suggest similarity between the granting or enforcement of the decree authorized by this statute to prevent *further* publication of malicious, scandalous and defamatory articles and the *previous restraint* upon the press by licensers as referred to by Blackstone and described in the history of the times to which he alludes.

He concluded his opinion not on constitutional grounds, but on pragmatic theory:

> It is well known, as found by the state supreme court, that existing libel laws are inadequate effectively to suppress evils resulting from the kind of business and publications that are shown in this case. The doctrine that measures such as the one before us are invalid because they operate as previous restraints to infringe freedom of press exposes the peace and good order of every community and the business and private affairs of every individual to the constant and protracted false and malicious assaults of any insolvent publisher who may have purpose and sufficient capacity to contrive and put into effect a scheme or program for oppression, blackmail or extortion.

The *Near* case put to rest any thought that judges would have power to make qualitative, content-based evaluations to determine which statements by the press should be subject to restraint and which should be protected under the Constitution. The balance is resolved, not in wholly satisfactory terms, to be sure, but in terms that best accommodate the principles upon which our constitutional democracy was founded. As Chief Justice Hughes concluded:

The fact that the liberty of the press may be abused by miscreant purveyors of scandal does not make any the less necessary the immunity of the press from previous restraint in dealing with official misconduct. Subsequent punishment for such abuses as may exist is the appropriate remedy, consistent with constitutional privilege.

Thus, the truth or falsity of what the "scandalous press" publishes must be treated as irrelevant if the command against prior restraint is to have full meaning. No law can define truth in all circumstances. False charges of official corruption or misconduct are undoubtedly harmful and potentially injurious. That this risk of injury may well, among other things, keep some of our best people out of public life, as is often argued, must be weighed on one side of the scales. But centuries of experience in the common law has resolved that the balance must be struck, as the Supreme Court of the United States did strike it, in favor of protection of expression—with only rare exceptions where national security is at stake. It is safe to note that in the half century following the narrow vote in the *Near* case, the Supreme Court has consistently followed the views of Chief Justice Hughes as to the invalidity of prior restraints.

CHAPTER FOURTEEN

MINNESOTA IGNORES THE CONTRACT CLAUSE

....

Home Building & Loan Association v. Blaisdell, 1934

While emergency does not create power, emergency may furnish the occasion for the exercise of power.

—Chief Justice Charles Evans Hughes,
for the Court in *Blaisdell*, 1934

If the provisions of the Constitution be not upheld when they pinch as well as when they comfort, they may as well be abandoned.

—Justice George Sutherland,
dissenting in *Blaisdell*, 1934

THE DAY WAS MARCH 6, 1933. America was in the middle of the worst worldwide depression in modern history. The mood among farmers in America was grim; corn was selling for 10 cents per bushel, wheat for 30 cents, oats for 9 cents, and barley for 15 cents. With those prices, farmers in the Midwest were claiming it would be impossible to pay even taxes and the interest on their debts, let alone any principal. The *Farm Holiday News*, a St. Paul, Minnesota, publication, warned that there was

plenty of social dynamite in the farm debt situation. The farmers of Lexington started things in 1776. The spirit of "76" is sweeping the farms of America today, and for causes immeasurably more serious than those that led to the Revolution and American freedom from the British tyranny of that time.

In other midwestern communities farmers had physically blocked the foreclosure sales of their neighbors' property. Farmers in Ohio and Iowa had recently showed up with rope in hand at the foreclosure sale of their neighbors' property and proceeded figuratively to "lynch" the sale itself; seldom did a foreclosure sale continue after such a demonstration. There were even reports from England that 200,000 farmers there had been in open revolt, "jeering the parsons and stoning the auctioneers." The farmers in Minnesota were equally determined to retain their homes, farms, and livelihoods. The implications were serious: some declared that a farm revolt was in order.

Early in the afternoon of Monday, March 6, 1933, a crowd began to gather in the open area in front of the State Capitol in St. Paul, one of Cass Gilbert's legacies to classical architecture. The crowd, which the local papers estimated at two thousand, grew and soon filled the entire plaza. Most were dressed in the working clothes of farmers. The mob moved up the long marble steps leading to the entrance to the Capitol. The protestors entered the building and soon filled its halls. Several hundred crowded into the chamber of the House of Representatives. Some sat on desks, others in the legislators' seats, feet up; some smoked in violation of House rules. They laughed and poked fun at the rich formality of the setting, which was quite different from their barns and haylofts.

The protestors had made their point. The foreclosure of a mortgage on a farm took away more than a home; it took away the farmer's livelihood as well. It destroyed him economically. What would be done about it? Two weeks later, another protesting crowd, this time twenty thousand people, gathered at the Capitol asking the same question. Few of these men knew of Shays' Rebellion in the summer of 1786, but perhaps some of the members of the Minnesota legislature remembered their history lessons well enough to recall it. The motives of the Minnesota farmers in 1933 and those of Daniel Shays and his friends in 1786 were similar. Resistance to foreclosures by creditors in time of great economic stress was not uncommon, as Shays' Rebellion had demonstrated.

The Minnesota farmers, of course, used different, and more democratic, tactics. Shays had attacked public arsenals to get arms, and his rebellion threatened to end in bloodshed. The Minnesota farmers, on the other hand, did not carry weapons and were not ready to employ violence to get the government to attend to their problem. Instead they rested on the First Amendment guarantees of the right to assemble and to petition their government, even if they did so perhaps more aggressively than the First Amendment contemplated.

Minnesota's Communists were gleeful. In the 1930s Minnesota was second only to New York in the number of members of the Communist party, with California third. Was this perhaps the beginning of "Der Tag"—the day they often talked of when they would take over? Was this the way the great 1917 Revolution began in Russia—peoples' protests, stirred up of course by the Party? This was even better, a spontaneous outburst. Active Party members openly gloated. This did not escape the attention of the Minnesota legislature. Something had to be done. The left-leaning, politically ambitious Governor Floyd Olson agreed.

The Minnesota legislature responded. It unanimously provided the protestors with relief in the form of the Mortgage Moratorium Law, which was approved on April 18, 1933:

> Whereas, the severe financial and economic depression[,] . . . low prices for the products of the farms and the factories, . . . unemployment, [and] an almost complete lack of credit for farmers, business men and property owners . . . [have rendered them] unable to meet all payments . . . [and have] threatened [them] with loss of such properties through mortgage foreclosure, . . . the Legislature of Minnesota hereby declares its belief, that [these] conditions . . . [have] created an emergency of such nature that justifies and validates legislation for the extension of the time of redemption from mortgage foreclosure and execution sales . . . .

Under the law, mortgagors could apply to the state courts for an extension of up to two years in the time allowed them to redeem their property after foreclosure. Was the law constitutional, or did it violate the constitutional mandate in Article I, Section 10, that "[n]o State shall . . . pass any . . . Law impairing the Obligation of Contracts"? Cases squarely presenting that issue quickly hit the state courts.

In 1928 John and Rosella Blaisdell had mortgaged their Minneapolis home for a $3,800 loan from the Home Building and Loan Association. They defaulted on the loan in 1932 and the bank foreclosed. Under state law at the time, the bank would have acquired full title to the property in 1933, when the redemption period expired, but the Blaisdells petitioned the state court for an extension under the moratorium law. The bank challenged the law as contrary to the Contract Clause of the Constitution. The Minnesota courts had never encountered the issue before, but the state trial court in Minneapolis declared the moratorium law unconstitutional. The judge reasoned that the law impaired contracts under the *Dartmouth College* case of 1819 (discussed in Chapter Eight), deprived the mortgage lenders of property without due process of law, and exceeded the state's police powers, all in violation of both the United States and Minnesota constitutions. The state court in St. Paul also found the law unconstitutional in another case.

Both cases were appealed to the Minnesota Supreme Court. Such cases aroused great public passions. About the same time that *Blaisdell* headed to the state supreme court, a judge in North Dakota was facing a recall election campaign for declaring unconstitutional a moratorium on foreclosures proclaimed by that state's governor. A Minnesota newspaper editorial opined that North Dakota Governor William Langer's action was constitutional under the police power, which "embraces the right of the Governor, in cases of great emergencies such as the present financial panic, to issue and enforce such proclamations he deems necessary to protect and secure people of the State in their homes and means of livelihood." In other words, the editor reasoned, in times of emergency a governor's police powers have no constitutional limits at all. The article criticized the North Dakota judge and found it "hard to understand a judge who will ballyhoo about 'upholding the Constitution' and still go contrary to the Governor's proclamation that has for its purpose to save the homes of the state." And speaking of the situation in Minnesota, the president of a farm association asked in an article,

"How long, O Lord, is the farmer to be crucified because of the perfidy and the treason of those who are supposed to represent him?"

The Minnesota Supreme Court reversed the two lower state courts and upheld Minnesota's Mortgage Moratorium Law. Only one justice out of seven, Associate Justice Royal Stone, dissented. The majority held that the law was a valid exercise of the state's police powers, did not violate the Contract Clause of the United States Constitution, and was constitutional in all other respects. Justice Stone, widely regarded as the ablest justice of the Minnesota Supreme Court, relied on the Contract Clause and Chief Justice Marshall's opinion in the *Dartmouth College* case in support of his view.

From there, the case went to the United States Supreme Court, which rendered its decision on January 8, 1934. The Court upheld the Minnesota law by a margin of one vote—with four justices vigorously dissenting.

Chief Justice Charles Evans Hughes delivered the opinion of the Court, which some scholars have called "ambivalent." Taken as a whole, however, Hughes' opinion relies on powers implied rather than expressed in the Constitution. In the words of Hughes' biographer Merlo Pusey, Hughes was "overjoyed by his success in swinging the court . . . into line" in *Blaisdell*, and his opinion for the Court "spoke in deliberate, judicial terms the language that was on the lips of legislators, editors, and leaders of the Roosevelt Administration." Hughes' opinion contained one particular statement that has above all else in the opinion been most challenged:

> While emergency does not create power, emergency may furnish the occasion for the exercise of power.

In the context of Hughes' opinion, that statement seems, at the very least, internally inconsistent. As the four dissenters asked, how can a power that has not been created be validly exercised, especially in light of the specific limitation of the Contract Clause?

Hughes elaborated:

> [I]t does not follow that conditions may not arise in which a temporary restraint of enforcement may be consistent with the spirit

and purpose of the constitutional provision and thus be found to be within the range of the reserved power of the State to protect the vital interests of the community. . . . The reservation of state power appropriate to such extraordinary conditions may be deemed to be as much a part of all contracts, as is the reservation of state power to protect the public interest in the other situations to which we have referred.

That analysis does little, however, to show why the statute did not violate the Contract Clause.

Hughes, apparently concerned that the answer was clear—and contrary to his—from the perspective of the framers of the Constitution, went on to state:

It is no answer to say that this public need [for a mortgage moratorium] was not apprehended a century ago, or to insist that what the [Contract Clause] of the Constitution meant to the vision of that day it must mean to the vision of our time. . . . "The case before us must be considered in the light of our whole experience and not merely in that of what was said a hundred years ago."

Hughes, who was generally a follower of the "original intent" school of constitutional interpretation—which relies on what the framers of the Constitution intended it to mean, as indicated by both the text and contemporary historical sources—thus apparently rejected the application of original intent in *Blaisdell*. But to suggest that the delegates in Philadelphia could not have anticipated precisely what the Minnesota farmers were suffering missed the mark not by yards but by miles. The "public need" of which Hughes spoke was certainly "apprehended" by the men who wrote and ratified the Constitution. Justice Stone's dissent in the Minnesota Supreme Court made exactly that point:

Repudiation of private and public contract debts was the main factor, the most alarming manifestation of chaos and near anarchy, which prevailed increasingly in the American colonies from the end of the Revolution in 1781 to the going into effect

of the Constitution in 1788. It was the whole animus of Shays'
Rebellion in Massachusetts, a disturbance which although local-
ized, was most alarming. It was distinctly a rebellion of militant
debtors against their creditors, and against courts and the judges
thereof sworn to enforce all law, including the law of contracts. . . . We need not go far in recent local experience for phe-
nomena exactly parallel.

Indeed, the Contract clause was the Constitution's answer to the difficulties produced by local efforts at debt relief, such as Shays' Rebellion.

It is puzzling that a great justice and a man who knew his history,
as Hughes surely did, came to such a dubious conclusion. Thurman
Arnold, who plainly liked Hughes' result, had this to say:

It is intriguing to examine the lengths to which [Hughes]
stretched to establish the proposition of valid state legislation creating debtor relief. From a different perspective, one familiar
with the Federal Convention and the early development of Supreme Court doctrine will see in *Blaisdell* an extraordinarily odd
decision.

The explanation may be that Hughes felt his position so weak that he
was groping for every possible argument in support.

In that quest, Chief Justice Hughes resorted to words reminiscent
of John Marshall, his greatest predecessor:

The question is not whether the legislative action affects contracts
incidentally, or directly or indirectly, but whether the legislation
is addressed to a legitimate end and the measures taken are reasonable and appropriate to that end.

Although Hughes' words echoed those of Chief Justice Marshall in
M'Culloch v. *Maryland*, his reasoning did not. Since when, we should
ask, does every remedy for a public need become constitutional simply
because it is good and necessary? When Marshall discussed the connection between reasonable means and legitimate ends, he was construing the broad grant of power in the Necessary and Proper Clause,

not an express constitutional limitation, such as the Contract Clause, on the means available to pursue certain ends. Indeed, Marshall allowed, in the pursuit of legitimate ends, only those means "which are not prohibited, but consist with the letter and spirit of the constitution." Hughes forgot, or more likely ignored, that caveat. Although Hughes did not rely on the writings of Thomas Jefferson in his opinion, he might have, in a fit of candor, quoted from Jefferson's justification for the Louisiana Purchase (discussed in Chapter Nine), which Jefferson conceded was unconstitutional but defended on the basis of necessity.

Justice George Sutherland, speaking for four dissenters, answered in terms that must have pained Chief Justice Hughes to the extent that he still believed in faithfulness to the framers' "original intent":

> The provisions of the Federal Constitution, undoubtedly, are pliable in the sense that in appropriate cases they have the capacity of bringing within their grasp every new condition which falls within their meaning. But, their *meaning* is changeless; it is only their *application* which is extensible.

Justice Sutherland said that the Court's decision raised the specter of "gradual but ever-advancing encroachments" upon the sanctity of contracts:

> Few questions of greater moment than that just decided have been submitted for judicial inquiry during this generation. He simply closes his eyes to the necessary implications of the decision who fails to see in it the potentiality of future gradual but ever-advancing encroachments upon the sanctity of private and public contracts. The effect of the Minnesota legislation, though serious enough in itself, is of trivial significance compared with the far more serious and dangerous inroads upon the limitations of the Constitution which are almost certain to ensue as a consequence naturally following any step beyond the boundaries fixed by that instrument. . . .
>
> A provision of the Constitution, it is hardly necessary to say, does not admit of two distinctly opposite interpretations. It does

not mean one thing at one time and an entirely different thing at another time.

Justice Sutherland's attack on the majority opinion continued with devastating impact. First, he cited a number of precedents for the proposition that the terms of the Constitution cannot be "suspended" in the face of an emergency and for the proposition that the Constitution must be construed now as it was when it was written. Second, Sutherland criticized the majority's interpretation of the Contract Clause; he expressed the view that "[a] candid consideration of the history and circumstances which led up to and accompanied the framing and adoption of this clause will demonstrate conclusively that it was framed and adopted with the specific and studied purpose of preventing legislation designed to relieve debtors *especially* in time of financial distress." Sutherland then traced the problems that arose from indebtedness following the American Revolution and the ill-advised attempts by state legislatures to provide for various forms of debtor relief, and he described how the delegates to the Constitutional Convention in 1787 sought to remedy these difficulties by limiting the ability of the states to interfere with the value of contracts. Sutherland concluded his historical survey:

> If it be possible by resort to the testimony of history to put any question of constitutional intent beyond the domain of uncertainty, the foregoing [history] leaves no reasonable ground upon which to base a denial that the clause of the Constitution now under consideration was meant to foreclose state action impairing the obligation of contracts *primarily and especially* in respect of such action aimed at giving relief to debtors *in time of emergency* (emphasis in original).

Sutherland supported his interpretation with citations to a long line of Supreme Court cases striking down similar state legislative schemes in the face of Contract Clause challenges, relying primarily upon Chief Justice Marshall's opinion in the *Dartmouth College* case.

Sutherland then cut to the heart of the matter—the majority's reliance upon the idea of "emergency" to support its decision. He acknowledged that some powers might, depending on their nature and the intent of the Constitution with respect to them, be exercised in an emergency,

> [b]ut we are here dealing not with a power granted by the Federal Constitution, but with the state police power, which exists in its own right. Hence the question is not whether an emergency furnishes an occasion for the exercise of that state power, but whether an emergency furnishes an occasion for the relaxation of the restrictions upon the power imposed by the contract impairment clause [of the federal Constitution]; and the difficulty is that the contract impairment clause forbids state action under any circumstances, if it have the effect of impairing the obligation of contracts.

The Minnesota statute impairs the obligation of contracts, Sutherland said, because it does not merely alter the remedy available to the creditor: "A statute which materially delays enforcement of the mortgagee's contractual right of ownership and possession does not modify the remedy merely; it destroys, for the period of delay, *all* remedy so far as the enforcement of that right is concerned." Furthermore, he said, the Minnesota statute could not be justified as legislation to promote the public health or public morals, because it did not render the affected contracts unlawful—in contrast, for example, to the situation where the sale of alcoholic beverages is outlawed and contracts for the sale of such beverages are effectively nullified—but instead the statute simply changed the terms of the contracts. Justice Sutherland bluntly concluded for the four dissenters with the following: "If the provisions of the Constitution be not upheld when they pinch as well as when they comfort, they may as well be abandoned."

There is, of course, nothing new about the enactment of emergency legislation or the suspension of constitutional guarantees in times of crisis—one need look no further than the aftermath of the 1861 attack on Fort Sumter or the 1941 attack on Pearl Harbor to appreciate that extraordinary circumstances often demand extraordinary measures. But those suspensions have occurred in only the most extreme circumstances. The question comes down to whether legislative action which raises serious constitutional questions is the *only* way to deal with a perceived need. Hughes was praised by liberal commentators for his "humanism," and his opinion is often cited in support of emergency governmental measures that are of doubtful constitutionality. For example, Hughes' opinion was cited with warm approval by Chief Justice Fred Vinson writing for the dissenters in the *Steel Seizure Case* in 1952 (discussed in the following chapter). Were there not other legislative means that Minnesota could have employed to achieve the same end? Why couldn't the Minnesota legislature have created a bank, for example, to purchase all the mortgages of distressed debtors, and thus provided direct relief to debtors without impairing preexisting contract rights?

Not surprisingly, Minnesota Governor Floyd Olson, whose politics were as far left as a Socialist would go, was enthusiastic about Hughes' opinion:

> The decision represents more than a triumph of the police power clause of the constitution over the due process of law and obligation of contract clause; it really represents a triumph of human rights over property rights. It also indicates that we can change the system under which we live in any manner we desire and keep with the constitution.

Olson's radicalism would have given legislatures and executive officers unreviewable power. Several federal judges, however, were more skeptical of the extent of "emergency" powers. The highly regarded Circuit Judge John J. Parker, who had been nominated to the Supreme Court by President Herbert Hoover but rejected by the Senate, acknowledged in a speech to the American Bar Association that although legislative power was enhanced by crises, he rejected the "heresy that unconstitutional acts may be justified because of an emergency. I hold to no such destructive and revolutionary doctrine." A federal district judge stated, in regard to the exercise of such power by Congress rather than a state: "The national emergency doctrine goes no further than that an emergency may call into activity a power which already exists. It may not speak into life that which is dead or never existed."

The debate over Hughes' opinion continues, at least in scholarly circles. Was this Hughes the accomplished jurist, which surely he was; was this Hughes the former governor of New York, the largest state at the time; was this Hughes the almost-president; or was this Hughes the statesman following Thomas Jefferson's "higher law"? Perhaps what ultimately saved Hughes' opinion was that the Mortgage Moratorium Law was truly temporary emergency legislation, which expired by its own terms several years after it was enacted. And as we will see in the next chapter, the Court did not often take as generous a view of "emergency" powers.

CHAPTER FIFTEEN

THE *STEEL SEIZURE CASE*

....

Youngstown Sheet & Tube Co. v. Sawyer, 1952

WHEREAS American fighting men and fighting men of other nations of the United Nations are now engaged in deadly combat with the forces of aggression in Korea, and forces of the United States are stationed elsewhere overseas for the purpose of participating in the defense of the Atlantic Community against aggression . . . .

. . . The Secretary of Commerce is hereby authorized and directed to take possession of all or such of the plants, facilities, and other property of the companies named in the list attached hereto, or any part thereof, as he may deem necessary in the interests of national defense . . . .

—President Harry S. Truman,
in Executive Order No. 10340,
April 8, 1952

[T]he use of the seizure technique to solve labor disputes in order to prevent work stoppages was not only unauthorized by any congressional enactment; prior to this controversy, Congress had refused to adopt that method of settling labor disputes. . . .

The order cannot properly be sustained as an exercise of the President's military power as Commander in Chief of the Armed Forces.

—Justice Hugo Black, for the
Court in the *Steel Seizure Case,*
June 2, 1952

161

NORTH KOREA'S INVASION of South Korea in 1950 alarmed the world community and led to concerted action by the United Nations, especially the United States. Many Americans opposed the massive commitment of U.S. troops, and challenged President Truman's constitutional authority to commit them. As is often the case, however, that issue never reached the courts. Instead, the major constitutional battle of the Korean War arose out of Truman's seizure of steel mills in 1952, in the face of a strike that could have impeded the war effort. The seizure gave rise to a seminal political, constitutional, and legal debate, focusing on the constitutional scope of the executive's power in an "emergency." This action became important because it helped to mark the perimeters of presidential authority, to define what was a "national emergency," and to assess the impact of such an emergency on the president's constitutional powers.

The North Koreans carried on their war against South Korea with massive support from the People's Republic of China and the Soviet Union, both of which were intent on expanding the Communist empire and blunting America's prestige. The Korean conflict, as President Truman correctly said, was part of the Cold War that the Communists launched after World War II when the open policy of the Soviet Union was to seek power everywhere. In Europe, Africa, Asia, and Latin America, the Soviet Union sent money, weapons, political agents, and surrogate troops in its drive to expand Communist power.

Clearly underlying the Korean War was the conflict not just between two great world powers, the United States and the Communist world, but between two fundamentally different ideas about how human beings should be governed. With "two Koreas," the world would soon see the graphic difference between a people divided on purely political lines: one part governed by Communist doctrine, the other by democratic concepts and a market economy. The result is that forty years later the per capita gross national product of South Korea is more than seven times that of its northern counterpart. Proportionally, the disparity between Taiwan and mainland China is even greater.

Truman seems to have decided that the sooner a check was put upon the Communists the better it would be not only for both world peace and prosperity but for the long-range interests of the United

States as well. But Truman decided that rather than acting through the Congress, of which he had once been a part, he would operate through the United Nations to check the Communists.

President Truman met with congressional leaders and proposed that the United States seek joint action with the United Nations to help defend South Korea, which could not defend itself effectively against the Communist forces. Congressional leaders acquiesced in Truman's program. Significantly, although Truman's party controlled Congress, Truman did not seek explicit war-making authority from Congress, as President George Bush did in the recent Gulf War.

Taking his case to the United Nations, Truman secured its approval to use force in the name of a United Nations order to check Communist North Korea's attack on South Korea. Truman placed General Douglas MacArthur in command and insisted that sending troops to Korea to implement the United Nations actions did not require a declaration of war inasmuch as it was a "police action" designed to thwart an "international bandit."

Had the police action succeeded as swiftly as the Gulf War in 1991, perhaps the country would have accepted this limited policy. But the Korean police action was prolonged and painful. By late 1950, only a few months into the war, it had become clear that Truman had underestimated what it would take to deal with North Korea's invasion. The massive miscalculations of the war potential of North Korea, supported by China and the Soviet Union, are clear in hindsight. The conflict far across the Pacific was to be a long and drawn-out one.

As the police action dragged on, it became the subject of heated debate in Congress and throughout the country. Military action in a continent far away so soon after World War II aroused increasingly bitter reactions. Senator Robert A. Taft of Ohio, who was a leading candidate for the Republican nomination for president in 1952, denounced the president's action as illegal. Other congressional leaders equivocated; some supported Truman, while others, including many influential Democrats, backed Taft's denunciation of going to war without a congressional declaration. With a national election looming, politics naturally entered into the picture. In 1952 members of the House of Representatives in particular, with a campaign for reelection only months away, were apprehensive about a "non-declared war," the duration and outcome of which had become far from certain. The police action was not popular among the voters, as was demonstrated in the fall of that year when Dwight Eisenhower won the presidency, based in part on his campaign pledge to "go to Korea" immediately upon his election—a masterful political stroke—and to "get us out of Korea."

Whatever its name, the Korean conflict was surely a war, and Truman was in a political box. Truman's police action policy became a great handicap when it was necessary to get the support of the Congress for a large-scale military operation, especially in far-away Asia. Once the Congress of the United States exercises its constitutional power "to declare War," an enormous momentum develops which almost ensures that the legislative branch will support the executive branch in whatever appears necessary to prosecute the war successfully. But in 1952, although Americans were fighting and dying just as they had in any declared war, Congress did not feel the same urge to support President Truman's police action. Truman obtained from Congress some authority over wages and prices, which experience had shown was needed in wartime. But Truman's political decision to have a "war without a war" left him with few options.

The steel industry posed a particular problem. The steel "sinews of war" were essential for the Korean conflict. But a dispute that had been brewing for some time threatened to interfere with steel production. Efforts to negotiate a wage settlement between the steel companies and the angry labor unions dragged on. The unions were ready to strike over wages and hours, Korea notwithstanding, and they declared their intention to do so on April 5, 1952. Truman decided quickly that seizing the steel mills and placing them under direct control of the federal government was the only way to avoid their closing by a strike. On April 8, 1952, he signed and issued Executive Order No. 10340 taking over the steel industry, which was to be operated under the direction of Secretary of Commerce Charles Sawyer.

Congressional reaction was heated. C. P. Trussell, a leading commentator for *The New York Times*, later noted that fifteen measures were introduced in a House Judiciary subcommittee "seek[ing] to impeach President Truman [or] to censure him," and a joint resolution was introduced to amend the Constitution to provide that "[t]he President shall not have power to seize or order the seizure of private property unless such action has been previously authorized or consented to by the Congress by statute or concurrent resolution." The legislative anger probably gave Truman little concern, because as a former senator he knew that Congress sometimes reacts viscerally to the executive's policies. But the president had more immediate concerns.

Lord Bryce once said that, sooner or later, all major political conflicts end up in the Supreme Court. Although that was not true of Truman's constitutional authority to prosecute the Korean War, it was true of his authority to seize the steel mills. The issue was ultimately settled by the Supreme Court in the case of *Youngstown Sheet & Tube Co. v. Sawyer.*

Within hours after Truman announced the seizure to a national television and radio audience on April 8, lawyers for the steel companies sought an injunction against the seizure in federal court. On April 29, the United States District Court in Washington, D.C., enjoined the seizure.

The case came to the High Court on direct appeal from the district court, making the length of time for the appeal relatively short. The Supreme Court stayed the effect of the district court's decision, thus temporarily leaving the steel mills in the hands of the government, and set the case for argument on May 12. Distinguished advocates represented both sides in the dispute. Youngstown Sheet & Tube Company and the other steel companies were represented by one of the foremost oral advocates of the twentieth century, John W. Davis. Davis was making his 139th argument before the Court—more than any other lawyer but two, one of whom was the great Daniel Webster. The United States was represented by Solicitor General Philip B. Perlman, who had served in that capacity for five years.

Media and political speculation flourished as the steel companies sped to the Supreme Court to make their case against the Truman administration. In 1950 the composition of the Supreme Court was the subject of much attention. Chief Justice Fred Vinson was a leading Democrat and a close friend and longtime political ally of Truman. He

had left the United States Court of Appeals for the District of Columbia Circuit to become director of the Office of Economic Stabilization
in 1943, and he had served as secretary of the treasury under Truman.
The senior associate justice, Hugo Black, had been a staunch Democrat
and an avid supporter of the New Deal in the Senate before Franklin D. Roosevelt put him on the Court. Justice Felix Frankfurter, next
in seniority, was another staunch Democrat and adviser to both Roosevelt and Truman. The next senior justice was William O. Douglas,
an ardent liberal Democrat, and after him was Robert H. Jackson,
who had served as solicitor general and attorney general under President Roosevelt. Harold Burton, a onetime Republican senator, had
been appointed to the Court by Truman, when the Court had none
but Democrats. Next in line was Justice Tom Clark, another leading
Democrat, who had also been attorney general under President Roosevelt; Justices Stanley Reed and Sherman Minton, both Democrats,
followed.

How would a Court with eight Democratic members and a former
Republican senator appointed by a Democratic president decide the
case? Many assumed, as Truman probably did, that they would back
Truman's executive order seizing the steel mills, thereby avoiding
steel-plant closings that would impede the police action effort. But the
Court proved the prognosticators wrong. The Court announced its
judgment on June 2, 1952, less than three months after Truman's
seizure order. The justices voted 6 to 3 against the president, which in
effect lifted the executive order and restored the steel mills to their
owners. Justice Black wrote the majority opinion, but, uncharacteristi-
cally, each of the other four justices who joined his opinion also wrote
concurring opinions. Justice Clark concurred only in the judgment,
not the reasoning of Justice Black's opinion for the Court or the other
justices' concurring opinions. Chief Justice Vinson wrote the opinion
for the three dissenters.

The vote made clear that with the Constitution in question, party
lines, personal friendships, and old loyalties were forgotten. As Arthur
Krock, the venerable *New York Times* columnist, noted at the time, of
those justices who joined the majority opinion, "five were controversial figures in partisan politics before they were appointed to the

court." Despite that, however, they had set a valuable nonpartisan precedent:

> The steel case has given rise to a Supreme Court decision far more important than the immediate production or non-production of steel. We have, in the opinion delivered by Justice Black yesterday and sustained by five other justices, a redefinition of the powers of the President. . . .
>
> The Court was faced by something more serious than the immediate controversy between the union and the steel companies. The issue was the balance of power between the legislative and the executive branches. . . .
>
> We need a balance of powers to keep ourselves both free and effective. The Supreme Court majority yesterday struck a blow for that balance.

Justice Black's majority opinion was terse and to the point, albeit perhaps less than clear on the constitutional issues. Black first noted that there was no statute authorizing the president's action, so "if the President had the authority to issue the order he did, it must be found in some provision of the Constitution." He then rejected reliance on the president's power as Commander in Chief and various other powers, and concluded that "[t]he Founders of this Nation entrusted the law-making power to the Congress alone in both good and bad times."

Justice Frankfurter's twenty-two-page concurring opinion, with another dozen pages of appendix, explained the result more fully than Justice Black's opinion. It was Frankfurter at his best, and must be regarded by jurists, lawyers, and historians as an important restatement of the relevant constitutional background. Frankfurter opened his concurring opinion with something of an essay on history and political science—to the delight of historians, no doubt. Frankfurter stated:

> A constitutional democracy like ours is perhaps the most difficult of man's social arrangements to manage successfully. Our scheme of society is more dependent than any other form of government on knowledge and wisdom and self-discipline for the achieve-

ment of its aims. For our democracy implies the reign of reason on the most extensive scale.

From that opening, Frankfurter went on:

> For the [Founding Fathers] the doctrine of separation of powers was not mere theory; it was a felt necessity. . . . The experience through which the world has passed in our own day has made vivid the realization that the Framers of our Constitution were not inexperienced doctrinaires. These long-headed statesmen had no illusion that our people enjoyed biological or psychological or sociological immunities from the hazards of concentrated power.

Frankfurter reminded his colleagues that when the wartime seizure of power conferred on the president during World War II expired on December 31, 1946, Congress explicitly declined to renew that authority. When it enacted the Labor Management Relations Act of 1947—the Taft-Hartley Act—Congress again declined, as Justice Black had written, "to adopt that method of settling labor disputes."

Justice Douglas' concurring opinion reflected some discomfort and suggested that the case was closer than Frankfurter had acknowledged. He began his opinion sympathetically to the president and paraphrased Chief Justice Hughes' enigmatic words in support of implied emergency powers in *Blaisdell*. Douglas wrote:

> There can be no doubt that the emergency which caused the President to seize these steel plants was one that bore heavily on the country. But the emergency did not create power; it merely marked an occasion when power should be exercised.

The question for Douglas was, who should exercise that power—the president or Congress? Noting that the executive and legislative powers of the government were placed in different branches, in the words of Justice Louis D. Brandeis, "not to promote efficiency but to preclude the exercise of arbitrary power," Douglas forcefully stated his long-held opposition to arbitrary power:

We therefore cannot decide this case by determining which branch of government can deal most expeditiously with the present crisis. The answer must depend on the allocation of powers under the Constitution. That in turn requires an analysis of the conditions giving rise to the seizure and of the seizure itself.

Considering those factors, Douglas concluded that the power to seize the steel mills was legislative, and so had to be authorized by Congress.

Justice Jackson's concurring opinion contained an extensive treatment of the history of presidential exercises of emergency powers. He brushed off Truman's claim that other presidents had made comparable seizures without congressional approval. That some presidents had gotten away with it was no basis for a claim of true constitutional power. Jackson referred to Jefferson's unilateral execution of the Louisiana Purchase. Jackson might well have noted that Jefferson himself later acknowledged that he had neither constitutional nor legislative authority for that historic act. Jefferson, it will be remembered, wrote with respect to the purchase of the Louisiana Territory that sometimes a leader must in effect "rise above the law" in the national interest. For Jackson's purposes, however, it was enough to note that the Louisiana Purchase concerned not the allocation of powers between Congress and the president—the purchase was accomplished by a treaty ratified by the Senate—but rather whether the Constitution authorized the national government to expand the nation's boundaries. Jackson concluded his opinion with a realistic statement of how a democratic government really works:

> With all its defects, delays and inconveniences, men have discovered no technique for long preserving free government except that the Executive be under the law, and that the law be made by parliamentary deliberations.

In his concurring opinion, Justice Burton, the only Republican on the Court, pointed to the failure of the president to use the eighty-day-injunction provisions of the 1947 Taft-Hartley Act. Justice Clark, in his opinion concurring in the Court's judgment, also emphasized the failure to comply with various laws that touched on the labor crisis and the steel mills:

> [T]he hard fact remains that neither the Defense Production Act nor Taft–Hartley authorized the seizure challenged here, and the Government made no effort to comply with the procedures established by the Selective Service Act of 1948, a statute which expressly authorizes seizures when producers fail to supply necessary defense matériel.

Justice Clark did not, however, as readily as the majority reject the existence of implied emergency powers. He stated:

> [T]he Constitution does grant to the President extensive authority in times of grave and imperative national emergency. In fact, to my thinking, such a grant may well be necessary to the very existence of the Constitution itself.

In Justice Clark's view, however, "the President's independent power to act depends on the gravity of the situation confronting the nation." Does this mean that if General MacArthur's armies were being pushed into the sea, Clark might have gone along with Truman's order? His emphasis on Truman's failure to use the statutory tools at his disposal suggests not, but as we have seen in previous chapters, circumstances, timing, and the cold facts as well as the law can play a role in judicial decision making—even on constitutional issues.

In a forty-four-page dissent, Chief Justice Vinson was joined by Justices Reed and Minton. All three had extensive experience in government: Vinson and Minton had been close associates of Truman in Congress; Vinson had been a major force in Truman's White House as well; and Reed had been solicitor general and was almost a career man in government. The essence of Vinson's dissent emerges in the opening statement:

> Those who suggest that this is a case involving extraordinary powers should be mindful that these are extraordinary times. A world not yet recovered from the devastation of World War II has

been forced to face the threat of another and more terrifying global conflict.

He added his fear that the supply of steel for arms in Korea might otherwise be cut off, pointing out that Secretary of Defense Lovett in testimony before Congress had stated that "a work stoppage in the steel industry will result immediately in serious curtailment of production of essential weapons and munitions of all kinds."

In the obvious frustration of a man who sat at the elbow of a wartime president, the Chief Justice added:

> Accordingly, if the President has any power under the Constitution to meet a critical situation in the absence of express statutory authorization, there is no basis whatever for criticizing the exercise of such power in this case.

To bolster his case, he offered a dramatic example from World War II:

> Some six months before Pearl Harbor, a dispute at a single aviation plant at Inglewood, California, interrupted a segment of the production of military aircraft. In spite of the comparative insignificance of this work stoppage to total defense production as contrasted with the complete paralysis now threatened by a shutdown of the entire basic steel industry, and even though our armed forces were not then engaged in combat, President Roosevelt ordered the seizure of the plant "pursuant to the powers vested in him by the Constitution and laws of the United States, as President of the United States of America and Commander in Chief of the Army and Navy of the United States."

Chief Justice Vinson reminded his colleague Justice Jackson, who had been President Roosevelt's attorney general at the time of that incident, that Jackson had argued that the president had the moral duty to keep the nation's defense effort going. The Chief Justice made it equally clear that Jackson's moral justification of President Roosevelt's actions had been coupled with "a legal justification equally well stated." He quoted Jackson's opinion as attorney general:

"The Presidential proclamation rests upon the aggregate of the Presidential powers derived from the Constitution itself and from statutes enacted by the Congress.

"The Constitution lays upon the President the duty 'to take care that the laws be faithfully executed.' . . . For the faithful execution of such laws the President has back of him not only each general law-enforcement power conferred by the various acts of Congress but the aggregate of all such laws plus that wide discretion as to method vested in him by the Constitution for the purpose of executing the laws.

"The Constitution also places on the President the responsibility and vests in him the powers of Commander in Chief of the Army and of the Navy. . . . [T]he implication is clear that he should not allow [the Nation] to become paralyzed by failure to obtain supplies for which Congress has appropriated the money and which it has directed the President to obtain."

Aiming at both Justices Jackson and Clark, Vinson noted that their views on presidential power as attorneys general would have supported President Roosevelt's authority to seize properties of Montgomery Ward throughout the country even though that company was only "a retail department store and mail-order concern," not an instrument of wartime production. Vinson also cited with approval Chief Justice Hughes' dubious language in *Home Building & Loan Association* v. *Blaisdell*, discussed in the previous chapter: "While emergency does not create power, emergency may furnish the occasion for the exercise of power." Just how a power not created could provide a basis for the "exercise of power," Chief Justice Hughes never explained, and Chief Justice Vinson did not fill that void.

Vinson concluded his dissent by stating that President Truman had authority to issue the executive order seizing the steel mills:

The diversity of views expressed in the six opinions of the majority, the lack of reference to authoritative precedent, the repeated reliance upon prior dissenting opinions, the complete disregard of the uncontroverted facts showing the gravity of the emergency and the temporary nature of the taking all serve to demonstrate how far afield one must go to affirm the order of the District Court.

The *Steel Seizure Case* has been the subject of at least one book, many articles, and much political debate over the years. It aroused strong feelings at the time. In deciding the case, the Supreme Court laid down no great new principle of constitutional law but merely re-peated some well-established propositions. Qualified observers see this case as being closer than those in the majority indicated. Vinson in his strong, bitter opinion should not be seen as a jurist whose loyalty ran to his old friend in the White House. Rather, he was writing as a jurist who, like Chief Justice Hughes, knew intimately the pressures of exec-utive decision making from his years as an "assistant to the president." Vinson knew the pressures of presidential decision making in a crisis, and he believed the Constitution should be interpreted to reflect that urgent necessity. One must wonder whether Vinson would have been writing for the majority if, as mentioned, General MacArthur's armies were being pushed into the sea.

In all, this case illustrates vividly that the Constitution, remarkable as it is, fails to sharply define and limit separation of powers in a man-ner that would cover every contingency. In the words of Chief Justice Marshall, it establishes only the "great outlines." It did, however, cre-ate a structure that can adapt to the stresses of crises, not always effi-ciently and smoothly but in a way that leaves "elbow room" to those who must act in times of crisis. The extent of that elbow room is left to be determined through the system of checks and balances among the three branches of government.

In retrospect, Truman's perception of the world political scene was more accurate than that of the Congress, but his interpretation of the Constitution was flawed. The president nevertheless kept his pledge to abide by whatever the Court decided. Before the Court had adjourned for the day, Truman wrote to Secretary Sawyer:

Dear Mr. Secretary:

In view of today's decision by the Supreme Court, you are hereby directed to take appropriate steps to relinquish immediately possession of plants, facilities, and other property of the steel companies which have been in the possession of the Government under Executive Order No. 10340 of April 8, 1952.

Short of openly defying the Supreme Court, President Truman had no choice: it was so ordered.

EPILOGUE

....

T HE CASES REVIEWED in this book offer a quick sketch, albeit in-
complete, of the evolution of the Supreme Court and help explain how it reached its present position in American life as the
interpreter and defender of the United States Constitution. The cases
also show how the Court established the judiciary as a co-equal branch
of our government. An underlying theme is the emergence of John
Marshall's vision for America as he spelled it out in the first thirty years
of his unparalleled thirty-four-year tenure as Chief Justice. In the view
of some commentators, Marshall is identified as a "conservative." But,
surprisingly, it was actually Jefferson, the "liberal," who was the "strict
constructionist" and hence more "conservative" in some respects in his
interpretation of the powers of both the Congress and the president
under the Constitution. It was Jefferson, for example, who twice
strongly opposed the creation of a national bank because there was no
express provision for such an institution in the Constitution.

In its two-hundred-year history, the Court reached its high point
under Marshall, and its nadir following *Dred Scott* and *Plessy* v. *Ferguson*. The Court experienced a rise in public esteem beginning with
Chief Justice Taft, and its reputation continued to improve with some
noteworthy cases in this century, such as the *Steel Seizure Case*. Marshall's major opinions demonstrate that he viewed the Constitution not
only as a limit on the powers of the federal government but also as a
guide to their exercise. In his view, the brevity of the Constitution revealed the draftsmen's intent to rely on powers that could reasonably
be implied from the express language of the document. This broad

view of implied powers disturbed men like Patrick Henry and George Mason and led them to demand that a "harness" be placed on national power in the form of a Bill of Rights. It also explains the basis for the demand of Mason and others for the Tenth Amendment, limiting federal powers vis-à-vis the states. Although James Madison and others sitting in Philadelphia thought that such limits were unnecessary because the Constitution created a government of expressly delegated powers and any powers not delegated were reserved to the states and the people, that principle was later written into the Bill of Rights and stands today, even if it is not often relied upon.

Young John Marshall, an active participant in the 1788 Virginia ratification convention, had no problems with the addition of a Bill of Rights, including the Ninth Amendment, which provides that the enumeration of certain rights in the Constitution does not "deny or disparage others retained by the people," and the Tenth Amendment, which provides that powers that the Constitution neither gives to the federal government nor denies to the states "are reserved to the States respectively, or to the people." It is an interesting footnote to history that Madison also proposed what would have been the Second Amendment, limiting the power of Congress to increase the salaries of its members. It was ratified by only six states at the time and sat in the files for two hundred and three years before the necessary three fourths of the states, now thirty-eight out of fifty, ratified it in 1992, making it the Twenty-Seventh Amendment to the Constitution.

When the principle of judicial review of congressional acts was confirmed in *Marbury* v. *Madison* in 1803, following on the 1796 decision in *Ware* v. *Hylton*, which involved judicial review of state legislation, the Marshall Court positioned itself to guard against encroachments on the Constitution and the authority of the federal government by either Congress or the states. These decisions helped make possible the unparalleled economic growth and development that took place in the early years of the young republic. Marshall's opinion in the *Dartmouth College* case in 1819 made clear to the world that the Contract Clause of the Constitution meant what it said, and that states could not tamper with contract rights. The Court's decision stimulated interstate and international trade and commerce and the nation's businesses prospered. That same year Marshall's opinion in *M'Culloch* v. *Maryland* broadly interpreted the Necessary and Proper Clause. By sustaining the constitutionality of the national bank and limiting the states' power to tax a federal instrumentality, the Supreme Court greatly strengthened the foundation for a stable economy. In the Necessary and Proper Clause Marshall found "the supple tool of power," in the words of Justice Oliver Wendell Holmes a century later. Then, in 1824, Marshall's opinion in *Gibbons* v. *Ogden* made clear that states could not employ protectionist measures that hampered interstate transportation and commerce, allowing Alexander Hamilton's genius and America's "common market" to bear rich fruit.

Seen through the eyes of Thomas Jefferson and the early anti-Federalist Republicans, many of these cases were examples of judicial legislation. But from Hamilton's and the Federalists' point of view—a point of view clearly shared by Chief Justice Marshall—the best way to promote the development of commerce was to eliminate barriers to trade. As the Constitution contemplated, commerce demanded more roads and more canals as well as a national monetary policy and a stable currency, objectives that were promoted by the national bank Jefferson opposed.

It is difficult to reconcile the strict constructionist views of Jefferson—which were essentially conservative—with the broad outlook that led him to consummate the Louisiana Purchase in 1803 and to send Lewis and Clark on their pioneering exploration of the Northwest. Jefferson, of course, viewed the Louisiana Purchase as beyond his constitutional power—but necessary.

Although the Federalist and the early anti-Federalist Republican views toward commerce and other issues differed, it is clear beyond doubt that there was virtual unanimity among the Founding Fathers that matters such as public education and intrastate roads should be funded and controlled by state and local governments. Jefferson and his early Republicans were even more determined to limit federal power. They feared that if the national government "funded" what was thought of as a state and local responsibility, federal control would follow the dollars. Only in the twentieth century was that fear realized.

A shift in the distribution of powers in our federal structure—a flow of more, and at times excess, power to Washington—came about as the result of two pivotal events in our history: the Civil War and the

Great Depression. Prior to the Civil War, states' rights were at the forefront of the concerns of Southern leaders. But that view was a thin cover for the underlying issue of the day—slavery. In the mid-nineteenth century, this country was deeply divided over slavery. Neither the Congress, the president, nor the Supreme Court could resolve the issue to the satisfaction of both the North and the South. Indeed, it was not long before the outbreak of hostilities between North and South that the Court rendered perhaps the most infamous decision in its history—*Dred Scott.* The decision was obviously popular among those who supported slavery, but for those who opposed it, the decision was completely unacceptable. It was an abandonment by the Court of the noble principles of the Declaration of Independence.

With the election of Abraham Lincoln as president in 1860, it soon became clear that the issues of slavery and state sovereignty would be resolved only through war. After America suffered four bloody years of Civil War, the Constitution was amended to abolish slavery. The modern concept of federalism began to emerge through the national government's increased involvement in affairs, such as civil rights, within the confines of the individual states.

Federal power was sharply expanded in the 1930s when the greatest worldwide depression in modern history vaulted Franklin D. Roosevelt to the presidency. When Roosevelt sent proposed legislative programs to Congress, he frequently urged Congress to lay aside any concerns about constitutionality to "get the job done." Legislation like the National Industrial Recovery Act, the Public Works Act, and other sweeping emergency measures were products of this sentiment. And the hungry, unemployed people and impoverished farmers gave no thought to whether the legislation violated the Constitution—as some of it surely did. One of the cases discussed—*Home Building & Loan Association* v. *Blaisdell*—illustrates this. The Roosevelt Revolution was a response of a people not noted for their patience with adverse economic and social conditions.

Roosevelt's improvisations in the interests of "getting the job done," rather than any grand philosophical plan, significantly altered our concepts of federalism and brushed aside one hundred and fifty years of tradition. Ironically, that tradition included old attitudes on the limits on government that had been advocated by Jefferson, the spiritual founder of the modern Democratic party. Faced with the crisis of the Great Depression and then World War II, Roosevelt, a president proclaiming himself a dedicated follower of Jefferson's, ultimately rejected Jefferson's idea of limited national government and narrow construction of constitutional powers, and instead adopted Jefferson's Louisiana Purchase approach, so that for fifty years after the New Deal, this country has practiced a form of federalism that Jefferson in his day would have loathed.

Looking back on history, it is clear that not only Jefferson but also Washington, Madison, and Marshall—but Marshall less so—would have been shocked by the expansion of federal authority that has evolved. Even though Marshall made the broad sweep of the Commerce Clause clear in *Gibbons* v. *Ogden*, when he stated that "[t]he power over commerce, including navigation, was one of the primary objects for which the people of America adopted their government," he certainly did not envision the day when Congress exercised control, directly or indirectly, over the financing of schools, the building of intrastate highways, the construction of public housing, and the working conditions in local businesses, among many other things. Yet for half a century it has been commonplace for governors and mayors alike to go begging for funds from Congress. Marshall's view of the Necessary and Proper Clause would have made it easier to accept these changes.

Our Founding Fathers would surely recognize—if they were here today—that changes in transportation, travel, and communications have placed some of our problems in a very different light. When Marshall postulated his concept of a "living Constitution," he could not have foreseen the advent of radio, television, airplanes, video recorders, and more recently, personal computers and the fax machine—but he left the door open. These changes have added to the complexity of the problems faced by this country since the 1930s and have also led to a consolidation of powers in Washington. The result is that the national government has, in some respects, become the "monster" that virtually all the eighteenth-century leaders opposed and feared. This modern conception of federalism would be anathema to the Founders, especially to Jefferson.

Even with the weaknesses in our federal system, it is nothing short of a miracle that America has become the nation that it is in such a short period of time. Only two hundred years ago, our new nation was forged from thirteen independent, truly sovereign states. In one broad constitutional sweep, the fragmentation—or, as is particularly appropriate today given the situation in the former Yugoslavia, the "balkanization"—of the United States was avoided. We owe our swift success in large part to those who drafted our Constitution and particularly to Marshall, who saw its potential. In the Constitution the Founders conceived of a new and workable system, not perfect by any means, but better than anything that had gone before. Washington, the revered leader; Madison, the architect; Hamilton, the technician and economist; and Marshall, the shaper and teacher, gave meaning to it all. Henry Steele Commager's statement again comes to mind: "Nothing in all history . . . ever succeeded like America . . . ." Despite its problems, America became and remains a model for people the world over.

The unfolding of recent events in Eastern Europe makes clear that, with all of their genius, the Founders' task was aided by a number of factors. The three million people who inhabited the colonies during the revolutionary era were not burdened with centuries of ancient ethnic and religious conflicts. They spoke a common language, shared common religious beliefs, and had nearly two hundred years of experience with town meetings, practicing democracy at the local level. They left the ancient conflicts behind when they left the "old country."

The emerging democracies of the former Soviet republics and Eastern Europe, on the other hand, freed from the heavy hand of Moscow and the KGB, have far greater burdens than were encountered by the thirteen former colonies from 1776 to 1787. The people of the former Soviet republics lack the common bonds shared by the peoples who inhabited the eastern edge of the American continent. Following the "Gorbachev-Yeltsin Revolution," for example, the world has witnessed extreme and deadly violence within the republic of Georgia and between the republics of Armenia and Azerbaijan, with the roots of these conflicts dating back centuries. With the fear of Communist repression removed, the ancient and long-suppressed ethnic and religious prejudices of the people of these countries have erupted again.

These tumultuous events are the latest reminder that the form of government envisioned by the Founding Fathers has led to remarkable political stability and economic prosperity in this country. Part of that system of government is the structured process the Constitution created for resolving conflicts, patterned on what England's and the colonies' common law had taught. As our courts developed, certain rules reflecting fundamental values became codified as the law of the land. Certain rights were confirmed as "unalienable." Americans generally accept the idea that the judiciary, and the Supreme Court in particular, has the responsibility of saying what those rules mean.

Some of the Supreme Court's decisions inevitably have been wrong. The Supreme Court has the final word on what the law means, but justices are human and their collective word has not always been correct. In cases like *Blaisdell*, for example, the Supreme Court ratified many state and federal emergency measures that led to our present form of federalism. Historians might well draw the conclusion that the Supreme Court at times has assumed a legislative role to meet what it perceives to be "crises" or "emergencies" that are not susceptible to prompt political resolution or that have occasioned defaults or errors by the political branches. *Blaisdell*, by failing to follow the Constitution's Contract Clause as construed in the *Dartmouth College* case, gave support to the view that the Court sometimes indulged in "judicial legislation"—to meet an emergency.

Other cases such as *Dred Scott* and *Plessy* constitute further evidence that the Supreme Court is not infallible. One cannot look back and see the egregious errors of the Supreme Court, few as they have been, without expressing some concern about "who will watch the watchman?" Who reviews the nine justices when they interpret the Constitution? In his dissenting opinion in *United States* v. *Butler* in 1936, Chief Justice Harlan Fiske Stone reminded his colleagues that "while unconstitutional exercise of power by the executive and legislative branches of the government is subject to judicial restraint, the only check upon our own exercise of power is our own sense of self-restraint." For the most part, that check has performed extraordinarily well for two centuries.

In the end, given that self-restraint is in large measure the only check upon the Supreme Court, it is even more remarkable that the manifest errors of the Court have been so few. The one hundred and eight justices who over the past two hundred years have drafted numerous distinguished opinions, working within the framework of judicial self-restraint, have brought the Court back from the depths of *Dred Scott* and *Plessy*. One cannot fully appreciate the significant decisions the Court has rendered, however, without understanding the setting within which those decisions were made. It is my hope that the stories in this book will have given the reader some insight into the Court and the justices whose task it has been to give meaning to the Constitution.

CASES CITED

....

Boyce v. *Anderson*, 27 U.S. (2 Pet.) 150 (1829)

Bracken v. *Visitors of William & Mary College*, 7 Va. (3 Call) 495 (1790)

Brown v. *Board of Education*, 347 U.S. 483 (1954)

Brown v. *Maryland*, 25 U.S. (12 Wheat.) 419 (1827)

Civil Rights Cases, 109 U.S. 3 (1883)

The Daniel Ball, 77 U.S. (10 Wall.) 557 (1871)

Dred Scott v. *Sandford*, 60 U.S. (19 How.) 393 (1857)

Gibbons v. *Ogden*, 22 U.S. (9 Wheat.) 1 (1824)

Home Building & Loan Association v. *Blaisdell*, 290 U.S. 398 (1934)

Marbury v. *Madison*, 5 U.S. (1 Cranch) 137 (1803)

M'Culloch v. *Maryland*, 17 U.S. (4 Wheat.) 316 (1819)

Near v. *Minnesota ex rel. Olson*, 283 U.S. 697 (1931)

Patterson v. *Colorado ex rel. Attorney General*, 205 U.S. 454 (1907)

Plessy v. *Ferguson*, 163 U.S. 537 (1896)

Scott v. *Emerson*, 15 Mo. 576 (1852)

Slaughter-House Cases, 83 U.S. (16 Wall.) 36 (1873)

Strader v. *Graham*, 51 U.S. (10 How.) 82 (1851)

Stuart v. *Laird*, 5 U.S. (1 Cranch) 299 (1803)

Terrett v. *Taylor*, 13 U.S. (9 Cranch) 43 (1815)

Trustees of Dartmouth College v. *Woodward*, 17 U.S. (4 Wheat.) 518 (1819)

United States v. *Aaron Burr*, 25 F. Cas. 30 (C.C.D. Va. 1807) (No. 14,692d)

United States v. *Butler*, 297 U.S. 1 (1936)

United States v. *Fisher*, 6 U.S. (2 Cranch) 358 (1805)

United States v. *Smith and Ogden*, 27 F. Cas. 1192 (C.C.D.N.Y. 1806) (No. 16,342)

Ware v. *Hylton*, 3 U.S. (3 Dall.) 199 (1796)

Youngstown Sheet & Tube Co. v. *Sawyer*, 343 U.S. 579 (1952)

THE DECLARATION OF INDEPENDENCE

Action of Second Continental Congress, July 4, 1776

The unanimous Declaration of the thirteen United States of America

WHEN in the Course of human Events, it becomes necessary for one People to dissolve the Political Bands which have connected them with another, and to assume among the Powers of the Earth, the separate and equal Station to which the Laws of Nature and of Nature's God entitle them, a decent Respect to the Opinions of Mankind requires that they should declare the causes which impel them to the Separation.

WE hold these Truths to be self-evident, that all Men are created equal, that they are endowed by their Creator with certain unalienable Rights, that among these are Life, Liberty, and the Pursuit of Happiness—That to secure these Rights, Governments are instituted among Men, deriving their just Powers from the Consent of the Governed, that whenever any Form of Government becomes destructive of these Ends, it is the Right of the People to alter or to abolish it, and to institute new Government, laying its Foundation on such Principles, and organizing its Powers in such Form, as to them shall seem most likely to effect their Safety and Happiness. Prudence, indeed, will dictate that Governments long established should not be changed for light and transient Causes; and accordingly all Experience hath shewn, that Mankind are more disposed to suffer, while Evils are sufferable, than to right themselves by abolishing the Forms to which they are accus-

tomed. But when a long Train of Abuses and Usurpations, pursuing in-
variably the same Object, evinces a Design to reduce them under absolute Despotism, it is their Right, it is their Duty, to throw off such
Government, and to provide new Guards for their future Security.
Such has been the patient Sufferance of these Colonies; and such is
now the Necessity which constrains them to alter their former Systems
of Government. The History of the present King of Great-Britain is a
History of repeated Injuries and Usurpations, all having in direct Object the Establishment of an absolute Tyranny over these States. To
prove this, let Facts be submitted to a candid World.

HE has refused his Assent to Laws, the most wholesome and necessary for the public Good.

HE has forbidden his Governors to pass Laws of immediate and
pressing Importance, unless suspended in their Operation till his Assent
should be obtained; and when so suspended, he has utterly neglected to
attend to them.

HE has refused to pass other Laws for the Accommodation of large
Districts of People, unless those People would relinquish the Right of
Representation in the Legislature, a Right inestimable to them, and
formidable to Tyrants only.

HE has called together Legislative Bodies at Places unusual, un-
comfortable, and distant from the Depository of their public Records,
for the sole Purpose of fatiguing them into Compliance with his
Measures.

HE has dissolved Representative Houses repeatedly, for opposing with manly Firmness his Invasions on the Rights of the
People.

HE has refused for a long Time, after such Dissolutions, to cause
others to be elected; whereby the Legislative Powers, incapable of An-
nihilation, have returned to the People at large for their exercise; the
State remaining in the mean time exposed to all the Dangers of Invasion from without, and Convulsions within.

HE has endeavoured to prevent the Population of these States; for
that Purpose obstructing the Laws for Naturalization of Foreigners; refusing to pass others to encourage their Migrations hither, and raising
the Conditions of new Appropriations of Lands.

HE has obstructed the Administration of Justice, by refusing his Assent to Laws for establishing Judiciary Powers.

HE has made Judges dependent on his Will alone, for the Tenure of their Offices, and the Amount and Payment of their Salaries.

HE has erected a Multitude of new Offices, and sent hither Swarms of Officers to harrass our People, and eat out their Substance.

HE has kept among us, in Times of Peace, Standing Armies, without the consent of our Legislatures.

HE has affected to render the Military independent of and superior to the Civil Power.

HE has combined with others to subject us to a Jurisdiction foreign to our Constitution, and unacknowledged by our Laws; giving his Assent to their Acts of pretended Legislation:

FOR quartering large Bodies of Armed Troops among us:

FOR protecting them, by a mock Trial, from Punishment for any Murders which they should commit on the Inhabitants of these States:

FOR cutting off our Trade with all Parts of the World:

FOR imposing Taxes on us without our Consent:

FOR depriving us, in many Cases, of the Benefits of Trial by Jury:

FOR transporting us beyond Seas to be tried for pretended Offences:

FOR abolishing the free System of English Laws in a neighbouring Province, establishing therein an arbitrary Government, and enlarging its Boundaries, so as to render it at once an Example and fit Instrument for introducing the same absolute Rule into these Colonies:

FOR taking away our Charters, abolishing our most valuable Laws, and altering fundamentally the Forms of our Governments:

FOR suspending our own Legislatures, and declaring themselves invested with Power to legislate for us in all Cases whatsoever.

HE has abdicated Government here, by declaring us out of his Protection and waging War against us.

HE has plundered our Seas, ravaged our Coasts, burnt our Towns, and destroyed the Lives of our People.

HE is, at this Time, transporting large Armies of foreign Mercenaries to compleat the Works of Death, Desolation, and Tyranny, already begun with circumstances of Cruelty and Perfidy, scarcely paralleled in the most barbarous Ages, and totally unworthy the Head of a civilized Nation.

HE has constrained our fellow Citizens taken Captive on the high Seas to bear Arms against their Country, to become the Executioners of their Friends and Brethren, or to fall themselves by their Hands.

HE has excited domestic Insurrections amongst us, and has endeavoured to bring on the Inhabitants of our Frontiers, the merciless Indian Savages, whose known Rule of Warfare, is an undistinguished Destruction, of all Ages, Sexes and Conditions.

IN every stage of these Oppressions we have Petitioned for Redress in the most humble Terms: Our repeated Petitions have been answered only by repeated Injury. A Prince, whose Character is thus marked by every act which may define a Tyrant, is unfit to be the Ruler of a free People.

NOR have we been wanting in Attentions to our British Brethren. We have warned them from Time to Time of Attempts by their Legislature to extend an unwarrantable Jurisdiction over us. We have reminded them of the Circumstances of our Emigration and Settlement here. We have appealed to their native Justice and Magnanimity, and we have conjured them by the Ties of our common Kindred to disavow these Usurpations, which, would inevitably interrupt our Connections and Correspondence. They too have been deaf to the Voice of Justice and of Consanguinity. We must, therefore, acquiesce in the Necessity, which denounces our Separation, and hold them, as we hold the rest of Mankind, Enemies in War, in Peace, Friends.

WE, therefore, the Representatives of the UNITED STATES OF AMERICA, in GENERAL CONGRESS, Assembled, appealing to the Supreme Judge of the World for the Rectitude of our Intentions, do, in the Name, and by Authority of the good People of these Colonies, solemnly Publish and Declare, That these United Colonies are, and of Right ought to be, FREE AND INDEPENDENT STATES; that they are absolved from all Allegiance to the British Crown, and that all political Connection between them and the State of Great-Britain, is and ought to be totally dissolved; and that as FREE AND INDEPENDENT STATES, they have full Power to levy War, conclude Peace, contract Alliances, establish Commerce, and to do all other Acts and Things which INDE-PENDENT STATES may of right do. And for the support of this Declaration, with a firm Reliance on the Protection of divine Providence, we mutually pledge to each other our Lives, our Fortunes, and our sacred Honor.

JOHN HANCOCK

New Hampshire

JOSIAH BARTLETT,   MATTHEW THORNTON.
WM. WHIPPLE,

Massachusetts Bay

SAML. ADAMS,   ROBT. TREAT PAINE,
JOHN ADAMS,   ELBRIDGE GERRY.

Rhode Island

STEP. HOPKINS,   WILLIAM ELLERY.

Connecticut

ROGER SHERMAN,   WM. WILLIAMS,
SAM'EL HUNTINGTON,   OLIVER WOLCOTT.

New York

WM. FLOYD,   FRANS. LEWIS,
PHIL. LIVINGSTON,   LEWIS MORRIS.

New Jersey

RICHD. STOCKTON,   JOHN HART,
JNO. WITHERSPOON,   ABRA. CLARK.
FRANS. HOPKINSON,

Pennsylvania

ROBT. MORRIS,   JAS. SMITH,
BENJAMIN RUSH,   GEO. TAYLOR,
BENJA. FRANKLIN,   JAMES WILSON,
JOHN MORTON,   GEO. ROSS.
GEO. CLYMER,

Delaware

CAESAR RODNEY,   THO. M'KEAN.
GEO. READ,

Maryland

SAMUEL CHASE,   CHARLES CARROLL OF
WM. PACA,   Carrollton.
THOS. STONE,

Virginia

GEORGE WYTHE,   THOS, NELSON, JR.,
RICHARD HENRY LEE, FRANCIS LIGHTFOOT
TH. JEFFERSON,   LEE,
BENJA. HARRISON,   CARTER BRAXTON.

North Carolina

WM. HOOPER,   JOHN PENN.
JOSEPH HEWES,

South Carolina

THOS. HEYWARD,   THOMAS LYNCH, JUNR.,
 JUNR.,
EDWARD RUTLEDGE,   ARTHUR MIDDLETON.

Georgia

BUTTON GWINNETT,   GEO. WALTON.
LYMAN HALL,

THE ARTICLES OF CONFEDERATION

To all to whom these Presents shall come, we the undersigned Delegates of the States affixed to our Names send greeting

Whereas the Delegates of the United States of America in Congress assembled did on the fifteenth day of November in the Year of our Lord One Thousand Seven Hundred and Seventyseven, and in the Second Year of the Independence of America agree to certain articles of Confederation and perpetual Union between the States of Newhampshire, Massachusettsbay, Rhodeisland and Providence Plantations, Connecticut, New York, New Jersey, Pennsylvania, Delaware, Maryland, Virginia, North-Carolina, South-Carolina and Georgia in the Words following, viz.

"Articles of Confederation and perpetual Union between the States of Newhampshire, Massachusettsbay, Rhodeisland and Providence Plantations, Connecticut, New-York, New-Jersey, Pennsylvania, Delaware, Maryland, Virginia, North-Carolina, South-Carolina and Georgia.

ARTICLE I. The stile of this confederacy shall be "The United States of America."

ARTICLE II. Each State retains its sovereignty, freedom and independence, and every power, jurisdiction and right, which is not by this confederation expressly delegated to the United States, in Congress assembled.

ARTICLE III. The said States hereby severally enter into a firm league of friendship with each other, for their common defence, the security of their liberties, and their mutual and general welfare, binding

191

themselves to assist each other, against all force offered to, or attacks made upon them, or any of them, on account of religion, sovereignty, trade, or any other pretence whatever.

ARTICLE IV. The better to secure and perpetuate mutual friendship and intercourse among the people of the different States in this Union, the free inhabitants of each of these States, paupers, vagabonds and fugitives from justice excepted, shall be entitled to all privileges and immunities of free citizens in the several States; and the people of each State shall have free ingress and regress to and from any other State, and shall enjoy therein all the privileges of trade and commerce, subject to the same duties, impositions and restrictions as the inhabitants thereof respectively, provided that such restrictions shall not extend so far as to prevent the removal of property imported into any State, to any other State of which the owner is an inhabitant; provided also that no imposition, duties or restriction shall be laid by any State, on the property of the United States, or either of them.

If any person guilty of, or charged with treason, felony, or other high misdemeanor in any State, shall flee from justice, and be found in any of the United States, he shall upon demand of the Governor or Executive power, of the State from which he fled, be delivered up and removed to the State having jurisdiction of his offence.

Full faith and credit shall be given in each of these States to the records, acts and judicial proceedings of the courts and magistrates of every other State.

ARTICLE V. For the more convenient management of the general interests of the United States, delegates shall be annually appointed in such manner as the legislature of each State shall direct, to meet in Congress on the first Monday in November, in every year, with a power reserved to each State, to recall its delegates, or any of them, at any time within the year, and to send others in their stead, for the remainder of the year.

No State shall be represented in Congress by less than two, nor by more than seven members; and no person shall be capable of being a delegate for more than three years in any term of six years; nor shall any person, being a delegate, be capable of holding any office under the United States, for which he, or another for his benefit receives any salary, fees or emolument of any kind.

Each State shall maintain its own delegates in a meeting of the States, and while they act as members of the committee of the States.

In determining questions in the United States, in Congress assembled, each State shall have one vote.

Freedom of speech and debate in Congress shall not be impeached or questioned in any court, or place out of Congress, and the members of Congress shall be protected in their persons from arrests and imprisonments, during the time of their going to and from, and attendance on Congress, except for treason, felony, or breach of the peace.

ARTICLE VI. No State without the consent of the United States in Congress assembled, shall send any embassy to, or receive any embassy from, or enter into any conference, agreement, alliance or treaty with any king, prince or state; nor shall any person holding any office of profit or trust under the United States, or any of them, accept of any present, emolument, office or title of any kind whatever from any king, prince or foreign state; nor shall the United States in Congress assembled, or any of them, grant any title of nobility.

No two or more States shall enter into any treaty, confederation or alliance whatever between them, without the consent of the United States in Congress assembled, specifying accurately the purposes for which the same is to be entered into, and how long it shall continue.

No State shall lay any imposts or duties, which may interfere with any stipulations in treaties, entered into by the United States in Congress assembled, with any king, prince or state, in pursuance of any treaties already proposed by Congress, to the courts of France and Spain.

No vessels of war shall be kept up in time of peace by any State, except such number only, as shall be deemed necessary by the United States in Congress assembled, for the defence of such State, or its trade; nor shall any body of forces be kept up by any State, in time of peace, except such number only, as in the judgment of the United States, in Congress assembled, shall be deemed requisite to garrison the forts necessary for the defence of such State; but every State shall always keep up a well regulated and disciplined militia, sufficiently armed and accoutered, and shall provide and constantly have ready for use, in public stores, a due number of field pieces and tents, and a proper quantity of arms, ammunition and camp equipage.

No State shall engage in any war without the consent of the United States in Congress assembled, unless such State be actually invaded by enemies, or shall have received certain advice of a resolution being formed by some nation of Indians to invade such State, and the danger is so imminent as not to admit of a delay, till the United States in Congress assembled can be consulted: nor shall any State grant commissions to any ships or vessels of war, nor letters of marque or reprisal, except it be after a declaration of war by the United States in Congress assembled, and then only against the kingdom or state and the subjects thereof, against which war has been so declared, and under such regulations as shall be established by the United States in Congress assembled, unless such State be infested by pirates, in which case vessels of war may be fitted out for that occasion, and kept so long as the danger shall continue or until the United States in Congress assembled shall determine otherwise.

ARTICLE VII. When land-forces are raised by any State for the common defence, all officers of or under the rank of colonel, shall be appointed by the Legislature of each State respectively by whom such forces shall be raised, or in such manner as such State shall direct, and all vacancies shall be filled up by the State which first made the appointment.

ARTICLE VIII. All charges of war, and all other expenses that shall be incurred for the common defence or general welfare, and allowed by the United States in Congress assembled, shall be defrayed out of a common treasury, which shall be supplied by the several States, in proportion to the value of all land within each State, granted to or surveyed for any person, as such land and the buildings and improvements thereon shall be estimated according to such mode as the United States in Congress assembled, shall from time to time direct and appoint.

The taxes for paying that proportion shall be laid and levied by the authority and direction of the Legislatures of the several States within the time agreed upon by the United States in Congress assembled.

ARTICLE IX. The United States in Congress assembled, shall have the sole and exclusive right and power of determining on peace and war, except in the cases mentioned in the sixth article—of sending and receiving ambassadors—entering into treaties and alliances, provided that no treaty of commerce shall be made whereby the legislative power of the respective States shall be restrained from imposing such imposts and duties on foreigners, as their own people are subjected to, or from prohibiting the exportation or importation of any species of goods or commodities whatsoever—of establishing rules for deciding in all cases, what captures on land or water shall be legal, and in what manner prizes taken by land or naval forces in the service of the United States shall be divided or appropriated—or granting letters of marque and reprisal in times of peace—appointing courts for the trial of piracies and felonies committed on the high seas and establishing courts for receiving and determining finally appeals in all cases of captures, provided that no member of Congress shall be appointed a judge of any of the said courts.

The United States in Congress assembled shall also be the last resort on appeal in all disputes and differences now subsisting or that hereafter may arise between two or more States concerning boundary, jurisdiction or any other cause whatever; which authority shall always be exercised in the manner following. Whenever the legislative or executive authority or lawful agent of any State in controversy with another shall present a petition to Congress, stating the matter in question and praying for a hearing, notice thereof shall be given by order of Congress to the legislative or executive authority of the other State in controversy, and a day assigned for the appearance of the parties by their lawful agents, who shall then be directed to appoint by joint consent, commissioners or judges to constitute a court for hearing and determining the matter in question: but if they cannot agree, Congress shall name three persons out of each of the United States, and from the list of such persons each party shall alternately strike out one, the petitioners beginning, until the number shall be reduced to thirteen; and from that number not less than seven, nor more than nine names as Congress shall direct, shall in the presence of Congress be drawn out by lot, and the persons whose names shall be so drawn or any five of them, shall be commissioners or judges, to hear and finally determine the controversy, so always as a major part of the judges who shall hear the cause shall agree in the determination: and if either party shall neglect to attend at the day appointed, without showing reasons, which Congress shall judge sufficient, or being present shall refuse to strike, the Congress shall proceed to nominate three persons out of each State, and the Secretary of Congress shall strike in behalf of such party absent or refusing; and the judgment and sentence of the court to be appointed, in the manner before prescribed, shall be final and conclusive; and if any of the parties shall refuse to submit to the authority of such court, or to appear or defend their claim or cause, the court shall nevertheless proceed to pronounce sentence, or judgment, which shall in like manner be final and decisive, the judgment or sentence and other proceedings being in either case transmitted to Congress, and lodged among the acts of Congress for the security of the parties concerned: provided that every commissioner, before he sits in judgment, shall take an oath to be administered by one of the judges of the supreme or superior court of the State where the cause shall be tried, "well and truly to hear and determine the matter in question, according to the best of his judgment, without favour, affection or hope of reward:" provided also that no State shall be deprived of territory for the benefit of the United States.

All controversies concerning the private right of soil claimed under different grants of two or more States, whose jurisdiction as they may respect such lands, and the States which passed such grants are adjusted, the said grants or either of them being at the same time claimed to have originated antecedent to such settlement of jurisdiction, shall on the petition of either party to the Congress of the United States, be finally determined as near as may be in the same manner as is before prescribed for deciding disputes respecting territorial jurisdiction between different States.

The United States in Congress assembled shall also have the sole and exclusive right and power of regulating the alloy and value of coin struck by their own authority, or by that of the respective States.—fixing the standard of weights and measures throughout the United States.—regulating the trade and managing all affairs with the Indians, not members of any of the States, provided that the legislative right of any State within its own limits be not infringed or violated—establishing and regulating post-offices from one State to another, throughout all the United States, and exacting such postage on the papers passing thro' the same as may be requisite to defray the expenses of the said office—appointing all officers of the land forces, in the service of the United States, excepting regimental officers—appointing all the officers of the naval forces, and commissioning all officers whatever in the service of the United States—making rules for the government and regulation of the said land and naval forces, and directing their operations.

The United States in Congress assembled shall have authority to appoint a committee, to sit in the recess of Congress, to be denominated "a Committee of the States", and to consist of one delegate from each State; and to appoint such other committees and civil officers as may be necessary for managing the general affairs of the United States under their direction—to appoint one of their number to preside, provided that no person be allowed to serve in the office of president more than one year in any term of three years; to ascertain the necessary sums of money to be raised for the service of the United States, and to appropriate and apply the same for defraying the public expenses—to borrow money, or emit bills on the credit of the United States, transmitting every half year to the respective States an account of the sums of money so borrowed or emitted,—to build and equip a navy—to agree upon the number of land forces, and to make requisitions from each State for its quota, in proportion to the number of white inhabitants in such State; which requisition shall be binding, and thereupon the Legislature of each State shall appoint the regimental officers, raise the men and cloath, arm and equip them in a soldier like manner, at the expense of the United States; and the officers and men so cloathed, armed and equipped shall march to the place appointed, and within the time agreed on by the United States in Congress assembled: but if the United States in Congress assembled shall, on consideration of circumstances judge proper that any State should not raise men, or should raise a smaller number than its quota, and that any other State should raise a greater number of men than the quota thereof, such extra number shall be raised, officered, cloathed, armed and equipped in the same manner as the quota of such State, unless the legislature of such State shall judge that such extra number cannot be safely spared out of the same, in which case they shall raise, officer, cloath, arm and equip as many of such extra number as they judge can be safely spared. And the officers and men so cloathed, armed and equipped, shall march to the place appointed, and within the time agreed on by the United States in Congress assembled.

The United States in Congress assembled shall never engage in a war, nor grant letters of marque and reprisal in time of peace, nor enter into any treaties or alliances, nor coin money, nor regulate the value thereof, nor ascertain the sums and expenses necessary for the defence and welfare of the United States, or any of them, nor emit bills, nor borrow money on the credit of the United States, nor appropriate money, nor agree upon the number of vessels of war, to be built or purchased, or the number of land or sea forces to be raised, nor appoint a commander in chief of the army or navy, unless nine States assent to the same; nor shall a question on any other point, except for adjourning from day to day be determined, unless by the votes of a majority of the United States in Congress assembled.

The Congress of the United States shall have power to adjourn to any time within the year, and to any place within the United States, so that no period of adjournment be for a longer duration than the space of six months, and shall publish the journal of their proceedings monthly, except such parts thereof relating to treaties, alliances or military operations, as in their judgment require secrecy; and the yeas and nays of the delegates of each State on any question shall be entered on the journal, when it is desired by any delegate; and the delegates of a State, or any of them, at his or their request shall be furnished with a transcript of the said journal, except such parts as are above excepted, to lay before the Legislatures of the several States.

ARTICLE X. The committee of the States, or any nine of them, shall be authorized to execute, in the recess of Congress, such of the powers of Congress as the United States in Congress assembled, by the consent of nine States, shall from time to time think expedient to vest them with; provided that no power be delegated to the said committee, for the exercise of which, by the articles of confederation, the voice of nine States in the Congress of the United States assembled is requisite.

ARTICLE XI. Canada acceding to this confederation, and joining in the measures of the United States, shall be admitted into, and entitled to all the advantages of this Union: but no other colony shall be admitted into the same, unless such admission be agreed to by nine States.

ARTICLE XII. All bills of credit emitted, monies borrowed and debts contracted by, or under the authority of Congress, before the assembling of the United States, in pursuance of the present confederation, shall be deemed and considered as a charge against the United States, for payment and satisfaction whereof the said United States, and the public faith are hereby solemnly pledged.

ARTICLE XIII. Every State shall abide by the determinations of the United States in Congress assembled, on all questions which by this confederation are submitted to them. And the articles of this confederation shall be inviolably observed by every State, and the Union shall be perpetual; nor shall any alteration at any time hereafter be made in any of them; unless such alteration be agreed to in a Congress of the United States, and be afterwards confirmed by the Legislatures of every State.

And whereas it has pleased the Great Governor of the world to incline the hearts of the Legislatures we respectively represent in Congress, to approve of, and to authorize us to ratify the said articles of confederation and perpetual union. Know ye that we the undersigned delegates, by virtue of the power and authority to us given for that purpose, do by these presents, in the name and in behalf of our respective constituents, fully and entirely ratify and confirm each and every of the said articles of confederation and perpetual union, and all and singular the matters and things therein contained: and we do further solemnly plight and engage the faith of our respective constituents, that they shall abide by the determinations of the United States in Congress assembled, on all questions, which by the said confederation are submitted to them. And that the articles thereof shall be inviolably observed by the States we re[s]pectively represent, and that the Union shall be perpetual.

In witness whereof we have hereunto set our hands in Congress. Done at Philadelphia in the State of Pennsylvania the ninth day of July in the year of our Lord one thousand seven hundred and seventy-eight, and in the third year of the independence of America.

On the part & behalf of the State of New Hampshire

JOSIAH BARTLETT,   JOHN WENTWORTH, JUNR.,
August 8th, 1778.

On the part and behalf of the State of Massachusetts Bay

JOHN HANCOCK,   FRANCIS DANA,
SAMUEL ADAMS,   JAMES LOVELL,
ELBRIDGE GERRY,   SAMUEL HOLTEN.

On the part and behalf of the State of Rhode Island and Providence Plantations

WILLIAM ELLERY,   JOHN COLLINS.
HENRY MARCHANT,

On the part and behalf of the State of Connecticut

ROGER SHERMAN,   TITUS HOSMER,
SAMUEL HUNTINGTON,   ANDREW ADAMS.
OLIVER WOLCOTT,

On the part and behalf of the State of New York

JAS. DUANE,   WM. DUER,
FRA. LEWIS,   GOUV. MORRIS.

On the part and in behalf of the State of New Jersey, Novr. 26, 1778

JNO. WITHERSPOON.   NATHL. SCUDDER.

On the part and behalf of the State of Pennsylvania

ROBT. MORRIS,   WILLIAM CLINGAN,
DANIEL ROBERDEAU,   JOSEPH REED, 22D
JONA. BAYARD SMITH,   July, 1778.

On the part & behalf of the State of Delaware

THO. M'KEAN, FEBY.   NICHOLAS VAN DYKE.
   12, 1779.
JOHN DICKINSON,
   May 5th, 1779.

On the part and behalf of the State of Maryland

JOHN HANSON,   DANIEL CARROLL,
   March 1, 1781.   Mar. 1, 1781.

On the part and behalf of the State of Virginia

RICHARD HENRY LEE,   JNO. HARVIE,
JOHN BANISTER,   FRANCIS LIGHTFOOT
THOMAS ADAMS,   LEE.

On the part and behalf of the State of No. Carolina

JOHN PENN,   CORNS. HARNETT,
   July 21st, 1778.   JNO. WILLIAMS.

On the part & behalf of the State of South Carolina

HENRY LAURENS,   RICHD. HUTSON,
WILLIAM HENRY   THOS. HEYWARD, Junr.
   DRAYTON,
JNO. MATHEWS,

On the part & behalf of the State of Georgia

JNO. WALTON, 24th   EDWD. TELFAIR,
   July, 1778.   EDWD. LANGWORTHY.

THE CONSTITUTION OF THE UNITED STATES

We the People of the United States, in Order to form a more perfect Union, establish Justice, insure domestic Tranquility, provide for the common defence, promote the general Welfare, and secure the Blessings of Liberty to ourselves and our Posterity, do ordain and establish this Constitution for the United States of America.

Article. I.

Section. 1. All legislative Powers herein granted shall be vested in a Congress of the United States, which shall consist of a Senate and House of Representatives.

Section. 2. The House of Representatives shall be composed of Members chosen every second Year by the People of the several States, and the Electors in each State shall have the Qualifications requisite for Electors of the most numerous Branch of the State Legislature.

No Person shall be a Representative who shall not have attained to the Age of twenty five Years, and been seven Years a Citizen of the United States, and who shall not, when elected, be an Inhabitant of that State in which he shall be chosen.

[Representatives and direct Taxes shall be apportioned among the several States which may be included within this Union, according to their respective Numbers, which shall be determined by adding to the whole Number of free Persons, including those bound to Service for a Term of Years, and excluding Indians not taxed, three fifths of all other Persons.]★ The actual Enumeration shall be made within three Years after the first Meeting of the Congress of the United States, and within

★Changed by Section 2 of the Fourteenth Amendment.

every subsequent Term of ten Years, in such Manner as they shall by Law direct. The number of Representatives shall not exceed one for every thirty Thousand, but each State shall have at Least one Representative; and until such enumeration shall be made, the State of New Hampshire shall be entitled to chuse three, Massachusetts eight, Rhode-Island and Providence Plantations one, Connecticut five, New-York six, New Jersey four, Pennsylvania eight, Delaware one, Maryland six, Virginia ten, North Carolina five, South Carolina five, and Georgia three.

When vacancies happen in the Representation from any State, the Executive Authority thereof shall issue Writs of Election to fill such Vacancies.

The House of Representatives shall chuse their Speaker and other Officers; and shall have the sole Power of Impeachment.

Section. 3. The Senate of the United States shall be composed of two Senators from each State, [chosen by the Legislature thereof,]★ for six Years; and each Senator shall have one Vote.

Immediately after they shall be assembled in Consequence of the first Election, they shall be divided as equally as may be into three Classes. The Seats of the Senators of the first Class shall be vacated at the Expiration of the second Year, of the second Class at the Expiration of the fourth Year, and of the third Class at the Expiration of the sixth Year, so that one third may be chosen every second Year; [and if Vacancies happen by Resignation, or otherwise, during the Recess of the Legislature of any State, the Executive thereof may make temporary Appointments until the next Meeting of the Legislature, which shall then fill such Vacancies.]★

No Person shall be a Senator who shall not have attained to the Age of thirty Years, and been nine Years a Citizen of the United States, and who shall not, when elected, be an Inhabitant of that State for which he shall be chosen.

The Vice President of the United States shall be President of the Senate, but shall have no Vote, unless they be equally divided.

The Senate shall chuse their other Officers, and also a President pro

★Changed by the Seventeenth Amendment.

tempore, in the Absence of the Vice President, or when he shall exercise the Office of President of the United States.

The Senate shall have the sole Power to try all Impeachments. When sitting for that Purpose, they shall be on Oath or Affirmation. When the President of the United States is tried, the Chief Justice shall preside: And no Person shall be convicted without the Concurrence of two thirds of the Members present.

Judgment in Cases of Impeachment shall not extend further than to removal from Office, and disqualification to hold and enjoy any Office of honor, Trust or Profit under the United States: but the Party convicted shall nevertheless be liable and subject to Indictment, Trial, Judgment and Punishment, according to Law.

Section. 4. The Times, Places and Manner of holding Elections for Senators and Representatives, shall be prescribed in each State by the Legislature thereof; but the Congress may at any time by Law make or alter such Regulations, except as to the Places of chusing Senators.

The Congress shall assemble at least once in every Year, and such Meeting shall be [on the first Monday in December,]* unless they shall by Law appoint a different Day.

Section. 5. Each House shall be the Judge of the Elections, Returns and Qualifications of its own Members, and a Majority of each shall constitute a Quorum to do Business; but a smaller Number may adjourn from day to day, and may be authorized to compel the Attendance of absent Members, in such Manner, and under such Penalties as each House may provide.

Each House may determine the Rules of its Proceedings, punish its Members for disorderly Behaviour, and, with the Concurrence of two thirds, expel a Member.

Each House shall keep a Journal of its Proceedings, and from time to time publish the same, excepting such Parts as may in their Judgment require Secrecy; and the Yeas and Nays of the Members of either House on any question shall, at the Desire of one fifth of those Present, be entered on the Journal.

Neither House, during the Session of Congress, shall, without the

*Changed by Section 2 of the Twentieth Amendment.

Consent of the other, adjourn for more than three days, nor to any other Place than that in which the two Houses shall be sitting.

Section. 6. The Senators and Representatives shall receive a Compensation for their Services, to be ascertained by Law, and paid out of the Treasury of the United States. They shall in all Cases, except Treason, Felony and Breach of the Peace, be privileged from Arrest during their Attendance at the Session of their respective Houses, and in going to and returning from the same; and for any Speech or Debate in either House, they shall not be questioned in any other Place.

No Senator or Representative shall, during the Time for which he was elected, be appointed to any civil Office under the Authority of the United States, which shall have been created, or the Emoluments whereof shall have been encreased during such time; and no Person holding any Office under the United States, shall be a Member of either House during his Continuance in Office.

Section. 7. All Bills for raising Revenue shall originate in the House of Representatives; but the Senate may propose or concur with Amendments as on other Bills.

Every Bill which shall have passed the House of Representatives and the Senate, shall, before it becomes a Law, be presented to the President of the United States; If he approve he shall sign it, but if not he shall return it, with his Objections to that House in which it shall have originated, who shall enter the Objections at large on their Journal, and proceed to reconsider it. If after such Reconsideration two thirds of that House shall agree to pass the Bill, it shall be sent, together with the Objections, to the other House, by which it shall likewise be reconsidered, and if approved by two thirds of that House, it shall become a Law. But in all such Cases the Votes of both Houses shall be determined by yeas and Nays, and the Names of the Persons voting for and against the Bill shall be entered on the Journal of each House respectively. If any Bill shall not be returned by the President within ten Days (Sundays excepted) after it shall have been presented to him, the Same shall be a Law, in like Manner as if he had signed it, unless the Congress by their Adjournment prevent its Return, in which Case it shall not be a Law.

Every Order, Resolution, or Vote to which the Concurrence of the Senate and House of Representatives may be necessary (except on a question of Adjournment) shall be presented to the President of the United States; and before the Same shall take Effect, shall be approved by him, or being disapproved by him, shall be repassed by two thirds of the Senate and House of Representatives, according to the Rules and Limitations prescribed in the Case of a Bill.

Section. 8. The Congress shall have Power To lay and collect Taxes, Duties, Imposts and Excises, to pay the Debts and provide for the common Defence and general Welfare of the United States; but all Duties, Imposts and Excises shall be uniform throughout the United States;

To borrow Money on the credit of the United States;

To regulate Commerce with foreign Nations, and among the several States, and with the Indian Tribes;

To establish an uniform Rule of Naturalization, and uniform Laws on the subject of Bankruptcies throughout the United States;

To coin Money, regulate the Value thereof, and of foreign Coin, and fix the Standard of Weights and Measures;

To provide for the Punishment of counterfeiting the Securities and current Coin of the United States;

To establish Post Offices and post Roads;

To promote the Progress of Science and useful Arts, by securing for limited Times to Authors and Inventors the exclusive Right to their respective Writings and Discoveries;

To constitute Tribunals inferior to the supreme Court;

To define and punish Piracies and Felonies committed on the high Seas, and Offenses against the Law of Nations;

To declare War, grant Letters of Marque and Reprisal, and make Rules concerning Captures on Land and Water;

To raise and support Armies, but no Appropriation of Money to that Use shall be for a longer Term than two Years;

To provide and maintain a Navy;

To make rules for the Government and Regulation of the land and naval Forces;

To provide for calling forth the Militia to execute the Laws of the Union, suppress Insurrections and repel Invasions;

To provide for organizing, arming, and disciplining, the Militia, and for governing such Part of them as may be employed in the Service of the United States, reserving to the States respectively, the Appointment of the Officers, and the Authority of training the Militia according to the discipline prescribed by Congress;

To exercise exclusive Legislation in all Cases whatsoever, over such District (not exceeding ten Miles square) as may, by Cession of particular States, and the Acceptance of Congress, become the Seat of the Government of the United States, and to exercise like Authority over all Places purchased by the Consent of the Legislature of the State in which the Same shall be, for the Erection of Forts, Magazines, Arsenals, dock-Yards and other needful Buildings;—And

To make all Laws which shall be necessary and proper for carrying into Execution the foregoing Powers, and all other Powers vested by this Constitution in the Government of the United States, or in any Department or Officer thereof.

Section. 9. The Migration or Importation of such Persons as any of the States now existing shall think proper to admit, shall not be prohibited by the Congress prior to the Year one thousand eight hundred and eight, but a Tax or duty may be imposed on such Importation, not exceeding ten dollars for each Person.

The Privilege of the Writ of Habeas Corpus shall not be suspended, unless when in Cases of Rebellion or Invasion the public Safety may require it.

No Bill of Attainder or ex post facto Law shall be passed.

No Capitation, or other direct, Tax shall be laid, unless in Proportion to the Census or Enumeration herein before directed to be taken.*

No Tax or Duty shall be laid on Articles exported from any State.

No Preference shall be given by any Regulation of Commerce or Revenue to the Ports of one State over those of another: nor shall Vessels bound to, or from, one State, be obliged to enter, clear, or pay Duties in another.

No Money shall be drawn from the Treasury, but in Consequence of Appropriations made by Law; and a regular Statement and Account

*See Sixteenth Amendment.

of the Receipts and Expenditures of all public Money shall be published from time to time.

No Title of Nobility shall be granted by the United States: And no Person holding any Office of Profit or Trust under them, shall, without the Consent of the Congress, accept of any present, Emolument, Office, or Title, of any kind whatever, from any King, Prince, or foreign State.

Section. 10. No State shall enter into any Treaty, Alliance, or Confederation; grant Letters of Marque and Reprisal; coin Money; emit Bills of Credit; make any Thing but gold and silver Coin a Tender in Payment of Debts; pass any Bill of Attainder, ex post facto Law, or Law impairing the Obligation of Contracts, or grant any Title of Nobility.

No State shall, without the Consent of the Congress, lay any Imposts or Duties on Imports or Exports, except what may be absolutely necessary for executing its inspection Laws: and the net Produce of all Duties and Imposts, laid by any State on Imports or Exports, shall be for the Use of the Treasury of the United States; and all such Laws shall be subject to the Revision and Controul of the Congress.

No State shall, without the Consent of Congress, lay any Duty of Tonnage, keep Troops, or Ships of War in time of Peace, enter into any Agreement or Compact with another State, or with a foreign Power, or engage in War, unless actually invaded, or in such imminent Danger as will not admit of delay.

Article. II.

Section. 1. The executive Power shall be vested in a President of the United States of America. He shall hold his Office during the Term of four Years, and, together with the Vice President, chosen for the same Term, be elected, as follows

Each State shall appoint, in such Manner as the Legislature thereof may direct, a Number of Electors, equal to the whole Number of Senators and Representatives to which the State may be entitled in the Congress: but no Senator or Representative, or Person holding an Office of Trust or Profit under the United States, shall be appointed an Elector.

[The Electors shall meet in their respective States, and vote by Ballot for two Persons, of whom one at least shall not be an Inhabitant of the same State with themselves. And they shall make a List of all the Persons voted for, and of the Number of Votes for each; which List they shall sign and certify, and transmit sealed to the Seat of the Government of the United States, directed to the President of the Senate. The President of the Senate shall, in the Presence of the Senate and House of Representatives, open all the Certificates, and the Votes shall then be counted. The Person having the greatest Number of Votes shall be the President, if such Number be a Majority of the whole Number of Electors appointed; and if there be more than one who have such Majority, and have an equal Number of Votes, then the House of Representatives shall immediately chuse by Ballot one of them for President; and if no Person have a Majority, then from the five highest on the List the said House shall in like Manner chuse the President. But in chusing the President, the Votes shall be taken by States, the Representation from each State having one Vote; A quorum for this Purpose shall consist of a Member or Members from two thirds of the States, and a Majority of all the States shall be necessary to a Choice. In every Case, after the Choice of the President, the Person having the greatest Number of Votes of the Electors shall be the Vice President. But if there should remain two or more who have equal Votes, the Senate shall chuse from them by Ballot the Vice President.]*

The Congress may determine the Time of chusing the Electors, and the Day on which they shall give their Votes; which Day shall be the same throughout the United States.

No Person except a natural born Citizen, or a Citizen of the United States, at the time of the Adoption of this Constitution, shall be eligible to the Office of President; neither shall any person be eligible to that Office who shall not have attained to the Age of thirty five Years, and been fourteen Years a Resident within the United States.

[In Case of the Removal of the President from Office, or of his Death, Resignation, or Inability to discharge the Powers and Duties of the said Office, the Same shall devolve on the Vice President, and the Congress may by Law provide for the Case of Removal, Death, Resig-

*Changed by the Twelfth Amendment.

nation, or Inability, both of the President and Vice President, declaring what Officer shall then act as President, and such Officer shall act accordingly, until the Disability be removed, or a President shall be elected.]*

The President shall, at stated Times, receive for his Services, a Compensation, which shall neither be increased nor diminished during the Period for which he shall have been elected, and he shall not receive within that Period any other Emolument from the United States, or any of them.

Before he enter on the Execution of his Office, he shall take the following Oath or Affirmation:—"I do solemnly swear (or affirm) that I will faithfully execute the Office of President of the United States, and will to the best of my Ability, preserve, protect and defend the Constitution of the United States."

Section. 2. The President shall be Commander in Chief of the Army and Navy of the United States, and of the Militia of the several States, when called into the actual Service of the United States; he may require the Opinion, in writing, of the principal Officer in each of the executive Departments, upon any Subject relating to the Duties of their respective Offices, and he shall have Power to grant Reprieves and Pardons for Offenses against the United States, except in Cases of Impeachment.

He shall have Power, by and with the Advice and Consent of the Senate, to make Treaties, provided two thirds of the Senators present concur; and he shall nominate, and by and with the Advice and Consent of the Senate, shall appoint Ambassadors, other public Ministers and Consuls, Judges of the supreme Court, and all other Officers of the United States, whose Appointments are not herein otherwise provided for, and which shall be established by Law: but the Congress may by Law vest the Appointment of such inferior Officers, as they think proper, in the President alone, in the Courts of Law, or in the Heads of Departments.

The President shall have Power to fill up all Vacancies that may happen during the Recess of the Senate, by granting Commissions which shall expire at the End of their next Session.

Section. 3. He shall from time to time give to the Congress In-

*Changed by the Twenty-Fifth Amendment.

formation of the State of the Union, and recommend to their Consideration such Measures as he shall judge necessary and expedient; he may, on extraordinary Occasions, convene both Houses, or either of them, and in Case of Disagreement between them, with Respect to the Time of Adjournment, he may adjourn them to such Time as he shall think proper; he shall receive Ambassadors and other public Ministers; he shall take Care that the Laws be faithfully executed, and shall Commission all the Officers of the United States.

Section. 4. The President, Vice President and all civil Officers of the United States, shall be removed from Office on Impeachment for, and Conviction of, Treason, Bribery, or other high Crimes and Misdemeanors.

Article. III.

Section. 1. The judicial Power of the United States, shall be vested in one supreme Court, and in such inferior Courts as the Congress may from time to time ordain and establish. The Judges, both of the supreme and inferior Courts, shall hold their Offices during good Behaviour, and shall, at stated Times, receive for their Services, a Compensation, which shall not be diminished during their Continuance in Office.

Section. 2. The judicial Power shall extend to all Cases, in Law and Equity, arising under this Constitution, the Laws of the United States, and Treaties made, or which shall be made, under their Authority;—to all Cases affecting Ambassadors, other public Ministers and Consuls;—to all Cases of admiralty and maritime Jurisdiction;—to Controversies to which the United States shall be a Party;—to Controversies between two or more States;—[between a State and Citizens of another State;—]* between Citizens of different States,—between Citizens of the same State claiming Lands under Grants of different States, [and between a State, or the Citizens thereof, and foreign States, Citizens or Subjects.]*

In all Cases affecting Ambassadors, other public Ministers and Consuls, and those in which a State shall be Party, the supreme Court

*Changed by the Eleventh Amendment.

shall have original Jurisdiction. In all the other Cases before mentioned, the supreme Court shall have appellate Jurisdiction, both as to Law and Fact, with such Exceptions, and under such Regulations as the Congress shall make.

The Trial of all Crimes, except in Cases of Impeachment; shall be by Jury; and such Trial shall be held in the State where the said Crimes shall have been committed; but when not committed within any State, the Trial shall be at such Place or Places as the Congress may by Law have directed.

Section. 3. Treason against the United States, shall consist only in levying War against them, or in adhering to their Enemies, giving them Aid and Comfort. No Person shall be convicted of Treason unless on the Testimony of two Witnesses to the same overt Act, or on Confession in open Court.

The Congress shall have Power to declare the Punishment of Treason, but no Attainder of Treason shall work Corruption of Blood, or Forfeiture except during the Life of the Person attainted.

Article. IV.

Section. 1. Full Faith and Credit shall be given in each State to the public Acts, Records, and judicial Proceedings of every other State; And the Congress may by general Laws prescribe the Manner in which such Acts, Records and Proceedings shall be proved, and the Effect thereof.

Section. 2. The Citizens of each State shall be entitled to all Privileges and Immunities of Citizens in the several States.

A Person charged in any State with Treason, Felony, or other Crime, who shall flee from Justice, and be found in another State, shall on Demand of the executive Authority of the State from which he fled, be delivered up, to be removed to the State having Jurisdiction of the Crime.

[No Person held to Service or Labour in one State, under the Laws thereof, escaping into another, shall, in Consequence of any Law or Regulation therein, be discharged from such Service or Labour, but shall be delivered up on Claim of the Party to whom such Service or Labour may be due.]*

*Changed by the Thirteenth Amendment.

Section. 3. New States may be admitted by the Congress into this Union; but no new State shall be formed or erected within the Jurisdiction of any other State; nor any State be formed by the Junction of two or more States, or Parts of States, without the Consent of the Legislatures of the States concerned as well as of the Congress.

The Congress shall have Power to dispose of and make all needful Rules and Regulations respecting the Territory or other Property belonging to the United States; and nothing in this Constitution shall be so construed as to Prejudice any Claims of the United States, or of any particular State.

Section. 4. The United States shall guarantee to every State in this Union a Republican Form of Government, and shall protect each of them against Invasion; and on Application of the Legislature, or of the Executive (when the Legislature cannot be convened) against domestic Violence.

Article.V.

The Congress, whenever two thirds of both Houses shall deem it necessary, shall propose Amendments to this Constitution, or, on the Application of the Legislatures of two thirds of the several States, shall call a Convention for proposing Amendments, which, in either Case, shall be valid to all Intents and Purposes, as Part of this Constitution, when ratified by the Legislatures of three fourths of the several States, or by Conventions in three fourths thereof, as the one or the other Mode of Ratification may be proposed by the Congress; Provided that no Amendment which may be made prior to the Year One thousand eight hundred and eight shall in any Manner affect the first and fourth Clauses in the Ninth Section of the first Article; and that no State, without its Consent, shall be deprived of its equal Suffrage in the Senate.

Article.VI.

All Debts contracted and Engagements entered into, before the Adoption of this Constitution, shall be as valid against the United States under this Constitution, as under the Confederation.

This Constitution, and the Laws of the United States which shall be made in Pursuance thereof; and all Treaties made, or which shall be made, under the Authority of the United States, shall be the supreme Law of the Land; and the Judges in every State shall be bound thereby, any Thing in the Constitution or Laws of any State to the Contrary notwithstanding.

The Senators and Representatives before mentioned, and the Members of the several State Legislatures, and all executive and judicial Officers, both of the United States and of the several States, shall be bound by Oath or Affirmation, to support this Constitution; but no religious Test shall ever be required as a Qualification to any Office or Public Trust under the United States.

Article.VII.

The Ratification of the Conventions of nine States, shall be sufficient for the Establishment of this Constitution between the States so ratifying the Same.

done in Convention by the Unanimous Consent of the States present the Seventeenth Day of September in the Year of our Lord one thousand seven hundred and Eighty seven and of the Independence of the United States of America the Twelfth In Witness whereof We have hereunto subscribed our Names,

G? Washington—Presid.
and deputy from Virginia

New Hampshire   John Langdon
Nicholas Gilman

Massachusetts   Nathaniel Gorham
Rufus King

Connecticut   Wm. Saml. Johnson
Roger Sherman

New York   Alexander Hamilton

New Jersey   Wil: Livingston
David Brearley
Wm. Paterson
Jona: Dayton

Pennsylvania   B Franklin
Thomas Mifflin
Robt Morris
Geo. Clymer
Thos. FitzSimons
Jared Ingersoll
James Wilson
Gouv Morris

Delaware   Geo: Read
Gunning Bedford jun
John Dickinson
Richard Bassett
Jaco: Broom

Maryland   James McHenry
Dan of St Thos. Jenifer
Danl Carroll

Virginia   John Blair—
James Madison Jr.

North Carolina   Wm. Blount
Richd. Dobbs Spaight
Hu Williamson

South Carolina   J. Rutledge
Charles Cotesworth Pinckney
Charles Pinckney
Pierce Butler

Georgia   William Few
Abr Baldwin

Attest William Jackson Secretary

AMENDMENTS
TO THE CONSTITUTION
OF THE
UNITED STATES OF AMERICA

Amendment I [1791].

Congress shall make no law respecting an establishment of religion, or prohibiting the free exercise thereof; or abridging the freedom of speech, or of the press, or the right of the people peaceably to assemble, and to petition the Government for a redress of grievances.

Amendment II [1791].

A well regulated Militia, being necessary to the security of a free State, the right of the people to keep and bear Arms, shall not be infringed.

Amendment III [1791].

No Soldier shall, in time of peace be quartered in any house, without the consent of the Owner, nor in time of war, but in a manner to be prescribed by law.

Amendment IV [1791].

The right of the people to be secure in their persons, houses, papers, and effects, against unreasonable searches and seizures, shall not be violated, and no Warrants shall issue, but upon probable cause, supported by Oath or affirmation, and particularly describing the place to be searched, and the persons or things to be seized.

Amendment V [1791].

No person shall be held to answer for a capital, or otherwise infamous crime, unless on a presentment or indictment of a Grand Jury, except in cases arising in the land or naval forces, or in the Militia, when in actual service in time of War or public danger; nor shall any person be subject for the same offence to be twice put in jeopardy of life or limb, nor shall be compelled in any criminal case to be a witness against himself, nor be deprived of life, liberty, or property, without due process of law; nor shall private property be taken for public use without just compensation.

Amendment VI [1791].

In all criminal prosecutions, the accused shall enjoy the right to a speedy and public trial, by an impartial jury of the State and district wherein the crime shall have been committed; which district shall have been previously ascertained by law, and to be informed of the nature and cause of the accusation; to be confronted with the witnesses against him; to have compulsory process for obtaining witnesses in his favor, and to have the assistance of counsel for his defence.

Amendment VII [1791].

In Suits at common law, where the value in controversy shall exceed twenty dollars, the right of trial by jury shall be preserved, and no fact tried by a jury shall be otherwise re-examined in any Court of the United States, than according to the rules of the common law.

Amendment VIII [1791].

Excessive bail shall not be required, nor excessive fines imposed, nor cruel and unusual punishments inflicted.

Amendment IX [1791].

The enumeration in the Constitution of certain rights shall not be construed to deny or disparage others retained by the people.

Amendment X [1791].

The powers not delegated to the United States by the Constitution, nor prohibited by it to the States, are reserved to the States respectively, or to the people.

Amendment XI [1795].

The Judicial power of the United States shall not be construed to extend to any suit in law or equity, commenced or prosecuted against one of the United States by Citizens of another State, or by Citizens or Subjects of any Foreign State.

Amendment XII [1804].

The Electors shall meet in their respective states, and vote by ballot for President and Vice President, one of whom, at least, shall not be an inhabitant of the same state with themselves; they shall name in their ballots the person voted for as President, and in distinct ballots the person voted for as Vice-President, and they shall make distinct lists of all persons voted for as President, and of all persons voted for as Vice-President, and of the number of votes for each, which lists they shall sign and certify, and transmit sealed to the seat of the government of the United States, directed to the President of the Senate;—The President of the Senate shall, in the presence of the Senate and House of Representatives, open all the certificates and the votes shall then be counted;—The person having the greatest number of votes for President, shall be the President, if such number be a majority of the whole number of Electors appointed; and if no person have such majority, then from the persons having the highest numbers not exceeding three on the list of those voted for as President, the House of Representatives shall choose immediately, by ballot, the President. But in choosing the

President, the votes shall be taken by states, the representation from each state having one vote; a quorum for this purpose shall consist of a member or members from two-thirds of the states, and a majority of all the states shall be necessary to a choice. [And if the House of Representatives shall not choose a President whenever the right of choice shall devolve upon them, before the fourth day of March next following, then the Vice-President shall act as President, as in the case of the death or other constitutional disability of the President—]* The person having the greatest number of votes as Vice-President, shall be the Vice-President, if such number be a majority of the whole number of Electors appointed, and if no person have a majority, then from the two highest numbers on the list, the Senate shall choose the Vice-President; a quorum for the purpose shall consist of two-thirds of the whole number of Senators, and a majority of the whole number shall be necessary to a choice. But no person constitutionally ineligible to the office of President shall be eligible to that of Vice-President of the United States.

Amendment XIII [1865].

Section 1. Neither slavery nor involuntary servitude, except as a punishment for crime whereof the party shall have been duly convicted, shall exist within the United States, or any place subject to their jurisdiction.

Section 2. Congress shall have power to enforce this article by appropriate legislation.

Amendment XIV [1868].

Section 1. All persons born or naturalized in the United States and subject to the jurisdiction thereof, are citizens of the United States and of the State wherein they reside. No State shall make or enforce any law which shall abridge the privileges or immunities of citizens of the United States; nor shall any State deprive any person of life, liberty, or property, without due process of law; nor deny to any person within its jurisdiction the equal protection of the laws.

*Superseded by Section 3 of the Twentieth Amendment.

Section 2. Representatives shall be apportioned among the several States according to their respective numbers, counting the whole number of persons in each State, excluding Indians not taxed. But when the right to vote at any election for the choice of electors for President and Vice President of the United States, Representatives in Congress, the Executive and Judicial officers of a State, or the members of the Legislature thereof, is denied to any of the male inhabitants of such State, being twenty-one years of age, and citizens of the United States, or in any way abridged, except for participation in rebellion, or other crime, the basis of representation therein shall be reduced in the proportion which the number of such male citizens shall bear to the whole number of male citizens twenty-one years of age in such State.

Section 3. No person shall be a Senator or Representative in Congress, or elector of President and Vice President, or hold any office, civil or military, under the United States, or under any State, who, having previously taken an oath, as a member of Congress, or as an officer of the United States, or as a member of any State legislature, or as an executive or judicial officer of any State, to support the Constitution of the United States, shall have engaged in insurrection or rebellion against the same, or given aid or comfort to the enemies thereof. But Congress may by a vote of two-thirds of each House, remove such disability.

Section 4. The validity of the public debt of the United States, authorized by law, including debts incurred for payment of pensions and bounties for services in suppressing insurrection or rebellion, shall not be questioned. But neither the United States nor any State shall assume or pay any debt or obligation incurred in aid of insurrection or rebellion against the United States, or any claim for the loss or emancipation of any slave; but all such debts, obligations and claims shall be held illegal and void.

Section 5. The Congress shall have power to enforce, by appropriate legislation, the provisions of this article.

Amendment XV [1870].

Section 1. The right of citizens of the United States to vote shall not be denied or abridged by the United States or by any State on account of race, color, or previous condition of servitude.

Section 2. The Congress shall have power to enforce this article by appropriate legislation.

Amendment XVI [1913].

The Congress shall have power to lay and collect taxes on incomes, from whatever source derived, without apportionment among the several States, and without regard to any census or enumeration.

Amendment XVII [1913].

The Senate of the United States shall be composed of two Senators from each State, elected by the people thereof, for six years; and each Senator shall have one vote. The electors in each State shall have the qualifications requisite for electors of the most numerous branch of the State legislatures.

When vacancies happen in the representation of any State in the Senate, the executive authority of such State shall issue writs of election to fill such vacancies: *Provided,* That the legislature of any State may empower the executive thereof to make temporary appointments until the people fill the vacancies by election as the legislature may direct.

This amendment shall not be so construed as to affect the election or term of any Senator chosen before it becomes valid as part of the Constitution.

Amendment XVIII [1919].★

[Section 1. After one year from the ratification of this article the manufacture, sale, or transportation of intoxicating liquors within, the importation thereof into, or the exportation thereof from the United States and all territory subject to the jurisdiction thereof for beverage purposes is hereby prohibited.

Section 2. The Congress and the several States shall have concurrent power to enforce this article by appropriate legislation.

★Repealed by the Twenty-First Amendment in 1933.

Section 3. This article shall be inoperative unless it shall have been ratified as an amendment to the Constitution by the legislatures of the several States, as provided in the Constitution, within seven years from the date of the submission hereof to the States by the Congress.]

Amendment XIX [1920].

The right of citizens of the United States to vote shall not be denied or abridged by the United States or by any State on account of sex.

Congress shall have power to enforce this article by appropriate legislation.

Amendment XX [1933].

Section 1. The terms of the President and Vice President shall end at noon on the 20th day of January, and the terms of Senators and Representatives at noon on the 3d day of January, of the years in which such terms would have ended if this article had not been ratified; and the terms of their successors shall then begin.

Section 2. The Congress shall assemble at least once in every year, and such meeting shall begin at noon on the 3d day of January, unless they shall by law appoint a different day.

Section 3. If, at the time fixed for the beginning of the term of the President, the President elect shall have died, the Vice President elect shall become President. If a President shall not have been chosen before the time fixed for the beginning of his term, or if the President elect shall have failed to qualify, then the Vice President elect shall act as President until a President shall have qualified; and the Congress may by law provide for the case wherein neither a President elect nor a Vice President elect shall have qualified, declaring who shall then act as President, or the manner in which one who is to act shall be selected, and such person shall act accordingly until a President or Vice President shall have qualified.

Section 4. The Congress may by law provide for the case of the death of any of the persons from whom the House of Representatives may choose a President whenever the right of choice shall have devolved upon them, and for the case of the death of any of the persons from whom the Senate may choose a Vice President whenever the right of choice shall have devolved upon them.

Section 5. Sections 1 and 2 shall take effect on the 15th day of October following the ratification of this article.

Section 6. This article shall be inoperative unless it shall have been ratified as an amendment to the Constitution by the legislatures of three-fourths of the several States within seven years from the date of its submission.

Amendment XXI [1933].

Section 1. The eighteenth article of amendment to the Constitution of the United States is hereby repealed.

Section 2. The transportation or importation into any State, Territory, or possession of the United States for delivery or use therein of intoxicating liquors, in violation of the laws thereof, is hereby prohibited.

Section 3. This article shall be inoperative unless it shall have been ratified as an amendment to the Constitution by conventions in the several States, as provided in the Constitution, within seven years from the date of the submission hereof to the States by the Congress.

Amendment XXII [1951].

Section 1. No person shall be elected to the office of the President more than twice, and no person who has held the office of President, or acted as President, for more than two years of a term to which some other person was elected President shall be elected to the office of the President more than once. But this Article shall not apply to any person holding the office of President when this Article was proposed by the Congress, and shall not prevent any person who may be holding the office of President, or acting as President, during the term within which this Article becomes operative from holding the office of President or acting as President during the remainder of such term.

Section 2. This article shall be inoperative unless it shall have been ratified as an amendment to the Constitution by the legislatures of three-fourths of the several States within seven years from the date of its submission to the States by the Congress.

Amendment XXIII [1961].

Section 1. The District constituting the seat of Government of the United States shall appoint in such manner as the Congress may direct:

A number of electors of President and Vice President equal to the whole number of Senators and Representatives in Congress to which the District would be entitled if it were a State, but in no event more than the least populous State; they shall be in addition to those appointed by the States, but they shall be considered, for the purposes of the election of President and Vice President, to be electors appointed by a State; and they shall meet in the District and perform such duties as provided by the twelfth article of amendment.

Section 2. The Congress shall have power to enforce this article by appropriate legislation.

Amendment XXIV [1964].

Section 1. The right of citizens of the United States to vote in any primary or other election for President or Vice President, for electors for President or Vice President, or for Senator or Representative in Congress, shall not be denied or abridged by the United States or any State by reason of failure to pay any poll tax or other tax.

Section 2. The Congress shall have power to enforce this article by appropriate legislation.

Amendment XXV [1967].

Section 1. In case of the removal of the President from office or of his death or resignation, the Vice President shall become President.

Section 2. Whenever there is a vacancy in the office of the Vice President, the President shall nominate a Vice President who shall take office upon confirmation by a majority vote of both Houses of Congress.

Section 3. Whenever the President transmits to the President pro tempore of the Senate and the Speaker of the House of Representatives his written declaration that he is unable to discharge the powers and duties of his office, and until he transmits to them a written declaration to the contrary, such powers and duties shall be discharged by the Vice President as Acting President.

Section 4. Whenever the Vice President and a majority of either the principal officers of the executive departments or of such other body as Congress may by law provide, transmit to the President pro tempore of the Senate and the Speaker of the House of Representatives their written declaration that the President is unable to discharge the powers and duties of his office, the Vice President shall immediately assume the powers and duties of the office as Acting President.

Thereafter, when the President transmits to the President pro tempore of the Senate and the Speaker of the House of Representatives his written declaration that no inability exists, he shall resume the powers and duties of his office unless the Vice President and a majority of either the principal officers of the executive department or of such other body as Congress may by law provide, transmit within four days to the President pro tempore of the Senate and the Speaker of the House of Representatives their written declaration that the President is unable to discharge the powers and duties of his office. Thereupon Congress shall decide the issue, assembling within forty-eight hours for that purpose if not in session. If the Congress, within twenty-one days after receipt of the latter written declaration, or, if Congress is not in session, within twenty-one days after Congress is required to assemble, determines by two-thirds vote of both Houses that the President is unable to discharge the powers and duties of his office, the Vice President shall continue to discharge the same as Acting President; otherwise, the President shall resume the powers and duties of his office.

Amendment XXVI [1971].

Section 1. The right of citizens of the United States, who are eighteen years of age or older, to vote shall not be denied or abridged by the United States or by any State on account of age.

Section 2. The Congress shall have power to enforce this article by appropriate legislation.

Amendment XXVII [1992].

No law, varying the compensation for the services of the Senators and Representatives, shall take effect, until an election of Representatives shall have intervened.

INDEX